Margaret Ward

Unmanageable revolutionaries

Women and Irish nationalism

Pluto Press

First published in Great Britain in 1983 by
Pluto Press Limited,
The Works, 105a Torriano Avenue,
London NW5 2RX

and simultaneously in Ireland by
Brandon Book Publishers Ltd.
Dingle, Co. Kerry, Ireland

Cover designed by Marsha Austin

Set by Grassroots Typeset, London

Printed in Great Britain by St Edmundsbury Press,
Bury St Edmunds, Suffolk IP33 3TU
Bound by William Brendon Limited, Tiptree, Essex CO5 0HD

British Library Cataloguing in Publication Data
Ward Margaret
    Unmanageable revolutionaries.
    1. Women in politics—Ireland   2. Ireland—Politics and
    government—19th century
    3. Ireland—Politics and government—20th century
    I. Title
    324   HQ1236

ISBN 0-86104-700-1

For my mother

Contents

Acknowledgements

'Women are at once the boldest and most unmanageable revolutionaries'—Eamon de Valera in conversation with W.H. Van Voris, Dublin, 6 June 1976 (with thanks to Jacqueline Van Voris for this information)

The need to write this book developed out of my experiences as a socialist feminist living in Belfast. I owe a large debt to my sisters in the Socialist Women's Group and to the Belfast Women's Collective for sharing my excitement in my research and for helping me to understand its political significance. I have received advice and encouragement from many sources over the years. I would like to thank Marie-Therese McGivern for her critical comments and patience in reading endless drafts; Shelley Charlesworth for her optimism that I would eventually write it all down; Bill Rolston for his generous comments on the manuscript and for all his support; Mike Farrell, a source of invaluable information, for spurring me on; Frank Wright for much encouragement when I needed it most; Liz Steiner-Scott for sharing her work with me; Fiona Stephens for reading an early draft; Richard Chessum for his kindness in talking to Pluto Press about my research, and Paddy Hillyard, who gave me the determination to finish.

The support and hospitality of many other friends made life very pleasant. Love and gratitude to: Ann, Brigid, Bernadette, Marie, Paul, John, Vince, Ronnie, Gerry, Miriam, Marilyn, Marie, Dave, Joanna, Siobhan, Mick, Mary and Mari.

I would also like to acknowledge the financial support provided by the Department of Political Science, and the Institute of Irish Studies, Queen's University, Belfast.

I owe a special debt to Maire Comerford and Eithne Coyle

O'Donnell, whose patience in answering my questions fired my enthusiasm and redoubled my determination to write down their experiences. Sadly, Maire Comerford died on 15 December 1982. I deeply regret the fact that she never saw the outcome of those long conversations because, although Maire might have disagreed with many of my conclusions, I know how much she wanted women's contributions to be seriously examined. For Maire, and for all the women who went before her, their stories still untold, my warmest appreciation.

Introduction

> The entire history of women's struggle for self-
> determination has been muffled in silence over and over.
> One serious cultural obstacle encountered by any feminist
> writer is that each feminist work has tended to be received
> as if it emerged from nowhere; as if each of us had lived,
> thought, and worked without any historical past or con-
> textual present. This is one of the ways in which women's
> work and thinking has been made to seem sporadic, er-
> rant, orphaned of any tradition of its own.[1]

As women living in a country where the past often appears to be as
vivid as the present, many of us have been conscious of the fact that
buried somewhere in the abundant chronicles of Irish history was
evidence to show that women had also been politically active, and
that they too warranted serious consideration by historians. We
know about our 'great women'—like Countess Markievicz, dressed
for rebellion, proudly brandishing her revolver—but have continued to feel that they were only exceptionally striking instances of
a type of woman common to that era. The question is why have all
the other women disappeared into obscurity? Generally, the importance of women's contribution has been dismissed in a few
sentences as historians itemise what they consider to be the important events; events which have been evaluated in male terms. In
many instances, what has been significant for men has not
necessarily proved to be so for women, while on other occasions,
the same historical event often has an additional significance for
women. For that reason, writing women into history does not mean
simply tagging them onto what we already know; rather, it forces
us to re-examine what is currently accepted, so that a whole people
will eventually come into focus: our historical categories will have

to be revised. As a recent evaluator of the current stage of women's history has concluded:

> women's history challenges mainstream history not to substitute the chronicle of the female subject for that of the male, but rather to restore conflict, ambiguity and tragedy to the centre of historical process: to explore the varied and unequal terms upon which genders, classes and races participate in the forging of a common destiny.[2]

Because women have been so marginal in the consciousness of those who have researched events, their significance has remained hidden within historical records, waiting for the understanding of someone who wants to know what women did, what they thought, and how they were affected by the upheavals of the past century. Although women's history clearly reveals the importance of the powerless in contributing to the success of those who became powerful, this contribution has at times been deliberately played down, and not just simply undervalued. To give serious consideration to their role involves a reappraisal of the reasons for their subsequent exclusion from political and economic life and some soul-searching on the part of those who continue to uphold the primary importance of women's domestic role.

While women were undoubtedly valuable and valiant fighters within the nationalist movement, one important qualification needs to be kept in mind when reading about their activities: the high points of women's participation were also moments of exceptional political crisis, when women were either drawn into the movement because of the temporary (enforced) absence of men, or they were encouraged to participate because a strong, united front was desperately needed, and because women, when the military struggle began, were also needed for essential back-up services. At no stage were they accepted as equal members, as a closer examination of the role of those who seem to have transcended this limitation clearly demonstrates.

The one nationalist women's organisation which was completely independent—Inghinidhe na hEireann—was formed because of women's exclusion from all other groups, and it existed during a period of general regroupment, when women's mobilisation was not even contemplated. The members of Inghinidhe had to fight for the right of women to participate alongside men; in effect, to alter the dominant consciousness concerning women's role within society. Although they were successful, it was—like the formation of Cumann na mBan—only a partial victory in that women were then carefully consigned to the role of subordinates and given no real opportunity to influence the direction of the movement. Neither were they encouraged to put forward their own demands, in case these conflicted with, or diverted, the general thrust of nationalist concerns.

But there is another dimension to this study: the determined struggles that were waged by women on their own behalf, both by women within the nationalist movement and by those critical feminists who remained on the outside. The tensions this generated between opposing groups of women and, on occasion, between women and their male colleagues, are again echoed today as we live through another cycle of the nationalist struggle. And that, primarily, is why this book has been written.

The contradictions between nationalism and feminism continue to overwhelm us, as the debate over whether or not the campaign for political status waged by the women prisoners in Armagh jail was a feminist issue, so painfully confirmed. Many feminists were emotionally torn between their desire to support the sufferings endured by the women, and their concern lest this feminist solidarity be translated into unconditional support for the Provisionals. And, unhappily, women within Sinn Fein who are fighting for greater equality for women, isolated as they so obviously are, felt betrayed at the lack of public support by the feminist movement. If any realignment of feminists is ever to be achieved, we will have to start by honestly confronting these conflicting allegiances. One way to begin is to see what happened to our sisters of another generation. This book does not claim to contain the answers, but I hope it can provide a frame of reference by which we can begin to formulate the questions. I also hope that it provides a stimulus for other feminist historians, so that in the future a much fuller account of the history of Irish women will be available to us all.

1. The Ladies' Land League, 1881-82

On 31 January 1881 a remarkable event took place. On that day Irishwomen were asked by Irishmen to take control of the turbulent mass movement known as the Land League. The Land War was then at its height, with thousands of tenant farmers pledged to fight against rack rents and landlord power, and the League leaders knew it was only a matter of time before they were jailed. The formation of a female organisation, which would be outside the terms of the Coercion Act, was therefore essential. Although the men considered women capable only of providing a 'semblance' of organisation, the gesture would symbolise their determination not to submit meekly to coercion. So, for the first time in Irish history, women were given the opportunity to participate in a political movement and, in the absence of men, found themselves free to assert their own principles and to develop their own organisational skills. Although little had been expected of them, they quickly revealed a determination to provide far more than ineffectual defiance. For the next 18 months militant women directed the campaign and organised resistance on the ground. As Michael Davitt testified: 'Everything in the way of defeating the ordinary law and asserting the unwritten law of the League... was more systematically carried out under the direction of the ladies' executive than by its predecessor.'[1]

Yet very little has been written about this unique period and Anna Parnell, the driving force behind the Ladies' Land League, is known only as the sister of Charles Stewart Parnell, hero of the Land League and, at one time, the 'uncrowned king of Ireland'. The women's contribution was carefully expurgated from most contemporary accounts, and with good reason: to have given serious consideration to their work would have involved a more critical appraisal of the Land League itself, and that was something many of the male leaders, busy congratulating themselves upon their success, preferred not to do.

The women's assessment of the situation reveals an uncomfortably different picture, while their activities demonstrated that women were both fully capable of leading a mass movement and could be more efficient and strategically aware than their male colleagues. The rediscovery of Anna Parnell's history of the period—the caustically entitled 'The Land League: Tale of a Great Sham', written to stem this flood of male self-congratulation—has helped to redress the balance. It is a scrupulously impersonal narrative of events, in which she completely effaces her own contribution.[2] One historian has, although disagreeing with her conclusions, praised the 'crystal clarity and surgical precision' of her analysis.[3] Its long disappearance enabled a single interpretation of events to remain dominant, which has not only distorted historical understanding, but has led to repercussions of which later generations of women have been only partially aware. The uncompromising stance of the women left a bitter taste in the mouths of male politicians and they were determined to ensure that women would never again be given the power that had been handed to the Ladies' Land League. An awareness of the history of the Ladies' Land League places into perspective the difficulties encountered by other women who later fought for a full and active role within the nationalist movement.

The Parnell Sisters

The Parnells came from a Protestant landed family of moderate wealth. Out of eleven children, three—Anna, Fanny and Charles Stewart—were to devote their lives to the cause of Irish independence. It was an unusual path for members of the Protestant ascendancy in Ireland, but much of their inspiration came from their American mother, Delia, who was deeply anti-British. Fanny, a well-known writer of nationalist poetry, had attended O'Donovan Rossa's trial after the Fenian rising of 1867, and she retained a sympathy for Fenianism which was never shared by her brother. Her poems, in particular 'Hold the Harvest', described by Davitt as 'the Marseillaise of the Irish peasant', gave her a fame which lasted long after her death. Her poetry was published in newspapers in Ireland, England and America, while in Ireland lockets containing her portrait were sold for a shilling.[4] While Anna and Fanny did not entirely share the same political views—Anna realised that the physical force tradition completely excluded women from its ranks—they both felt the injustice of women's sexual oppression.

The period in which they lived offered few socially productive opportunities for women of their class. Ireland was a predominantly rural country with a peasant economy; the basic economic unit was the household, all the members of which worked on the land or in the declining cottage industries, which were adversely affected by the Industrial Revolution taking place in Britain. Only the north provided any large-scale wage labour for women: the Belfast linen industry had a 75 per cent female workforce. But for upper-class women, the role of governess was the only acceptable outlet, and that was a last resort for those without an inheritance.

The Parnell sisters' position as unmarried daughters from a relatively impoverished Protestant landed family had certain advantages: the family was not part of the conservative Irish Catholic tradition and neither did it hold a particularly important position in the social and economic structures of the country. Delia's American influence was also important: a contemporary account reveals that Anna was a regular reader of New York and Boston journals, and well acquainted with the views of the early American feminists who were fighting against slavery and for the rights of women.[5]

As a young girl living at home, she made friends with the Catholic daughters of a local miller, but broke off the friendship because she found them too conservative in their views, especially in their uncritical acceptance of church teaching on the natural inferiority of women. Her independence of mind made close relationships difficult; only Fanny shared her views.

Although Anna studied painting in Paris (where she was accompanied by her mother) and later attended art college in England, she had no hope of ever achieving financial independence. Her income consisted of a small allowance of £100 a year, derived from the Collure estate of another brother, John Howard, and provided by the terms of her father's will. All the boys inherited property while the girls of the family received identical allowances. Charles, as the inheritor of the family estate of Avondale, was responsible for the support of any member of the family living there. This economic dependence was a humiliation, and Anna wrote with bitterness of the custom of the upper classes of 'giving all, or nearly all, to the sons and little or nothing to the daughters'.[6] The allowances received by such women were usually at the mercy of the family fortunes—if these declined, then one of the first economies was to cut off these stipends. Anna empathised with the ignominy of their position, left to the mercy of charitable funds and 'little less the victims of the landlords than the tenants themselves'.

As a landlord—albeit a benevolent one—Charles Parnell remained unequivocally a member of his class. Anna, however, became more and more critical of the existing social structures. Her alienation was a consequence of her realisation that, as a dependant of her brother, she was simultaneously of the landlord class and estranged from and exploited by it. Her denunciation of her class was couched in terms which did not exclude her brother: 'if the Irish landlords had not deserved extinction for anything else, they would have deserved it for the treatment of their own women.' Few women of similar background saw so clearly the links between their sexual oppression and the class exploitation of labourers and small farmers which underpinned the social and economic structures.

Anna, because of her sex, was deprived of the right to vote or to take political office—a disenfranchisement she acutely resented, as her sardonically entitled *Notes From The Ladies' Cage* testifies. This was a series of articles, written for the *Celtic Monthly*, evaluating the Irish party's performance in the House of Commons at Westminster; this she witnessed from the secluded gallery where women were allowed to view the proceedings, but not to participate.[7] An Irish Suffrage Society had been formed in Dublin, in 1876, by two Quakers, Anna and Thomas Haslam, to campaign for women's right to vote in local government elections. Its limited aims and moderate views had little appeal for women who wanted a total reform of Irish society and the breaking of the enforced political and economic link with Britain. Anna's exclusion from political life had a paradoxically positive aspect, enabling her to analyse events unswayed by any considerations of future personal power. While Parnell was courted by the English Liberals, his sister became an uncompromising nationalist, refusing to surrender political principles for short-term personal or political gains.

The formation of the Land League

There had been movements centred around land distribution and high rents before, but none had welded small tenant farmers, large farmers, landless labourers, parliamentarians and politically committed women into a social force which would ultimately change a land system in which 800 landlords owned half the country. Different economic circumstances, combined with a change in political direction, were to create the conditions from which the Land League emerged.

The Great Famine of 1845 had left 800,000 dead while hundreds of thousands fled from the scene of such horror. This decimation of the population had many consequences. People were determined to prevent such a catastrophe from ever happening again, and the only way of doing that (in the absence of a revolutionary transformation of society) was to reduce the numbers of people dependent upon each plot of land. In the east and south of the country, the small farms had been consolidated into larger ranches, bought up by those who had survived, but in the west the peasants still scraped out a living on their tiny plots of land, the potato still their staple diet. Although it was, in some respects, a pre-Famine existence, they too postponed marriage to a later age and no longer subdivided the land for their sons and daughters, so afraid were they of the consequences of rearing large numbers of children on a food that had once been tainted with blight. Those who had emigrated wrote of the better land they had found, and dissatisfaction grew amongst those at home. Unlike before, the poorest sections of the peasantry were now aware of the disparities between their way of life and that of those who did not have to eke out a miserable living on barren soil, with no security of tenure, paying rents to often absent landlords for an amount far beyond their means. Gradually rising expectations, cruelly frustrated by a new series of disastrous harvests, focused their hopes upon the Land League.

The season of 1879 was the worst experienced by Irish farmers since the Famine. The potato crop, valued at £12,000,000 in 1876, plummeted to £3,500,000. The larger cattle farmers were also suffering as American competition in grain, which was now pouring out of the recently cultivated prairies, affected the whole of western Europe and Irish farmers were no longer able to sell their crops to the British market. Seasonal migrants couldn't find work in Scotland or England, a loss of earnings which in the west of Ireland alone was reckoned at £250,000.[8] As there was no work for them at home, their support for the Land League was inevitable. Shopkeepers and businessmen in the towns identified with the plight of the farming community, because if the farmers couldn't afford to buy, those who depended on their trade would be financially wiped out.

Social discontent was widespread, and it was at this point that an alliance was formed between those who believed in physical force, the Fenians, and a section of the Irish party at Westminster, led by Charles Stewart Parnell. Devoy, the leader of the American Fenians, together with Michael Davitt, a Mayo man recently released from jail, reached an agreement with Parnell in June 1879 by which the campaign on the land question would have as its central aim the demand for peasant proprietorship. The Fenians believed that no British government would concede this demand, so the League would eventually be forced to transform itself into a movement for national independence. Therefore, what appeared on the surface to be a purely economistic movement had the potential to become an instrument of revolutionary nationalism. For his part, Parnell wanted to form an all-class movement to campaign for Home Rule—a limited form of self-government—and he believed that this would only be achieved when the land question had been resolved. As far as he was concerned, the Land League was not a revolutionary challenge to the exploitative landlord system, but a vehicle to reform its most glaring abuses. Once that had been accomplished, landlords would unite with tenants to fight for Irish political independence. He was therefore careful not to offend the larger landed interests while aiming at this all-class alliance, and he avoided discussions on such radical problems as landless labourers or land redistribution. For the same reason, he was against calling for a full-scale rent strike, because the more prosperous farmers would not have agreed to any actions which would leave them liable to eviction—they were in secure possession of their farms and what they wanted was a reduction in rent. On the other hand, Anna Parnell and some of the more radical members of the Land League believed that in the early part of 1880, while the League was in the ascendant and morale was high, the policy of rent strike would have had some chance of success. It was certainly the only time when it could have been reasonably adopted as a tactic.

Davitt had formed the Mayo Land League on 16 August 1879. That summer, blight appeared in the potato fields and excessive rain ruined the harvest. The threat of eviction increased. A central body to direct and co-ordinate resistance was essential so, on 21 October, the Irish National Land League, with Parnell as its president, came into existence. Its objects were declared to be the reduction of rack rents and the ownership of the soil by the occupiers of the soil.[9]

The first battle against eviction took place at Carraroe, Connemara, on 5 January 1880, when bailiffs, escorted by armed police, attempted to evict impoverished peasants for failure to pay their rent. It was a 'bloody conflict', with the police using bayonets and firing volleys over the heads of the crowd. The 'fierce daring' women who led the resistance displayed what observers felt to be 'utter recklessness of life', and they forced the police and bailiffs to withdraw.[10] But although the people won that round of the battle the police were quick to alter their tactics so that bailiffs could complete eviction processes. The Land League needed an alternative method of resistance, one which did not depend on the willingness of peasants physically to resist the armed forces of the law.

There had been 1,238 evictions in 1879 and by the following year half the peasants in Connacht were in danger of eviction as a result of the failure of the potato crop for the fourth successive season. When the House of Lords rejected a bill which would have given compensation to those evicted as a result of bad harvests, the League decided upon a policy of obstruction. If the landlord didn't agree to a reduction in rent, the tenant was to pay only 'at the point of a bayonet'. This entailed holding out until the land was seized by the bailiffs, while at the same time making seizure as difficult as possible by hiding cattle and blocking roads. The Land League pledged itself to pay the legal costs incurred, while the tenant then paid the rent arrears. It was an expensive policy and one which did little to weaken the power of the landlord; the League was raising money which would ultimately go into the landlord's pocket. Although tenants were refusing to pay more than a 'fair rent', an average reduction of 20 per cent benefited only the larger farmers.[11] The uneconomical size of the holdings of the poorer peasants meant that they were simply unable to pay any rent. Although evictions were not prevented, linked to the obstructionist tactic was what became known as the 'boycott', which isolated land-grabbers and made life so unpleasant for them that it was hoped no one would want to buy up a farm after the previous tenant had been evicted, and the landlord would eventually be forced to take back the original occupant. By the end of 1880, as the Land League grew in strength, the numbers of evictions decreased.

The government decided to prosecute the League leaders for conspiracy in preventing payment of rent and with resisting eviction processes. At their trial in January 1881, Fanny Parnell's poem 'Hold the Harvest' constituted a major part of the prosecution's case, with its passionate appeal to the peasants to be 'bold and stern' in deed, 'and set your faces as a flint, and swear to hold your own'.[12]

Although the outcome was an acquittal, it was not a victory. The government's real intention had been to demonstrate that ordinary law was ineffectual in dealing with subversive movements and they now had the excuse they wanted to do away with the necessity for trial by jury. On 2 March, the Protection of Person and Property (Ireland) Bill, giving 'absolute power of arbitrary and preventative arrest', became law. This coercion act meant that the League would be proscribed and its leaders jailed. The Land Leaguers were faced with two options: either to allow the land agitation to die down for lack of leadership once the government had their leaders arrested, or to devise an alternative form of leadership. The latter meant that they would have, in other words, to enlist the help of women.

The origins of the Ladies' Land League

While the Land League was steadily growing in strength Delia, Fanny and Anna Parnell were living in America and working for the relief of famine in Ireland. The greater freedom of American society enabled them to work for the Irish cause in a public manner that was unknown in Ireland. Fanny had written a poem ('Ireland, Mother') describing the anguish of a woman wanting to participate, yet unable to do so—'I am a woman, I can do naught for thee, Ireland, mother!'—and now, at last, she had the opportunity. Parnell and John Dillon, another MP and Land League leader, had been on a tour of America which raised £60,000 for famine relief and £12,000 for the League, but the level of donations had slowed down since their departure. Fanny and Anna were working ten hours a day on the relief committee, but that alone was not enough. Fanny decided that what was required was to set the women to work, and by this 'much needed stimulus would be given to the men'.[13] On 12 August 1880, she wrote a letter to the *Irish World* and other American newspapers, describing the desperate situation in Ireland and calling for the formation of a sister organisation to support the Land League. A New York woman, Jane Byrne, answered Fanny's plea and the two of them decided to form a New York Ladies' Land League. The first meeting was held on 15 October and was attended by 50 women, including Ellen Ford, the daughter of the editor of the *Irish World*, who became vice-president of the League. Delia Parnell was elected president, a collection of $100 taken up and immediately sent off to Ireland, and the women settled down to plan an energetic programme of work.[14]

Branches soon sprang up in other parts of the country and Fanny embarked on an exhausting tour of the north-eastern states and Canada, raising thousands of dollars for relief. But she was only too well aware of the fact that fund-raising alone was insufficient and that the real solution lay in the agitation being carried out in Ireland. On 1 January 1881, the Dublin newspaper *Nation* published a letter from her in which she urged the women of Ireland to form a similar movement which could take over if the men were imprisoned. Although some women had written to her of their eagerness to take part in such a movement, they didn't respond to this appeal. Lacking the cooler, more analytical judgement of her sister, Fanny fretted over what she considered the timidity of Irishwomen. She lamented that 'not having any leader they remained feeble and obscure', while the situation worsened with the passing of the Coercion Act in March.[15]

Anna, on the other hand, appreciated the difficulties facing women who wished to become politically active; the situation in Ireland was entirely different from the ease of American life and their work would involve not only considerable danger, but also hostility from family and friends. When the Ladies' Land League (Ireland) came to be formed, Anna was the obvious choice for organising secretary, most of all because she understood the necessity of fostering women's confidence in their abilities. Davitt had persuaded the other leaders to agree to the formation of a female organisation and Anna was asked to undertake the work. With considerable misgivings about her own abilities, she returned to Ireland at the end of 1880. She was 28 years of age.

The formation of the Ladies' Land League

When Davitt broached his idea to the other leaders he had a hard time persuading them to agree. They feared they would be open to 'public ridicule' if they were seen relying on women to organise public agitation. Finally they accepted this 'most dangerous experiment', only because no one could think of a feasible alternative. Davitt, however, was full of enthusiasm and extolled the women's merits to his reluctant colleagues:

> No better allies than women could be found for such a task. They are, in certain emergencies, more dangerous to despotism than men. They have more courage, through having less scruples, when and where their better instincts are appealed to by a militant and just cause in a fight against a mean foe.[16]

Most of the men maintained their reservations about the advisability of this move, but there was one other man who, after meeting Anna, agreed without hesitation to the plan. This was Andrew Kettle, a man whose undeviating loyalty to Parnell makes his testimony to Anna's abilities even more convincing. He considered her to have:

> a better knowledge of the lights and shades of Irish peasant life, of the real economic conditions of the country, and of the social and political forces which had to be acted upon to work out the freedom of Ireland than any person, man or woman, I have ever met... Anna Parnell would have worked the Land League revolution to a much better conclusion than her great brother.[17]

Throughout her life Anna remained adamant that she had not been consulted beforehand about the formation of the Ladies' Land League. Soon after its inauguration she declared that 'Mr Davitt settled it all in his own mind, and then he informed the world that I was going to do it, to carry his ideas out, and never asked my consent at all.'[18] Her memoirs also insist that her only notification was a letter informing her of the decision and asking her to take charge of the office in Dublin.[19] This evidence that Anna never had the opportunity to discuss policy with the male leaders—she was simply handed the key to the office and left to her own devices—becomes, with the benefit of hindsight, extremely significant. No guidance was ever given as to the course of action to be undertaken and the women were left to discover for themselves the state of Land League affairs. The men, of course, didn't believe the women would be capable of a great deal—John Dillon, Parnell's fiery young lieutenant, who was MP for Tipperary, wanted the women to be a charitable group, although he had been outspoken in his calls for a rent strike. Even Davitt's initial expectations of their abilities was not much greater; as well as being the 'medium for charity', they would 'keep up a semblance of organisation during the attempted repression'.[20] But they hadn't reckoned on the formidable powers of Anna Parnell. Not only were the women going to take over the direction of the movement, they were going to infuse new life into the campaign of resistance and, indeed, redefine 'resistance' itself. Charity was insufficient—'the programme of a permanent resistance until the aim of the League shall be attained, was the only logical one', as Anna so forthrightly declared.

The Ladies' Land League begins to organise

On 31 January 1881, the Ladies' Land League was formally instituted. Davitt was rearrested the following day, his ticket of leave revoked, but he found comfort by thinking of the 'power that had been raised up for Mr Forster (Chief Secretary for Ireland) to grapple with.'[21] On 4 February, the executive council issued a call to their countrywomen which left no one in any doubt that the women were taking their new position seriously and were preparing to challenge the whole landlord system:

> You cannot prevent the evictions, but you can and must prevent them from becoming massacres. Form yourselves into branches of the Ladies' National Land League. Be ready to give information of evictions in your districts, to give advice and encouragement to the unhappy victims, to collect funds, and to apply those which may be entrusted to you as emergencies arise.[22]

Anna was only one of a remarkable group of women organisers who now emerged. In addition to Anna, those who put their names to that first address were: Clare Stritch, Hannah Lynch and Harriet Byrne—all secretaries of the League; Mrs Moloney and Miss O'Leary—treasurers; Mrs Dean, Dillon's aunt, was honorary president; among the organisers were Mrs Margaret Moore (an American), Miss Hanna Reynolds, Miss Mary O'Connor and Miss Yates. Helen Sullivan, whose husband owned the *Nation*, was a committee member, as was Jenny Wyse Power, the widow of a Fenian. The writer Katharine Tynan, also a member, although a self-confessed 'frivolous one', described them as having 'grown up among the writers, thinkers, orators, politicians, conspirators of their day'.[23] Ellen O'Leary's brother John had served a nine-year jail sentence for Fenian activities, Mary O'Connor's brother was one of the youngest MPs in the Irish party, while the Land League had been planned in the home of two other women activists—Bee and Margaret Walsh, from Balla, County Mayo. Hannah Lynch had gone to convent school abroad and travelled extensively as a governess, an experience the women were to find extremely useful. As well as the executive, there was a reserve executive of 21 women, prepared to take the place of anyone arrested. When the arrests did begin, Fanny sent over three American women to augment their forces.

Anna's misgivings about her ability to co-ordinate and inspire the Ladies' Land League were due mainly to her realisation of the difficulties involved in this unique opportunity now open to Irishwomen to work independently, without the guidance of those whom they had been accustomed to 'trust and to look to for help' (as she had once indignantly described women's dependent status). If women proved themselves capable of meeting the challenge, they would have succeeded in wresting a place for themselves in political life. She saw her first task as instilling self-confidence into the women who were beginning to offer their services—'You must learn to depend upon yourselves and to do things for yourselves and to organise yourselves.'[24] At a public meeting a few months later she had gained enough confidence to be able to remark, with barbed humour, 'I observe that we have succeeded today in getting rid of the men nearly entirely—and I am sure that we all feel much more comfortable in consequence.'[25]

Anna was also uncompromising in her refusal to be characterised in a traditional female role. When a resolution at a meeting applauded her for being 'prepared to work as well as weep', she retorted, with some asperity, that she would leave the weeping to the men.[26] Her unconcealed hostility towards men was reflected in the course the Land War now took. She urged women to pay for all groceries with cash, so that their husbands would be unable to save the money for rent payment. As women lacked any legal entitlements and therefore did not pay the rent (unless they were widows, or unmarried daughters left with the family farm), any blame for the conduct of resistance to rent must, in the women's eyes, fall upon the men.

Anna's initial dislike of the men had rapidly increased as a result of the frustration the women were experiencing in their efforts to bring some order to the chaos of League affairs. Their central office in Upper Sackville Street was shared with the Land League, and existing Land League branches were supposed to encourage the formation of women's branches. However, the women were left to their own devices in determining how best to continue the resistance to rent, the men's assistance confining itself to allowing the women access to the files containing the names and addresses of the principal local officials. This was not the greatest of help. The day before his arrest, Parnell had received a report from one of his organisers describing the demoralisation that was increasing daily and the confusion that existed in the League's affairs, with some active branches not being recorded in the files at all.[27] The women decided to start from scratch and began to compile a *Book of Kells*, which was a huge dossier of every estate in Ireland, containing records of tenants, rents, evictions, the character of the landlord and the morale of the people. 'The most perfect system that can be imagined', was Davitt's high praise.[28] Unfortunately, all the records of the Ladies' Land League were later destroyed, whether by themselves or by others is not known.[29]

One major difficulty was attracting women who would be able to tour the country, building up branches and directing resistance on the ground, because few families in those Victorian days were prepared to allow their daughters such a degree of freedom. The qualities required were daunting, particularly when one considers the lack of educational opportunities and social experience available to women. They were expected to deal with intricate legal and agricultural matters, while facing hostility from press and clergy and the armed force of army and police. Anna considered 'tact, firmness, commonsense... powers of observation and natural aptitude for judging character' to be indispensable, as well as youth, physical strength and endurance, because 'long distances were to be travelled; exposure to weather was inevitable; and in most parts of Ireland there was very poor accommodation for travellers.' While the tireless energies of this small group of full-time organisers more than compensated for their lack of numbers, their ranks were soon to be swelled by the addition of scores of women in local areas who volunteered their services to the League.

Their major task was to support the evicted and prevent land-grabbing. When notice was received from a local branch concerning threatened eviction, one of the organisers would then travel to the scene with a supply of money for immediate assistance. Whenever possible, a wooden hut was erected to shelter the evicted family; this had the added advantage of placing them in a position to deter potential land-grabbers. In one year they provided 210 huts,[30] although they were eventually forced to have them transported from Dublin as those built locally were, as a local secretary wrote to Anna, 'splendid monuments to the spirit of the people, but quite unfit for human habitation'. The men were never as keen on the erection of Land League huts as the women, possibly considering it too much bother and of little consequence to the overall campaign. The women, however, were not motivated solely by humanitarian considerations. They believed those crude wooden constructions powerfully symbolised that 'all power did not lie with the foreign enemy in possession of the country'. Parnell certainly never thought in those terms.

In her memoirs, Anna states her surprise at the reluctance of the Land League leaders to initiate an all-out resistance to rent payment. Although she had an 'uncomfortable feeling' that their preparations were less than adequate, at this stage it hadn't occured to her that preparations had not been made because the men had no intention of stepping up the campaign. An awareness of the true situation soon dawned upon her—the Ladies' Land League was only expected to maintain a 'semblance' of organisation because that was all that the Land League itself had achieved. She later bitterly remarked that if the faintest suspicion of this had crossed her mind, she would never have consented to undertake the work. But there was no going back, the men clung to them as 'Pharaoh clung to the children of Israel', and they were reluctant to throw the tenant farmers back on the mercy of the landlords.

Nevertheless, as the women's understanding of the situation grew, they became convinced that in attempting to build a genuine resistance they were reversing the policy of the League and 'raising forlorn hopes in the people'. Money was draining away so rapidly in eviction costs and in supporting those tenants who paid only when the sheriff arrived to remove them from the properties. This expenditure ensured that the 'point of a bayonet' policy could not continue indefinitely. The cost of resistance to rent payment was often greater than the rent itself, and as the rent was ultimately paid, in the case of those who could afford it, the League was doing little more than raise money for the landlord. Although the Land League frequently urged farmers to refuse all reductions in rent which did not include all the tenants on the same estate, if the landlord refused, the individual tenant paid up anyway, arguing that there was no point in rejecting his own arrangement as it wouldn't benefit the other tenants. The more prosperous tenants were therefore able to win a settlement while the poor went, as usual, to the wall. The class differences within the League were beginning to become apparent. As well as this, the women were shocked to discover that applications for relief were coming, not from those who had obeyed League policy and had suffered eviction for refusing to pay more than a reasonable rent, but from those who had simply been unable to pay any rent at all. If that continued, the League would lose all its agitational impetus and become yet another charitable agency.

When a Land League branch secretary wrote to them saying that there was not 'a single tenant in Ireland who would not pay the rent if he could', the true reality of the situation was inescapable. Over the next few months, the women struggled to establish control. Adequate preparation was almost impossible, due as much to the disarray of the organisation as to their limited resources; they could not spare enough women to travel around the country acquiring knowledge of local conditions. As a result, they had to be very liberal with their grants to evicted tenants, 'deserving' or otherwise, in order to boost people's morale and overcome their fear of the result of eviction. This was the reasoning behind their reliance upon Land League huts, and another reason for the men's lack of interest—the latter, not having a fighting strategy, were not particularly concerned in providing shelter to the victims of evictions. All this was necessary, but it was expensive, and when the time came for the men to insist upon the women's dissolution, their supposed extravagence was held up as a cardinal sin.

The women had barely begun to gather together their forces when the expected arrests of the men started. By the end of March, 40 arrests had been made; Dillon was arrested in April and, by May, Brennan, the League secretary, had joined him. In August, the British government passed legislation guaranteed to ensure the continued disintegration of the movement. This was a Land Act, containing provision for fair rent, fixity of tenure and free sale. But leaseholders and those in rent arrears were excluded, and the land courts, set up to implement the act, were weighted in favour of the landlord. The omission of leaseholders meant that one-sixth of the Irish peasantry were outside the benefit of the act, and the vital, radical question of land redistribution was ignored. Parnell had been forced to alter League policy from the discredited (and expensive) 'rent at the point of a bayonet' to letting the farms go. This meant that tenants who had not made substantial improvements to their farms, and who had not been offered a reduction in rent, would leave them to be snapped up by the landlord's agents. It was hoped that, because of the boycott system, the landlord would eventually be forced to take back the original tenants. Although this was potentially a sound strategy, it was doomed to failure once the Land Act came into operation. The Land Act exposed the contradictions contained in the all-class alliance of the League—those who abandoned their farms would not benefit from the Act, and the larger farmers refused to forfeit any possible gains.[31] The only groups to continue to have confidence in the League—perhaps because they had no alternative—were the small peasantry and the landless labourers.

The male leaders decided to 'test the Act' by bringing cases which would show up its inadequacies, while at the same time placating those farmers who did want to bring their claims to the land court. It was a tactical move to maintain unity while continuing to put pressure on the government. The women's attitude was quite different. Fanny wrote a poem about the Land Act which made her feelings plain:

Tear up the parchment lie!
Scatter its fragments to the hissing wind—
And hear again the People's first and final cry:
No more for you, O Lords, we'll dig and grind;

No more for you the Castle, and for us the Stye![32]

Anna's views were characteristically forthright: the act was absurd and worthless and the fight would go on.

Prime Minister Gladstone had no intention of allowing his act to be sabotaged, and the arrests continued. On 13 October, Parnell himself was interned in Kilmainham, and, on 20 October, the Land League was declared a proscribed organisation. After months of preparation for this eventuality, the women finally found themselves on their own.

On their own

Parnell's arrest had occurred at a fortunate political moment for him. In a letter to his mistress, Kitty O'Shea, he wrote, 'the movement is breaking fast and all will be quiet in a few months when I shall be released.'[33] Once in jail, he issued the 'No-Rent Manifesto', against the advice of more radical members of the League, who felt it was far too late. Anna was furious—the Ladies' Land League was placed in an impossible position by this manifesto, issued without their knowledge or consent, which was nothing more than a cover whereby the male leaders could withdraw from the impasse they had placed themselves in, while at the same time maintaining a fiction of a continued opposition. The implication of the 'No-Rent Manifesto' was that the League's money was now to go only to those tenants who were genuinely supporting the no-rent call, but it was becoming more and more difficult to determine when to pay out and when not to pay. At this point Anna took over control of finances, refusing to consult with the Land League treasurer, Egan, who had escaped jail by going to Paris.[34] The incarceration of the leaders saved their reputation by minimising their responsibility for failure, while the women were left with the unenviable task of trying to 'make ropes of sea sand'.

That July, in an effort to cut down the enormous expenses which were draining away funds, the Ladies' Land League had been forced to inform branches that the League could no longer pay costs for tenants buying in their farms—if they wanted, they could buy them at their own expense, but if they gave up their claim they would be supported by the League after eviction.

The women's workload was now doubled. Not only were they helping evicted families and supervising the building of Land League huts for those who had been left homeless, they also had to provide for the steadily increasing numbers of prisoners and their dependants. At the same time, they were also attempting to extend the campaign of resistance. Between October 1881 and May 1882, they paid out a total of nearly £70,000.[35] This was not undue extravagance: in June 1881, Thomas Sexton, another League leader, had pointed out that a large expenditure would be necessary for some time to come and, in that month alone, the Land League had spent almost £3,000.[36] By November, the amount of money required to provide one meal a day for all the prisoners was calculated at £400 a week. To cope with this, Anna established a separate Political Prisoners Aid Society, which was presided over at its first meeting by Helen Taylor, the step-daughter of John Stuart Mill.[37] As its officers were all prominent Ladies' Land League members, the women now had an additional burden. By Christmas, the society had collected £9,000—but the total cost of the prisoners during the lifetime of the Ladies' Land League was in excess of £21,000.

Newspapers were predictably scathing about the ability of women to direct a campaign. *The Times* sneered, 'when treason is reduced to fighting behind petticoats and pinafores it is not likely to do much mischief.'[38] This unheard of phenomenon of a group of women flouting all conventions by taking over a movement which was regarded as dangerous and subversive, excited the attention of the British and Irish press, but, as *The Times* reporter reassured his readers, although it would be impossible to refuse the 'lady agitators' a hearing, the women could hardly become part of the wider political movement because, 'it will hardly be to the ladies that the men will look for real advice and guidance in the crisis at which they now find themselves.' Underlying this assessment was a barely disguised fear that the women might, in the future, be consulted by the men. It was bad enough to have women carrying on in this way while the men were absent, but of much greater threat to all men—supporters or opponents of the League—was the prospect that the women would be given status as political equals.

The women were not getting a good press. Six months

earlier, they had provoked an hysterical outburst from Archbishop McCabe of Dublin, who condemned those women who were prepared to 'forget the modesty of their sex and the high dignity of their womanhood' by parading themselves 'before the public gaze in a character unworthy of a child of Mary'.[39] Although the individualistic Croke, Archbishop of Cashel, challenged the 'monstrous imputations' cast upon the women, the general violent antipathy towards the Ladies' Land League had the rare consequence of briefly uniting Protestant and Catholic. The (Protestant) *Belfast News-Letter* attacked the 'distasteful spectacle of women making a harangue from a public platform', with Anna being singled out for special condemnation. The editor made no bones about his views on women activists: 'Sensible people in the North of Ireland dislike to see woman out of the place she is gifted to occupy, and at no time is woman further from her natural position than when she appears upon a political platform.'[40]

Another revolutionary upheaval which the women's intervention had brought about affected that traditional feature of Irish political life—the mass meeting. It was an exclusively male practice, in terms both of speakers and audience. Few women attended noisy public gatherings and those who did, stayed at the back. But now that women had come into the public arena, observers noticed that the ordinary woman no longer viewed the proceedings 'at a respectful distance', but thronged around the platform as if she had a right to be there.[41] It was clearly a development that few men welcomed.

Although Anna addressed public meetings all around the country, she never concealed her distaste for the emotionalism they provoked. She regarded it as a peculiarly male form of demagoguery to incite crowds to frenzied cheers, regardless of the content of the speech. One report described her as 'a young lady of prepossessing appearance, who appeared in black, and who spoke slowly and quietly'.[42] She disliked mass meetings because they prevented any explanation or discussion upon issues, and always maintained that the most effective method of putting a message across was by holding meetings at the scene of an eviction, where the necessity of resisting landlordism was powerfully displayed, and where discussion could be generated and a common policy reached.[43] There was without any doubt a genuine spirit of co-operation amongst the women who worked together—Katharine Tynan, although only an addresser of envelopes and occasional letter writer, remembered her Ladies' Land League days with great fondness, as being like 'an agreeable picnic', with 'hot tea cakes, bread and butter, jam puffs', contributed by the father of one woman and the husband of another.[44] But as well as this, Katharine also remembered Anna working until after midnight each night, then walking home alone—something no 'respectable' woman would ever have done.

Resistance continues

Although farmers were beginning to take their cases to the land courts, pockets of resistance continued, especially in the poorest areas of the country. The women decided to concentrate their energies into strengthening direct action against landlord power. In August, Anna was a prominent figure at evictions in Mitchelstown, County Tipperary, where she accompanied the sheriff on his rounds, rushing ahead to all the cottages to urge the tenants to stand firm. The police adopted a policy of harassment, and the Land League paper *United Ireland* now began to list weekly reports of meetings broken up by the police. These were countered by a strong determination to remain unintimidated, as this account of Margaret Moore's (an organiser) refusal to be silenced by a constable indicates:

> I defy you to interfere with me. I know the law much better than you do. (applause) You and the like of you try to trample people in country places and you must be taught your position. I will speak to those ladies as long as I like; the law which took the men's arms could not touch the women's tongues. (laughter) If I am acting illegally I shall take the consequences; but I warn you, you are liable to prosecution as a trespasser in this room. (applause).[45]

It was not long before the press stopped sneering at the 'petticoats and pinafores' as they were unwillingly forced to report the successes of the women:

> Whatever else may be said of the Ladies' Land League, one thing will be admitted, that Miss Reynolds, its representative, is a smart female who today made the West Cork eviction a laughing stock and foiled them in their efforts to collect rents. She has, within a few hours, wrought a most remarkable change in the disposition of the people in these parts.[46]

Before Hanna Reynolds arrived, the *Express* added, the people were 'as mild as lambs', but an hour after her appearance, they 'assumed the air of wolves'. She undertook to build huts and supply them with all the necessities if they refused to pay their rent, and with this support, the tenants unanimously agreed to stand by the League. Eighteen new branches of the Ladies' Land League were formed in September; the 3 December edition of *United Ireland* listed 34 branch meetings, some having attendances of between 100 and 200 women. Branches were also formed in many parts of England, with Helen Sullivan establishing a London headquarters in the Westminster Palace Hotel.[47] Children's branches were instituted, their main function being to teach children Irish history. All members of the Ladies' Land League resolved 'to encourage home manufacture in every possible way... and purchase no foreign goods while Irish can be obtained.'[48] In many of the activities they foreshadowed the work of later Irish separatists.

More and more women in rural areas came forward to offer their support; perhaps the arrest of the male members of the family left them free to do so, as they no longer had to seek their male relatives' consent first. Hanna Reynolds reported, in September, that 64 branches had been formed, including Glasgow, London, Liverpool and Manchester. By the beginning of 1882, there were over 500 branches.[49]

The women were fast becoming heroines in many people's eyes. When a branch of the children's league was broken up by the police, the children paraded through their village, cheering for 'Miss Parnell and the Land League'.[50] When a meeting of the Ladies' Land League ended in Macroom, County Cork, 'an immense crowd of young men' collected on the street opposite the women's rooms and as they filed out greeted them with cheers for 'Parnell, the Land League and the Ladies'. In the face of such support, the police didn't interfere.[51] But the women were completely capable of challenging the police without male support. When, in November, a meeting of 200 women in Ballinascreen was forbidden by the police, the women marched to a church one mile away and said the rosary. Although they were followed by the police they declared that they would say the rosary at the same place on every Sunday at 4 p.m.[52] Neither was the Herbertstown branch quelled, as their bloodthirsty resolution proved:

> Resolved—that those gallant extinguishers of their
> country's liberty, the Royal (anti) Irish Constabulary do
> merit the recognition of their masters and we would sug-
> gest that they be rewarded with medals of lead—that
> metal representing the attributes for which they are most
> conspicuous.[53]

Newspaper coverage of their activities was gradually increasing; on 10 December, *United Ireland* gave them the ultimate accolade of a front page cartoon, showing women with banners facing Forster, the chief secretary, along with police and army, the caption reading: 'Mr Forster sets up his Buggabow to intimidate the ladies of the Land League but they march steadily onwards in the good work, their courage daily increasing, as well as their power.' A song was also written about 'The Land League Ladies of Erin', the chorus of which went:

> Then shout, boys, hurrah, and raise your voices well,
> Long life to Miss Reynolds and also Miss Parnell,
> May every Irish woman help the ranks to swell
> The Ladies' Land League of old Ireland.[54]

The women were in fact achieving a considerable notoriety. At this time, Anna was engaged in a speaking and fund-raising tour throughout Scotland and England and Kitty O'Shea wrote to Parnell that Anna had been burnt in effigy, along with the Pope, outside her gate on Guy Fawkes Day. The Ladies' Land League was now so well known that, at a meeting in Liverpool, Anna told the audience that tenant farmers in parts of Mayo were afraid to be seen speaking to strange women, for fear they might be representatives of the Land League![55]

Cowper, the lord lieutenant, supreme representative of the

British government in Ireland, was extremely annoyed to discover that the Land League was not so 'completely broken down as imagined, [because] the work has been taken up by women [who] go about the country conveying messages and encouraging disaffection.' He wanted the cabinet to agree to what he ominously termed 'new measures'.[56] These were finally agreed upon, and, on 16 December 1881, the Ladies' Land League was also suppressed. The inspector general of constabulary announced that 'Where any females are assembled... such meeting is illegal.' It was no idle threat—Hanna Reynolds was immediately sentenced to one month's imprisonment for inciting a tenant of the Earl of Bantry not to pay rent.[57]

Defying the government

The women immediately decided to fight this attempt at coercion. A defiant letter was sent by the executive to all branches, calling on members to hold a meeting at 1.30 p.m. on Sunday 1 January 1882. They were determined to start the new year as militantly as possible. If any arrests were made, the meetings were to be continued every Sunday for as long as the government attempted to treat the Ladies' Land League as an illegal organisation.[58]

The response was tremendous, with mass meetings held all over the country. Jenny Wyse Power, who was to become a veteran campaigner for national independence, justifiably claimed this stance as 'the first time when Britain's power to "proclaim" was not only questioned but defied.'[59] As one observer said, 'Five thousand ladies of Ireland were calling on the government to arrest them and were preaching Land League doctrines as they were never preached before.'[60]

Although the Ladies' Land League continued to counsel resistance, their organisers were steadily being arrested. In January, Miss McCormick of the Dublin branch was sentenced to three months for being seen talking to an old woman in Tulla who was about to be evicted.[61] Margaret Daly, Mary Wall, Ellen Hannigan and Annie McAuliffe of the Drumcollogher branch were all sentenced to one month for holding an illegal meeting of the League, but were released after two weeks. Two members of the Dunmanway branch—Mrs Crowley and Mary Ann Hurley—

were summonsed on charges of abusive behaviour, having called the police ruffians, perjurers, robbers and puppies.[62]

The women suffered the additional humiliation of being arrested under statutes designed to curb prostitution, rather than being treated as political prisoners like the men. T.P. O'Connor, Member of Parliament, visited his sister Mary, who was serving a six-month sentence in Mullingar jail. He was outraged at the severity of her treatment, which included being held in solitary confinement like the most 'degraded' of her sex. But he was even more astonished to find Mary 'quite collected and not in the least miserable', her only regret being 'the almost cowardly grief, as it appeared to her, with which her townspeople had followed her arrest and progress to gaol'.[63] The men were allowed almost free association, were secluded from the ordinary prisoners, and had so little restraint placed upon them that William O'Brien was able to continue editing *United Ireland* from his prison cell; the women were allowed no communication with each other at all. Even in the exercise yard they were forbidden the right of speaking as they walked round in single file. Of course, some of the male prisoners were Members of Parliament and men of status and their treatment reflected their privileged position—Parnell, who was getting all his food from the governor's kitchen, complained that he was getting fat. Women who challenged convention were not 'political' but outcasts from 'decent' society and treated as such—along with the prostitutes, pickpockets and vagrants.

The attempted repression backfired on the government as enthusiasm mounted and scores more women volunteered their services. An editorial in *United Ireland* indicated that the men felt deeply threatened by this implied loss of masculinity in having to depend on women, whose courageous stand put them to shame—the Land League after all had accepted its own proscription without a murmur:

> We only wish the men had done [their business] as stoutly, as regularly, and as fearlessly... Has Mr Forster any better means of coercing Irish men than those which Irish women laughed at? Are the suspects' prisons as bad as the solitary confinement which sensitive girls dared and went through with a smile? ...Is it easier to cow a nation

of men than a handful of women? Shall it be said that, while the Ladies' Land League met persecution by extending their organisation and doubling their activity and triumphing, the National Land League to which millions of men swore allegiance melted away and vanished the moment Mr Forster's policemen shook their batons at it?[64]

Many found this an ignominious reversal of role and an uneasiness with imprisonment—calmly accepted up to this time —began to develop.

Parnell had been over-hasty in his prediction to Kitty O'Shea of the rapid disintegration of the movement. Although nearing exhaustion, the women doggedly continued to battle on. They were now distributing *United Ireland*, which had a circulation of around 100,000. Hannah Lynch at one period managed to distribute 30,000 copies. The printers were eventually arrested and the women, not having printing as one of their 'accomplishments' (to use Anna's ironical phrase), had to rush over to Paris and arrange for the paper to be illicitly printed in France. Hannah Lynch, who undertook this work, found her previous experience as a governess in France of invaluable benefit in coping with the task. Few other women had the necessary language skills or contacts. It was a real achievement to maintain uninterrupted production as papers relating to League affairs had to be hidden all over the country and newspaper shops were constantly being raided. Mary Ann Hurley's abuse of the police had occurred when her father's shop was being raided for the paper.

The increase in repressive measures was gradually forcing the women to curtail their agitational activities. Their agents who attended evictions could not, without laying themselves open to immediate arrest, counsel resistance but had to confine themselves to making arrangements for shelter. But they were still imprisoned, as were the workmen who erected the shelters. One result of this imprisonment of the women who were able to travel around the countryside was that the League's sources of information were almost totally extinguished. Anna, on seeing the lord lieutenant ride down Westmoreland Street surrounded by an armed escort, gave vent to her frustration by leaping out and seizing the reins of his horse, angrily asking him to justify the decision of the government to prevent the building of Land League huts.[65]

For all their enthusiasm and commitment, the movement was losing cohesion as the more prosperous farmers applied to the land courts. Only the poor and the landless remained in wholehearted support of the League and they, in desperation, turned to violence as the only source of protest left. It was an attitude, if not encouraged by the women, certainly understood by them. They had done all that they could, only to see the movement no nearer its objective and confronted by a government that appeared able to resist their demands.

In the early days of 1882, the imprisoned male leaders had ordered the women to drop the no-rent call, but their instructions were ignored as the women decided that, ill-advised as the call had been, more harm would be done by suddenly changing policy. Parnell became increasingly alarmed that the League was being used 'not for the purposes he approved of, but for a real revolutionary end and aim', as Davitt scornfully remarked.[66] Forster was also alarmed, confessing to Gladstone that 'impunity from punishment is spreading like a plague.'[67] Although resistance to landlordism had decreased, agrarian crime soared—there had been 2,379 'outrages' in the ten months before the Coercion Act and this number increased to 3,821 in the next ten months.[68] The Ladies' Land League was given the credit for having instigated this new wave of crime and Davitt, in describing the effects of the women's handling of the situation, declared that the result was:

> more anarchy, more illegality, more outrages, until it began to dawn on some of the official minds that the imprisonment of the male leaders had only rendered confusion worse confounded for Dublin Castle, and made the country infinitely more ungovernable under the sway of their lady successors.[69]

He also charged them with having encouraged intimidation, and of characterising districts as 'courageous' or 'timid' according to how well they used the boycott—their financial help being dependent upon their approval of the fighting spirit of the area.

Anna later dismissed his book, *The Fall of Feudalism in Ireland* as 'a mass of lies', but Davitt wasn't condemning the women; on the contrary, he was one of the few allies they had. He does, however, overstate the degree to which the women were responsible for the violence—it was common practice in Ireland and there had always been plenty of secret societies to carry it out; still, the women's attitude towards it was certainly not the same as the men's. As a nationalist, Anna said simply that 'when people do not govern their own country, then responsibility for crime rests on the conqueror, i.e. England.'

The growing panic of both Parnell and the British government finally created a mutual bond between them: a desire to get rid of these unruly women. Negotiations began which eventually culminated in what became known as the 'Kilmainham Treaty' of 2 May 1882. By this, the government agreed to release the prisoners, deal with the question of rent arrears, and amend the Land Act by extending the fair rent provision to leaseholders. Parnell in return promised to use his influence to prevent further 'outrages'. He and other prisoners were released on 4 May. Forster and Cowper both refused to be a party to this deal and they resigned their offices of chief secretary and lord lieutenant, respectively.

The dissolution of the Ladies' Land League

Forster believed the government had suffered a major defeat by not forcing Parnell to give a public promise to obey the law. He was wrong—it was a Parnellite surrender—but the resignations gave the 'treaty' the appearance of a Land League victory. In reality, Parnell had disowned agrarian agitation and was secretly preparing to co-operate with the Liberals. The Ladies' Land League had become an acute embarrassment to him and was now expendable.

The Land League was euphoric, but the women did not believe that the government had been defeated. Anna felt 'this period of fictitious triumph to be even more unsatisfactory than the cold atmosphere of censure we had for so long been used to.' When the victorious Parnell first met the women after his release, he was infuriated to be brusquely told that he should have stayed in Kilmainham; there was no hero's welcome from that quarter.

Davitt and Parnell met on their release from jail. Davitt reported that Parnell was angry with the women and accused them of having done great harm to the movement, an allegation Davitt was quick to refute, 'the harm is evident in the fall of Forster and in the dropping of coercion and in our release.'[70] That defence of the women didn't help—Parnell was even more enraged at the suggestion that it had been them and not he himself who might have been responsible for the ending of repression. He told Davitt that the Ladies' Land League had to be suppressed, and if they were not, he threatened to leave public life.

But just as Parnell was congratulating himself on having brought Ireland to the verge of Home Rule as a result of his new understanding with Gladstone, an event occurred which allowed the government to enforce a new coercion policy and set back Parnell's parliamentary ambitions—the Phoenix Park murders. On 6 May, Lord Frederick Cavendish, the new lord lieutenant, and his under-secretary, Thomas Burke, were stabbed to death in the Phoenix Park, Dublin, by a secret group called the Invincibles. Many people were appalled by the tragedy and its consequences; Parnell sank into a deep depression, the incident fuelling his deep antagonism to the Ladies' Land League and confirming his resolve to be rid of them as soon as possible. As Katharine Tynan admitted, Parnell had always detested the organisation which, in the hands of 'the sister as like him as a woman can be like a man, had taken a course of its own and one in many ways opposed to his wishes and policy.'[71] He now had the freedom to reveal his feelings.

Three months of tortuous negotiations were now to ensue before the Ladies' Land League finally disappeared. It was a bizarre situation. The women, far from fighting to retain their organisation, had looked forward to their release from a 'long and uncongenial bondage', as Anna described it. Once the men were back on the scene the old antagonisms re-emerged and the women felt it to be 'morally impossible' to continue working with them. They demanded the right to disband 'without unnecessary delay', but reluctantly agreed to continue working during the confusion which the Phoenix Park murders had induced. Parnell wrote privately to Dillon that if the women were to resign now 'they will be acting very badly and may do considerable mischief.'[72] The release of suspects had been halted and evictions continued, so the work went on as usual.

June and July passed without the women receiving any indication of what had been decided. When they asked whether resistance to rent was to continue, their question was ignored; the men either unable to make up their minds, or unwilling to tell them what the policy should be. They were in a strange position: the men continued to be in daily communication with them, although constantly finding fault with their work—when the women sent them cases for consultation, they were simply returned. It was obvious that the men were not going to treat the women as political equals, and equally obvious that they were not yet prepared to make this plain. They seemed to have decided upon a cat-and-mouse strategy, and were not willing to release the impatient mice until they had formulated their plans in more detail.

When Davitt, who was now in New York, was asked what had become of the Ladies' Land League, he blandly replied that the political work had been resumed by the men and the ladies 'contented themselves with doing that which was charitable.'[73] But the 'ladies' were far from content and relations between themselves and the men reached ludicrous proportions. On one occasion, as Parnell and Dillon came up the stairs to the office, they were disconcerted to find themselves greeted by the women sarcastically singing Gilbert and Sullivan's 'Twenty Love-Sick Maidens We'.[74] It couldn't go on like this for much longer.

All League funds had been removed to Paris in 1881, so that they could not be impounded by the government. When the Ladies' Land League wrote, as was normal practice, for money to cover their continuing expenditure, all their requests were again, not refused, but ignored. Their bank manager told them he could not continue to cash their cheques. In exasperation, the executive decided to continue issuing cheques in the hope that if the bank dishonoured them, the Land League would be forced to come out into the open and reveal their plans for the future. Anna was in favour of unilaterally dissolving on the grounds of no funds, but the majority of her executive were against this for fear that dragging the quarrel into the open would adversely affect the credibility of the movement.

By August, their overdraft had reached £5,000 and the men finally revealed their scheme. The women's debts would not be discharged unless the heads of the Ladies' Land League signed a resolution guaranteeing that the organisation would disband, while the women would continue their work of considering applications for relief. They were all outraged at this blackmail—this had always been the most heartrending aspect of their work and now, without the benefit of having their own organisers on the ground to advise them, they were to become a 'perpetual petticoat screen behind which [the men] could shelter, not from the government but from the people.' They also had strong political objections to the policy of doling out relief unlinked to any programme of resistance. All fear of public discredit vanished and the women were unanimous in wanting to contest the ultimatum. They told the men they would hand over their records and provide secretarial assistance, but they refused to bind themselves to 'everlasting penal servitude'. Although the bank overdraft was far greater than their personal savings, they had little fear of having to pay from their own pockets. The previous year, on Anna's advice, they had all transferred their money abroad, so if proceedings were taken by the bank they would have to be conducted in America.

The affair did not, however, reach the law courts. According to Anna, a way out of the deadlock was arrived at by the women altering the wording on the document they had to sign so that they were responsible, not for Land League tenants, but for the *Ladies'* Land League tenants. Whether the men noticed the alteration at the time and decided to ignore it because it provided everyone with a face-saving way out of an impossible situation, remains a matter for speculation. By now Anna was referring to them as 'the enemy' and it was obvious that the women would never have agreed to those conditions. As the women had kept aside a small sum of money from subscriptions which were still coming in, they were able to cover their last obligations to evicted tenants.

At the next meeting of the executive, presided over by Mrs

Tilly of New York, the resolution to dissolve the Ladies' Land League was agreed upon. Clare Stritch moved the notice of dissolution, diplomatically avoiding all contentious issues: as circumstances had changed with the Coercion Act due to expire, the formation of a new tenants' organisation, and the setting up of the Mansion House Relief Committee, there was no longer any necessity for their continued existence. Hannah Lynch proposed the election of a working committee to supervise the final discharge of liabilities, and all branches were requested to send the committee any remaining funds. Although the central organisation had disbanded, Miss Kennedy, on behalf of the working committee, declared that the decision to dissolve was to be left to each branch to decide individually, 'as the circumstances in each locality are the only proper guide on this question.'[75] Although Parnell agreed to the winding-up committee, he was determined to keep the women under control and he told Dillon its only function was to act under the men's instructions. His suspicion and distrust could hardly have been greater.[76]

For the rest of August and throughout September, the pages of *United Ireland* were filled with notices of dissolution, often containing the heartbreakingly poignant pledge to 'come forward any time our country shall need our service'.

The disillusionment of Anna Parnell

Anna remained completely silent during these last days of the Ladies' Land League. She made no speeches and issued no statements and her memoirs contain no references to her feelings. All she says is that one organiser was now too ill to go to the office and two others had been forced to go to the seaside to recuperate from the strain. This terse statement conceals a tragedy in her personal life from which she never fully recovered. On 20 July, Fanny Parnell, at the young age of 33, died suddenly of heart failure. Her death came as a huge shock to Anna, who was already physically and emotionally exhausted by the strain of the past 18 months. The news of her sister's death precipitated an emotional collapse which forced her withdrawal from the executive, which had to fight the final battle without her. A report on her health at the beginning of August stated that, although she was recovering, it was unlikely she would again assume 'the heroic task she performed in the heat and burden of the life-and-death struggle of last winter'.[77] At least, not if the writer of the report (a member of the Land League), had anything to do with it.

One historian, assessing Anna as 'one of the most likeable, and possibly the most admirable of the Parnells', believes that she refused to be a party to the submission and tried to struggle on alone for as long as she could.[78] But her memoirs make it clear that she had no intention of continuing the thankless task of leading a movement, the direction of which would be determined not by the women, but by the men. She may not have wanted to give up without a fight and she certainly resented the high-handed way the men treated the women and the unscrupulous method they used finally to dispose of them, but there was no rational foundation for wanting to remain once the leaders had been released from jail. As well as a difference in aims, there was the unequal distribution of power of consider. The men, by virtue of their position as Members of Parliament, would always have been in a commanding position, able to subdue their recalcitrant female subordinates.

Parnell was preparing a political deal between the Irish party and the Liberal government, and so he wanted to drop the land agitation in order to concentrate on constitutional issues, conducted not in Ireland, but in the House of Commons. Those of his colleagues who disagreed and who wanted to continue the struggle were those who initially supported the Ladies' Land League's right to continue. But once Parnell agreed to a compromise of forming the more moderate Irish National League, which was not intended to be an agitational body, and which was described as 'an open organisation in which the ladies will not take part'(!), no one had any scruples in ignoring the fate of the women—who had only been pawns in a political power struggle. Anna rejected the whole idea of Irish people working alongside a British government for reform. Her vision had been the creation of a movement which would unite the most disadvantaged sections of the population into a force which would eventually win independence through its own activity, not through an act of parliament. She firmly believed the Liberal promise of support for a Home Rule bill to be mere fiction and her brother's subsequent move towards parliamentarianism a sell-out of national aspirations and a denial of the growing power of the mass movement. She unequivocally condemned the future strategy of the Irish party:

> When goods are paid before delivery, not once, but just as often as the manufacturer asks for payment, why should the manufacturer deliver them at all? We have no evidence that Mr Gladstone meant to pass Home Rule, but much ground for suspecting that he knew he could not pass it.

The veteran Fenian John O'Leary later told Maud Gonne that the Land League women may not have been right in the manner in which they pursued the Land War, but they were really suppressed because they were 'honester and more sincere than the men'.[79] This 'sincerity' stemmed from their very lack of bargaining power or political influence. Many of the women felt the most oppressed sections of the peasantry to be their natural allies, and this subjective identification with a similarly oppressed group led them to take a radical view of the land question. As nationalists *and* as women, the only organisation they could support would have to be a militant, open, mass movement—because this was the only means by which women could be involved in politics. In striving for this, they followed neither the conspiratorial tradition of Fenianism, nor the constitutionalism of the Irish party, both of which excluded women. The victory of Parnell and the increasing dominance of the Irish party in political life over the next decades was a major defeat for women's political aspirations. There can be no doubt that their subsequent exclusion was a direct consequence of the uncompromising radicalism of the Ladies' Land League.

Anna's personal history was equally exemplary and bleak. Her bitter reflection on her experience was that, as long as she lived, she would never again believe a word any Irishman said. She never spoke to her brother again, cutting him dead on the few occasions they met. She became a recluse after the disappointment of her hopes in the revolutionary potential of the land campaign and went to England, living in an artists' colony in

Cornwall. In the late 1890s she wrote an allegorical poem of her disillusionment, when 'a band of thieves' robbed her and 'cast me/All bleeding by the way'. The last stanza summarises the feelings of a woman without any cause into which to channel her formidable energies:

> And since that hour I have crawled,
> A cripple blind with tears,
> While each step I've made has cost me
> The pain and strain of years.[80]

However, she never severed her links with Ireland and was particularly supportive to Inghinidhe na hEireann, whose formation must have pleased her. Although almost destitute, she sent Maud Gonne a donation to her Patriotic Children's Treat, which had been organised in protest against Queen Victoria's visit to Ireland in 1900 (see pp.48-9). In 1907, she was invited by Sinn Fein to speak on behalf of their candidate in a by-election against the Irish party—the first occasion when the constitutionalists were opposed by the separatists.[81]

In September 1911, she was drowned while swimming in heavy seas near Ilfracombe, having characteristically (or deliberately) ignored warnings about the bad conditions. As she was living under the assumed name of Cerisa Palmer, it was some time before anyone realised who she was. No member of her family attended her funeral; Parnell probably would have, despite everything, but he had died 20 years earlier.

When some of the participants of the Land War came to write their memoirs of the period, they had the grace to admit that the women had played an important role, but they couched their acknowledgements very carefully. William O'Brien called the 'sweet girl graduates... as truly heroic a band of women as ever a country had the happiness to possess in an hour of stress' and he admitted that they had been responsible for breaking Forster's power 'when even pretty resolute men's hearts beat low'.[82] Tim Healy credited Anna for having been perceptive enough to 'scent surrender' when Parnell negotiated the 'Kilmainham Treaty',[83] but no one cared to explain fully why these same women were so rapidly excluded from subsequent political events. The memory of the Ladies' Land League was a male nightmare, and one they were determined to forget as quickly as possible. The subsequent playing down of the women's actual role was a calculated effort to discourage the next generation of women from believing that it might be possible for them to assume the mantle of the Ladies' Land League. For the next 20 years, no group of women activists emerged. When Maud Gonne found women who shared her anger at this exclusion, Inghinidhe na hEireann was born—but the legacy of the Ladies' Land League was the bitter realisation that if women wanted to be politically active, they had either to form their own organisation or accept subordinate status.

2. Inghinidhe na hEireann, 1900-14

The Gaelic revival

After the dissolution of the Land League and the collapse of the agrarian struggle, the Irish Parliamentary Party became the dominant force in Irish political life, its energies centred on the sole objective of persuading the British government to grant Home Rule. The Irish Republican Brotherhood (IRB), the physical-force tradition, desperately needed an influx of new members to restore its credibility, but this would not happen for another 20 years, and, in the meantime, no other militant separatist group existed.

In 1890, this period of unusual tranquillity was abruptly shattered when Captain O'Shea sued his wife Kitty for divorce, citing Parnell as co-respondant. The Irish party immediately disintegrated into factions, as long-suppressed political grievances came to the surface and found expression in the scandal of Parnell's personal life. The Parnellite split was reflected throughout the country as people took sides over the issue. The bitterness created would last for decades and the new generation of men and women, disillusioned by this revelation of the seamier side of politics, turned their energies into regenerating a national identity that had been almost destroyed by the increasing anglicisation of Irish society.

The Gaelic Athletic Association had been formed in 1884 to encourage the playing of traditional games, although their interest was not only in sports as the IRB was prominent amongst the membership and members carried hurleys at Parnell's funeral. That alone was obviously not enough to create a sense of being Irish, and so, in 1893, the Gaelic League was launched as the means whereby Irish would be re-established as the first language of Ireland. Padraic Pearse was to declare the League the 'most revolutionary influence that ever came into Ireland'. It was certainly revolutionary in its attitude to women, accepting women and men equally into classes and even occasionally holding ceilidhs (dances) where both sexes could socialise. The Catholic Church predictably reacted against such innovations, refusing to allow the League to use church halls if men and women attended together. The church's attack had serious consequences, especially in rural areas, as many young people were forced to withdraw from membership.[1] Even conservative nationalists reacted angrily against this disastrous clerical intervention; as Arthur Griffith said, the effect of such puritanism was to deprive those in the country of their one source of entertainment, and many emigrated to places where life was less dull.[2] Despite these set-backs, the Gaelic League was for a considerable number of years a source of inspiration to the new generation, and by 1902 it had succeeded in introducing the teaching of Irish into 13,000 national schools.

However, the Gaelic League was avowedly non-political and many young idealists began to realise that a forum for political agitation was also essential if Ireland was ever to recover its Gaelic heritage. In 1893, Willie Rooney, Griffith's closest friend, formed the Celtic Literary Society, to study and support the Irish language, history, music and literature. Its political policy became one of 'independent action' and they rejected the parliamentary approach. In fact, the founders of Sinn Fein would come from the Celtic Literary Society. But it was only one of a number of clubs now springing up in this flowering of the Celtic revival. One rather exclusive one (membership limited to 50, and later extended to 75), was the Contemporary Club, which had as members such notables as the old Fenian John O'Leary; John Butler Yeats, well-known artist and father of the poet; Douglas Hyde, president of the Gaelic League; George Russell (who wrote under the name of AE); and Dr George Sigerson. It had been founded by Charles Oldham, a Trinity College Home Ruler, as a fraternity which could debate all the issues of the day. Oldham was also to have the distinction of introducing Maud Gonne to the club, her first nationalist group.

Maud Gonne

Maud's father had been a colonel in the British army and had
spent a large part of his career stationed in Ireland. According to
his daughter he had, before his death, planned to resign his commission in order to stand for parliament as a Home Rule candidate. Maud had lived in Ireland during the time of the Land
League and in her autobiography she describes how she shed the
political views of her class after witnessing the eviction of
families by a landlord who was her host when she attended a
hunt ball.[3] All this is undoubtedly apocryphal, but her fabrication
of an early commitment to nationalism and her awarding of pos-
thumous nationalist credentials to her beloved father, Tommy,
doesn't necessarily signify an habitual liar so much as a person
unwilling to admit that she had not always been a nationalist.[4] In
Maud's rather blatant rewriting of her history she depicts an ex-
society beauty, now orphaned, impatiently waiting for the time
when she can lead an independent life. In 1886, a year after her
father's death, she was 21 and able to claim her inheritance. She
now had enough money to do as she pleased, despite the disapproval of her relatives.

Whatever the gloss Maud eventually placed upon her early
life, the fact remains that she devoted the next 60 years to the
Irish cause. She wanted to 'get to work for Ireland quickly', and
was advised by W.T. Stead, the crusading journalist, that the
best person to contact was Michael Davitt, the founder of the
Land League. Maud took Stead's advice and went to the House
of Commons to meet Davitt. He was understandably suspicious
of the fashionably dressed young woman who had impetuously
approached him with a request for work and who, in conversation
stated nothing Irishmen might do in retaliation for England's
presence in Ireland could be considered a crime. Fearing her to
be a spy, all Davitt offered Maud was a ticket for the ladies'
gallery in the Commons where, like Anna Parnell before her, she
fumed as she watched the all-male body settle the affairs of the
nation. She decided she would have to go to Ireland and find
work through her own efforts.[5]

Maud's next meeting was with John O'Leary who was introduced to her at a meeting of the Contemporary Club, to which

she had been invited by Oldham. He introduced her by declaring 'Maud Gonne wants to meet John O'Leary; I thought you would all like to meet Maud Gonne.' As she glanced round the 'cosy room' where 12 men sat smoking and drinking tea, Maud felt a little doubtful about the last part of the introduction, because she was well aware that women were not admitted to the club. It was only later that a monthly ladies' night was instituted, a concession to the growing number of women joining the nationalist movement.[6] Mary Macken, who went to the club after the "exclusive" males were good enough to admit [women] to a symposium every fourth Saturday', remembered that Maud's miniature always hung on the wall, even though her activities had by that stage gone far beyond the scope of that respectable gathering.[7] O'Leary was captivated by this beautiful, transparently sincere convert to Irish independence, and Maud was invited to remain for the meeting, which was a discussion on the Land League. Slightly in awe, she only ventured one question —what had happened to the Ladies' Land League?—and was answered by O'Leary in his famous rejoinder: 'They may not have been right, but they were suppressed because they were honester and more sincere than the men.' It was a comment that must have provided her with much food for thought over the ensuing years.

Although proud to be invited to attend any other meetings she wished, Maud was not content to confine her entrée into political life to the prestigious but rather tame Contemporary Club. The Celtic Literary Society graciously allowed women to attend (at the end of the sessions!), and Maud was invited to recite some poems of Thomas Davis. She was so pleased with the activities of the society that she enthusiastically told the secretary she wanted to join. He was extremely embarrassed by this request and Willie Rooney was called over to explain, as politely as he could, that the rules excluded women from membership. Maud had the presence of mind to retort that she would start a woman's society and would get all their sisters and sweethearts to join. She predicted that the men 'would have to look to their laurels then'.[8] As Padraic Colum later remarked, it sometimes seemed as if the Celtic Literary Society was only an adjunct to the women.[9]

But for the time being, her vow remained only a half-germinated idea, as Maud continued her attempts to gain entry into some part of the national movement, despite the disability of her sex. She next went to the offices of the National League (the more moderate successor to the Land League), where she told a secretary that she wanted to join the League and was willing to do any work suggested. Once again, an embarrassed man was forced to tell her that women were excluded from membership. 'How strange,' Maud replied, 'Surely Ireland needs all her children?' She was slowly being forced to conclude that 'Decidedly there was no place for women in the National movement.'[10]

Tim Harrington, head of the National League, paid Maud a visit the next day. As he was accompanied by two other MPs, Maud longed to ask whether they were his chaperons, but wisely refrained. The conversation not surprisingly centred on the exclusion of women from all nationalist groups, with Maud protesting that the Ladies' Land League had done splendid work and there was therefore no reason for insisting upon women's exclusion. Harrington bitterly replied that the Ladies' Land League 'did too good work, and some of us found they could not be controlled.' When Maud asked whether he disapproved of women in politics, he half-jestingly said a woman's place was in the home, but he was prepared to accept her as a worker. However, Maud was not fighting purely on her own behalf, but on a point of principle. If individual women were permitted to engage in political activity they were, she complained, confined to 'back-door influence'. Maud never scrupled about using her beauty in Ireland's cause, but she wanted the right to be part of an organisation, to be accepted by her adopted country as a patriot in common cause. Harrington was an astute politician who was able to exploit Maud's concern for the destitute. Well aware of her propaganda value, he advised her to go to Donegal, where evictions were taking place.

Her work in Donegal duplicated the past work of the women of the Land League: together with Pat O'Brien, MP, she ensured that Land League huts were built for those about to be evicted. There was no longer a mass movement, yet Maud threw herself into the work, nursing the sick and the dying, raising funds, writing letters to the press. The Donegal tenants called her 'The

Woman of the Sidhe', after mythical fairy-guardians.

She states that a warrant for her arrest put an end to the work, forcing her to escape to France, where she had established a home for herself. In fact, around five years earlier, Maud had begun a strange alliance with Lucien Millevoye, a French patriot who was a close associate of General Boulanger and, in January 1890, she gave birth to their first child, George, who died a few months later.[11] In October of that year, Maud sadly returned to Ireland sailing, by coincidence, on the same boat that carried Parnell's body home for burial. Maud's black dress, although appropriate for the occasion, was worn out of grief for her dead son.

She continued to work for famine relief, joining forces with James Connolly, and enlisting the support of Ellen Ford (who had started the Ladies' Land League in New York with Fanny Parnell) to open a fund for the victims.[12] Yet she fully realised that she was only a freelance and that the talents of many people remained untapped because no organisation existed which could harness their energies.

The *Shan Van Vocht*

In 1896, a national literary magazine was established in Belfast. Its name was the *Shan Van Vocht* (Poor Old Woman) and it was edited by two remarkable women poets, Alice Milligan and Anna Johnson (who wrote under the pseudonym of Ethna Carbery). The earliest writings of James Connolly were included within the varied pages of the journal, although the editors made it plain they disagreed with his socialism. Maud Gonne soon became firm friends with them and they obviously admired her greatly. There were strong protests when Maud's name was dropped from the council of the National Literary Society which she had helped W.B. Yeats set up in 1892. Maud, although bearing 'merely a woman's name', as the editors sarcastically noted, was invaluable because her continued presence 'would have served to connect the society in the eyes of the Irish race with what some of us hold to be the National Movement'.[13] Her reputation was obviously spreading; so was the participation of women within the nationalist movement.

In 1897, steps were taken to form an all-party alliance to celebrate the centenary of the United Irishmen's Rising of 1798. Parliamentarians—both pro- and anti-Parnellites—plus Fenians, were to share a common platform for all ceremonies. Continuous internal dissension made it appear that these moves towards unity would be still-born, while at the same time a separate woman's centenary union was formed. *Shan Van Vocht* hoped it would avoid the acrimony surrounding the men's organisation as women, lacking the vote and excluded from all groups, were not 'called upon to have any opinion whatever as to who has a right to speak for Ireland.' Despite the bitterness of the comment, this debarment was, for once, seen as a positive blessing.[14]

By September, the work of the Irishwomen's Centenary Union was well under way, unmarred by political wrangles, and *Shan Van Vocht* took great pleasure in hammering home the point. 'Is it not a fortunate thing that the better half (numerically of course, I mean) of the population of Ireland is not involved in these differences of the polling booths?' As well as honouring the spirit of 1798 by arranging an exhibition in Belfast, by decorating neglected graves of old heroes, selling home-produced goods and collecting money for memorials, the women considered their task to be that of giving men 'safe guidance out of the hurly-burly of the political faction fight into which they have wandered from the straight path.' Their lack of political experience was not regarded as a disadvantage. A recurrent theme in the history of Inghinidhe na hEireann would be their dismissal of any form of parliamentarianism as a corrupting influence, and their reaffirmation of the need to develop an authentic national spirit through the formation of organisations that sprang from the people, rejecting any necessity of looking cravenly across the Irish Sea. As many men in the north would, for business reasons, be unable to take part in the celebrations in case they alienated their Protestant customers, some of their female relatives announced that they would take their place.

Anna Johnson, Alice Milligan, Willie Rooney and Maud Gonne were part of a group who took the opportunity of the 1798 celebration to tour the countryside giving lectures on the United Irishmen. Maud concentrated her energies on the west, but came to Dublin for the concluding ceremony. By this time she had established herself, not as a political leader, but as an inspirational force: nationalists were succumbing to the hypnotic charm of this exceptionally beautiful woman.

The start of the Boer War in 1899 heralded Maud's appearance as a figure of primary importance at nationalist meetings. She was one of the founders of the Transvaal Committee, formed in October 1899 to support the efforts of the Boers. At a meeting of 20,000 in Dublin, addressed by O'Leary, Davitt and Maud, the crowd unyoked the horses from the brake the speakers were standing upon and, after dragging it through the streets, concluded their demonstration by giving 'ringing cheers for Miss Gonne and the Transvaal'.[15]

The Patriotic Children's Treat Committee

Shan Van Vocht folded in April 1899. The final edition explained that by steering clear of all sectional differences, they were deprived of the backing of any party and so had no choice but to cease publication. The editors sent their subscription list to Arthur Griffith, their rival, who had begun the publication of *United Irishman*. Griffith, who affectionately dubbed Maud 'Queen', was one of the many men to fall half in love with her—and also one of the many whose admiration she was able to redirect into support for her many projects. *United Irishman* reprinted many of Maud's articles from her newspaper *Irlande libre*, which she had established in 1897 to propagandise the Irish cause in France. Griffith also gave generous coverage to the activities of Inghinidhe na hEireann; indeed, it was Griffith who unwittingly provided the inspiration for the formation of the Inghinidhe.

There were several reasons why a group of women should have met in the rooms of the Celtic Literary Society after 12 o'clock mass on Easter Sunday 1900. One was that they wanted to raise a subscription for a 'nice strong blackthorn with a silver ring, bearing an Irish inscription', to compensate Griffith for the loss of his South African sjam-bok, which he had just broken over the editor of *Figaro*, a society journal which had published a defamatory article claiming Maud to be a British spy. (Griffith spent two weeks in jail for his chivalry; Maud later won a libel case.) The 15 women also discussed hair, the latest fashions (black and khaki because it was the year of the Boer War), and then someone raised the topic of Queen Victoria's visit to Ireland. Victoria had arrived in Dublin on 4 April and in her honour a free treat had been held in Phoenix Park for 5,000 children. An editorial comment in *United Irishman* had complained that nationalists had never exerted themselves over the question of giving children a nationalist education—for example, by organising an outing to a place of national significance. One girl mentioned this comment and they unanimously agreed it would be a good idea to organise a counter-treat for those children who had not attended Queen Victoria's.[16]

An *ad-hoc* committee, soon to be called the Patriotic Children's Treat Committee, was immediately formed, with Maud the unanimous choice for president. It was what she had been hoping for for years and finally she had found women like herself, who 'resented being excluded, as women, from National organisations'.[17] They were still excluded, but no longer prepared to acquiesce.

The children's treat was intended from the outset to be on as lavish a scale as possible. After the first meeting it was stated that the women hoped to entertain a large part of the 30,000 boys and girls they believed would be eligible. As enthusiasm mounted, increasing numbers of women began to attend the weekly meetings. On 28 April, *United Irishman* listed 31 women present; by 19 May, there were 59. Alice Furlong was elected vice-president, May O'Leary-Curtis and Judith Rooney were treasurers, and Annie Egan and Sarah White were secretaries. Anna Johnson came down from Belfast to attend meetings and Jenny Wyse Power, who had been a member of the Ladies' Land League, also joined the committee.

Donations of an exceptionally generous nature began to pour in. A Mr Cole guaranteed to supply 1,000 oranges; Messrs Kernan and Company promised 1,200 minerals; 20 tons of sweets came from the Grogans and 40,000 buns were to come from a variety of bakers, including John Daly of Limerick, an old Fenian himself, whose niece Kathleen was soon to marry the man he had been imprisoned with, Tom Clarke. Anna Parnell sent a donation of £1, which she could ill-afford. By the end of

June, £184 had been collected, mainly by the personal canvassing of the members of the committee. As the time agreed upon drew near, two members of the committee spent two hours each afternoon in the offices of the Celtic Literary Society, enrolling the names of the children.[18]

By 30 June, 25,000 names had been registered. It was decided that the original venue of Bodenstown, where there was an annual pilgrimage to the grave of Wolfe Tone, posed too many problems in terms of marshalling the children, so the committee accepted the offer of the owner of Clonturk Park to use his facilities. For the final four days before the treat, over 100 women and men packed and made up food in a shop in Talbot Street, which had been lent for that purpose. The date chosen was the Sunday following the Wolfe Tone commemoration.

Griffith enthused that 'Dublin never witnessed anything so marvellous as the procession through its streets last Sunday of the thirty thousand school children who refused to be bribed into parading before the Queen of England'. As they paraded through the Dublin streets, many held up green cards proclaiming 'Irish Patriotic Children's Treat—no Flunkeyism here'. Maud Gonne and Maire Quinn accompanied the procession in an open carriage while men from the Celtic Literary Society and the Gaelic Athletic Association (the only adults allowed) acted as marshals. Four platforms were erected in the park so that the children would be able to hear at least one speaker. Maud, Willie Rooney, Mr O'Leary-Curtis and a Mr O'Neill were the four chosen. Significantly, although women had organised the event, Maud was the only female speaker. At this stage, few women had the self-confidence to address such a large crowd—even though it was composed solely of children.

Maud's speech was characteristic. She told the children that their presence revived hopes in nationalists' hearts, which were sad from the long weary struggle. She hoped that Ireland would be free by the time they had grown up, so that they could put their energies into building up a free nation and not 'the arid task of breaking down an old tyranny'.[19] Forty years later, Maud was still meeting women and men who would come up to her and say 'I was one of the patriotic children at your party when Queen Victoria was over.'[20]

Letters of congratulation poured into the offices of the *United Irishman*. One of the most fervent came from Thomas Timmins, writing on behalf of the builders' labourers, 'there is no name that will ever shine out with greater prominence in the history of our country than that of our beloved lady, Miss Maud Gonne'.[21] However, Maud's most ardent admirer, W.B. Yeats, took a much more gloomy view of the success of the venture as he asked himself 'How many of these children will carry bomb or rifle when a little under or a little over thirty?'[22] He was more farsighted than he realised.

The formation of Inghinidhe na hEireann

When the Ladies' Committee met to settle the last accounts arising out of the Treat, they realised that they could not simply dissolve and again go their separate ways, unable to join any other group. Their success had discovered previously unexpressed talents and had proven women's capabilities. Mrs O'Leary-Curtis proposed a resolution that something should be done to educate little girls into an understanding of the national ideal. After some discussion, it was agreed to form a permanent National Women's Committee, whose work would include Irish history classes for girls. As many members would be away over the summer, it was decided to postpone any regular meetings until September. It was obvious that they already perceived their role to be far more than the educators of children, as two members—Jenny Wyse Power and Maire Quinn—were delegated to represent the committee at Franco-Irish celebrations being held in Paris that July. Maud Gonne and Annie Egan were attending on behalf of the National Irishwomen's Association.[23] Arthur Griffith and others from the Transvaal Committee also took part in the colourful events.

At the beginning of October 1900, the inaugural meeting of Inghinidhe na hEireann (Daughters of Erin) took place. Twenty-nine women were listed as having attended. Maud Gonne was elected president; Annie Egan, Anna Johnson, Jenny Wyse Power and Alice Furlong were joint vice-presidents; Maire Quinn, Dora Hackett and Elizabeth Morgan were the secretaries, and Sarah White and Margaret Quinn became treasurers. Among the names are reminders of the time when Irishwomen last had a political organisation: as well as Jenny Wyse Power, who now owned a restaurant in Dublin which had become a regular meeting place for nationalists, there was Annie, the wife of James Egan, a former 'Treason Felony' prisoner. And, of course, Anna Johnson was a former editor of *Shan Van Vocht*. Of the other members, Maire Quinn (later to marry actor Dudley Digges) was an actress; her sister Margaret ran a tea shop; Maire Killeen was Willie Rooney's fiancee; Molly Walker was to take the name Maire nic Shiubhlaigh and achieve fame as an actress; Sinead O'Flanagan, teacher and author, later married Eamon de Valera; Mary Macken became a professor of German; Sara Allgood and Maire O'Neill (the playwright Synge's fiancee), sisters who both became well-known actresses, were early members, as were the sisters of Griffith and Rooney. *Bean na hEireann*, Inghinidhe's paper, later declared them to be (with one exception—obviously Maud herself) all 'working girls', by which was meant, not that they were working class, but that they were independent women earning their own living without the financial support of their families.

St Brigid was to be the patron of the organisation. Unlike many other groups, the women were completely open in detailing what they hoped to achieve. It was an ambitious list:

The re-establishment of the complete independence of Ireland.

To encourage the study of Gaelic, of Irish literature, History, Music and Art, especially among the young, by organising the teaching of classes for the above subjects.

To support and popularise Irish manufacture.

To discourage the reading and circulation of low English literature, the singing of English songs, the attending of vulgar English entertainments at the theatres and music hall, and to combat in every way English influence, which is doing so much injury to the artistic taste and refinement of the Irish people.

To form a fund called the National Purposes Fund, for the furtherance of the above objects.

They pledged themselves to 'mutual help and support and to stand loyally by one another'.[24] The rules of membership were surprisingly strict. It was not to be a group where women could drift in and out as they pleased; they had to make a definite commitment. Candidates were to be proposed and seconded by two members and a week was to elapse between nomination and election by ballot. This was of course also a security measure; another precaution they took was the adoption of Gaelic names to conceal their identity and prevent victimisation by employers. As a nationalist organisation they had one other qualification— all members had to be of Irish birth or descent.

This initial meeting devised an energetic programme of work. Free classes in Irish, history and music for children over the age of nine were to be held between 7.30 p.m. and 9 p.m. each Thursday. As they had a surplus of £8 17s 3d from the Patriotic Children's Treat, they decided to organise a Christmas Treat for those attending. And as part of their aim of reviving the Irish traditions they instituted monthly ceilidhs (dances), to which were invited members of the Celtic Literary Society and other nationalist organisations. As well as music, dancing and songs, a member of Inghinidhe would read out a paper on a Celtic heroine. For the first ceilidh Maud gave a talk on 'The Goddess Brigid'—she was much more interested in Brigid as a goddess than as a saint; to redress the balance, Maire Killeen later read a paper on the saintlier aspects of Brigid's career. In keeping with the declared feminism of the group, Maud began her address, 'My sisters and friends'. The evenings were a great success. Arthur Griffith, a regular at these social occasions, wrote appreciatively that 'the refreshments... were of a first class and substantial character'. Mrs O'Beirne, a member of the group, also ran the Derrybawn Hotel, where the entertainments were held.[25]

The children's classes were also extremely popular, partly due to the fact that they were able to call on the services of a large number of talented people. Ella Young, poet and mystic, and a close friend of Maud's, agreed to teach history by retelling the sagas and hero tales. She had vivid memories of her experiences:

In a room perched at the head of a rickety staircase and

overlooking a narrow street, I have about eighty denizens
of untamed Dublin: newsboys, children who have played
in street alleys all their lives, young patriot girls and boys
who can scarcely write their own names. Outside there is
a continuous din of street cries and rumbling carts. It is
almost impossible to shout against it if the windows are
open, and more impossible to speak in the smother of
dust if the windows are shut. Everyone is standing, closely
packed—no room for chairs![26]

This education of the young was perceived by non-
nationalists to be a great threat and the malicious put about a
rumour that the children were being taught a grotesque parody
of the Catholic Church's catechism, beginning 'Who is the
origin of evil? England.' It certainly provided the Inghinidhe
with a golden opportunity to inculcate nationalist sentiments
into the future generation. As the women of the Ladies' Land
League had done 20 years earlier (when a similar rumour had
done the rounds concerning the alphabet they taught: 'A is the
army that covers the ground, B is the buckshot we're getting all
round,' etc.), they realised the importance of reaching out to
children. Perhaps it was still an extension of women's traditional
concerns? Maud captivated the hundreds of children who came
to the Christmas Treat. There was no difficulty in extracting
from them an enthusiastic promise never to join or consort with
members of the British army.[27]

Victoria's visit to Ireland had been designed to revive
recruitment figures, which had slumped drastically as a result of
the hostility evoked by Britain's war against the Boers. It was a
popular war in Britain, but not in Ireland. The annual report of
the inspector general of recruiting admitted that, while
recruiting in Britain had improved, it had badly declined in
Ireland. The *United Irishman* attributed this state of affairs to
the 'splendid work done by Miss Gonne and the Irish Transvaal
Committee'. While Maud continued her work with the Transvaal
Committee, the Inghinidhe decided upon what they described as
an intense campaign against enlistment in the British army.
Their technique was novel as they, like Anna Parnell before
them, decided to concentrate on direct action rather than public
meetings.

At that time O'Connell Street was divided into two zones—the west side frequented by the British military and their girlfriends, and the east by Dublin civilians. Leaflets were produced warning girls against 'consorting with the enemies of their country', and distributed to women who were seen walking with soldiers. The dangers of venereal disease and illegitimate babies were also graphically described, which was unusual, given the period and the religious background of most of the Inghinidhe.[28] The result of all this work was, as Maud recalled with relish, that 'almost every night there were fights in O'Connell Street', as the brothers and boyfriends of Inghinidhe members were called upon to defend the women against attack by irate soldiers, with passers-by often joining in the fray. Griffith hated it, although he dutifully took part. Another, even more hazardous method of conveying their anti-recruitment message, was to follow recruiting sergeants into pubs and then distribute leaflets stating the Catholic Church's doctrine on unjust wars.[29]

It must have been more of an adventure than anything else for these young women, who got a glimpse of a life that had been completely unknown to them. They had shown themselves to be imaginative propagandists, but revealed little awareness of the reasons why women were forced to resort to prostitution. However, a decade later Maud, on behalf of the Inghinidhe, appealed through the pages of *The Irish Worker* for men and women to come together 'without any false modesty' in order to see what could be done to prevent the system where 'women were forced to sell their body, mind and soul'. She admitted that the Inghinidhe until recently had simply 'appealed to girls as sisters to keep out of temptation's way and to help them to keep others out', but they had come to realise that they had no alternative to offer—they couldn't get non-existent, or atrociously paid factory jobs for the women—and they appealed to the working class, men and women, to organise with them in order to alleviate the situation.[30] The passionate concern of this entreaty disclosed a maturity of understanding that simply didn't exist when Inghinidhe na hEireann was young and its members delighting in daring escapades.

Inghinidhe na hEireann and the birth of the Irish theatre

The forms of entertainment prevalent in Dublin infuriated not only nationalists, but anyone with any pretensions to cultural interests. Not only were they wholly British in character, the most popular were music hall frolics which, as a reviewer complained in *United Irishman*, 'sought to make women unthinking dolls' instead of 'intelligent comrades'.[31] W.B. Yeats had for years been dreaming of establishing an Irish theatre which would both form a new identity for Irish people and provide the impetus for a new generation of Irish writers. If Ireland would not read literature, it might listen to it, he hoped.[32] The Inghinidhe had deliberately included within their manifesto a pledge to combat the English influence they considered so injurious to 'artistic taste' and now, with so many talented women joining the group and enthusiasm and confidence in their abilities at its height, they decided to use whatever meagre resources came to hand. While Yeats continued to anguish about financial backing for his 'hopeless' plan, Maud's never failing optimism reassured the Inghinidhe that the necessary support would eventually materialise.

Their first venture required little financial outlay. Male actors were obtained from willing volunteers in the Celtic Literary Society and the two groups co-operated in devising a programme of *tableaux vivants* (living pictures), illustrating such legends as the Children of Lir, Brian at Clontarf, and Queen Maeve. The performance, held in the Antient Concert Rooms, over the Easter holidays, was as usual given rapturous praise by the *United Irishman* ('no Irish entertainment we have witnessed for years has at all compared with the one which astounded and delighted Dublin'), and the women were congratulated for having 'as usual, shown us the way to work successfully'.[33]

Several more *tableaux* were staged and interest in developing these rudimentary theatrical attempts was expressed by many people. The Inghinidhe discovered a host of budding playwrights only too willing to write for an indigenous Irish theatre. Their next series of performances was timed to coincide with horse-show week in Dublin, the intention being to show the Anglo-Irish that nationalist Dublin was capable of providing a strong counter-attraction to the yearly ritual in Ballsbridge. In addition to a new series of tableaux, three plays were presented, all under the inspired direction of the Fay brothers. Alice Milligan wrote two—*The Deliverance of Red Hugh* and *The Harp that Once*—while the other, *Eilis agus Bhean Deirce*, by P.T. MacGinley, became the first play in Irish to be produced in Dublin. The roles of this were taken by Maire Perolz and Miss Waters, both Inghinidhe members, and Maire Quinn's brother, a member of the Celtic Literary Society. Maud read out the legend of Red Hugh at the beginning of that play; Ella Young said of her that 'the quality of her beauty dulled the candle-flames'. Although the first two nights were badly attended, they were playing to packed houses by the end of the week. The proceeds of £20 went to the Wiliam Rooney Memorial Fund, as Rooney had recently died at the tragically early age of 26.[34]

After Yeats had watched a performance of *Red Hugh*, he came away, he said, with his 'head on fire', wanting to hear his own plays spoken with a Dublin accent.[35] This newly awakened ardour delighted Maud, who had for years been trying to convince him that he should devote his talents into providing propaganda for the nationalist cause. From this union of poetic emotion and nationalist fervour there emerged *Kathleen ni Houlihan*. Maud promised to act in the title role if Yeats gave the rights of production to her group, under the direction of the Fays. At the same time AE (George Russell) gave them his play *Deirdre*, in which Maire Quinn, Helen Laird and Maire nic Shiubhlaigh acted.

On 2 April 1902, in the tiny St Theresa's Hall, the Irish National Theatre Company (as the young group now called itself) gave the first performance of the two plays. In front of the footlights, the banner of the Inghinidhe—a golden sunburst on a blue background—was displayed in all its glory. Yeats wrote ecstatically to Lady Gregory that Maud had played the part of Kathleen 'magnificently and with weird power',[36] and Maire nic Shiubhlaigh, who was later to model her interpretation on Maud's portrayal, described the impact she made as the old woman with 'the walk of a queen', symbolising the image of a free nation: 'In her, the youth of the country saw all that was magnificent in Ireland. She was the very personification of the figure she portrayed on the stage.'[37]

Yeats was also delighted by the acting of *Deirdre*. Although the youthful players showed some signs of inexperience, it was 'grave and simple'. The theatre was packed each night, 'gleaming shirt fronts' mingling with the 'less resplendent garb of the Dublin worker', as Maire nic Shiubhlaigh described the audience. Griffith believed the plays could have continued for three weeks rather than three nights, but limited finances prevented a longer run. Nevertheless, nationalist opinion was agreed that an Irish theatre was near to fruition now that the combined efforts of Inghinidhe na hEireann and the Celtic Literary Society had made it possible to dispense with English actors. Only six months earlier, *Diarmuid and Grania*, a play written jointly by Yeats and George Moore, had had to be performed solely by English actors, Mr Benson and his Company. Frank Fay had found the performance an excruciating experience, calling attention in his review to the 'execrable acting' performed in the presence of 'Ireland's greatest daughter, Miss Maud Gonne' and 'Ireland's greatest poet, Mr W.B. Yeats'.[38]

The impetus provided by Inghinidhe na hEireann led to the formation of a professional theatre group, out of which came the Abbey Theatre. Individual members of the Inghinidhe were to join and make careers out of acting, but as a group the Inghinidhe felt that their work had been accomplished. Their efforts had shown it was possible to provide good drama; once that had been achieved, they felt free to return to their work of building up a political opposition to England's presence in Ireland.

An assessment of the first two years of the Inghinidhe

By the time *Kathleen ni Houlihan* was performed, Inghinidhe na hEireann was celebrating the end of its second year. The women were a valuable addition to the small network of clubs and societies and had their own modest expansion to contribute. Their branches in Cork, Limerick and Ballina, had all been formed in the tide of enthusiasm which occurred whenever Maud Gonne embarked on a lecture tour.[39] The Cork branch, which appears to have been the most vigorous of the off-shoots, was a smaller-scale replica of the parent body. The members had carried black flags in protest when King Edward VII's representative came to open an exhibition; they had 100 children in their language and history classes; they gave concerts; they promoted Irish manufacture and collected for the Irish Language Fund.[40] The president was a young woman called Margaret Goulding, who was later, as Margaret Buckley, to be an organiser of the Irish Women Workers' Union and president of Sinn Fein.

What they lacked, however, was the imaginative flair of Maud, who posssessed an unerring gift for knowing what actions were likely to result in the maximum amount of publicity. Commitments often took her outside Ireland: a second child, Iseult, had been born to Maud and Lucien Millevoye in 1894, and after their relationship ended, she married John MacBride, in 1903. She and MacBride separated in 1905, a year after the birth of their son, Sean, and, afterwards Maud spent a great deal of time in France, afraid of bringing Sean to Ireland in case the Mac-Brides sued for custody. Despite these enforced absences, however, her influence upon the other women cannot be overestimated. Sydney Gifford compared her to a 'goddess, a creature from another planet, and when she spoke you thought she must speak in oracles'.[41] Without this inspiration and, most importantly, her immense range of contacts amongst the various groups and personalities, it is unlikely that the Inghinidhe could have captured the wholehearted allegiance of so many women at a time when nationalists had little public presence and women were not expected to have any public presence at all.

The Inghinidhe were unique: they brought a new dimension to nationalist life, imbuing the movement with a theatrical element which stirred the imagination and aroused more emotion than a thousand meetings or earnest resolutions ever did. The effect of this whirlwind of activity is well illustrated by a columnist in the *United Irishman*, who, after reading their first annual report, concluded that 'woman rushes in where man fears to tread and makes him look foolish and fall back on the apple story to save himself'. He wished, not only that every town in Ireland had a branch, but that the world could be ruled by women: 'I am weary living in a world ruled by men with mouse-hearts and monkey-brains, and I want a change.'[42]

A contrast with the only other organisation to admit women, reveals the immense difference between the vivacious Inghinidhe and the earnest, staid Gaelic League; it also reveals the radical challenge that the Inghinidhe posed to the more conservative nationalists. Whereas the Inghinidhe addressed one another as 'sister' and sought to identify their movement with strong, independent women of the past, the ladies' branch of the Dun Laoghaire Gaelic League sent out a circular asking for the 'co-operation of all the principal ladies of our town... who, by the cradle and in the nursery, can instil good and noble thoughts into the youthful minds of the children entrusted to their tender care'.[43] That, of course, was the traditional view of women's interest in public life and social change. It's difficult to imagine that pompous appeal having much attraction for women who wanted a means of escaping from the confines of their usual roles. And its class bias would certainly have been repugnant to the more egalitarian-minded Inghinidhe. Although they did devote much time to the education of children, this was out of a commitment to nationalism and as a means of providing some stimulation for the children of the poor. It was undertaken in the role of political activist, and not as wife and mother.

Opposition to the king's visit, 1903

So far, the Inghinidhe activities had been individual efforts. Although they had received support from other groups, they had not yet really co-operated in a joint venture. King Edward's visit to Dublin was to provide such an opportunity, and it was also to show that the women were fully prepared to take the initiative when they believed the national interest to be at stake.

When Queen Victoria came to Dublin in 1900, Thomas Pile, then Lord Mayor, had read a loyal address and the Patriotic Children's Treat, although organised after the event, had been the only public show of dissent. Now, when rumours began that King Edward was shortly to visit Dublin, the Inghinidhe immediately took advantage of the forthcoming municipal elections to distribute an address to the *women electors* of Dublin, urging them to vote against anyone who had allowed the previous address of welcome to be passed. They were at pains to point out that as a 'purely national society', they were intervening solely because of the gravity of the issue, which implied a distinct lack of interest in local government issues, one of the few spheres where women had, since 1898, the right to vote, although still debarred from standing as candidates.[44] As their annual report later boasted, they were the first group to protest. Although they were premature because another year was to elapse before the king finally arrived, they had made their point. They were determined to ensure that Ireland's capital city would deny him the welcome his mother had received.

When confirmation of the king's visit came the following year, the playwright Edward Martyn was the first person to send a letter of protest to the press: 'It is for Nationalist Ireland to... tell the government with one voice that if they bring the King here under any other guise than as a restorer of our stolen constitution they will regret their rashness.'[45]

On 9 May, *United Irishman* published inside information which claimed that an address of welcome would be placed on the agenda of Dublin corporation while Tim Harrington, the Lord Mayor (and the same man who had advised Maud Gonne to work for the Donegal peasants), would arrange to be outside Dublin, appointing his Unionist deputy in his place. Maud cut short her honeymoon with Major MacBride so that she could mobilise opposition to the king. While Yeats was leading her to her train at Euston he showed her the article. Maud had assured Yeats that Harrington would not 'go on his knees to an English King', but the report shook her confidence. Her journey back to Ireland was spent in wondering how she could prevent this capitulation.[46]

Maud's account of the following two days says much for her own initiative, but very little about anyone else's. According to her version, she arrived in Dublin to see large posters announcing a meeting of the Irish Parliamentary Party in the Rotunda the following day, 18 May. As Harrington was billed to chair while Redmond, the party leader spoke, Maud had an idea: Harrington must be asked publicly to repudiate the statement published in the *United Irishman*. She immediately dispatched telegrams to Maire Quinn, the secretary of Inghinidhe, to Griffith, to Seamus

MacManus (widower of Anna Johnson, who had died the previous year), and to a few other reliable friends. The small group met that afternoon at Maud's house and agreed with her suggestion to go to the Rotunda to put one question to Harrington: was Dublin going to recognise the English king?

The delegation decided to call itself the People's Protection Committee, and Edward Martyn was chosen to act as spokesman. Maire Quinn, after giving Maud a great hug, went off to summon members of the Inghinidhe, plus friends and sweethearts, which was considered a prudent move in case violence erupted after they had taken up their 'strategic positions'. Maire thought the women would be equal to the occasion as they had gained experience through upsetting British propaganda plays. Maud thought it was all going to be 'great fun'.[47]

Although events were probably essentially as Maud has recounted them, there are a few discrepancies. First of all, Griffith had warned in the *United Irishman* of 16 May—the day before Maud returned to Ireland—that nationalists would be at the Rotunda to put their case. Second, the People's Protection Committee's press statement declared their inaugural meeting to have been held at 20 Rutland Square, whereas Maud stated they had come to her house in Coulson Avenue. Lastly, Maud's memoirs end shortly after her account of the Rotunda meeting and her marriage to MacBride, but in fact the People's Protection Committee was formed, not solely for the purpose of confronting Harrington, but with the expressed aim of preventing 'undue pressure' of the kind which had been brought to bear on the working class during Victoria's visit, which had 'compelled them to participate and to allow their children to participate in festivities and demonstrations of which they disapproved'.[48] In other words, they intended to ensure there was no repetition of the children's treat. One reason for Maud's omission of the later events could be that the counter-treat the Inghinidhe organised on this occasion failed to match the triumph of its predecessor.

The confrontation with Harrington was promptly christened 'The Battle of the Rotunda' by the newspapers. Martyn and Maud made their way on to the platform occupied by the speakers and demanded that Harrington should answer their question. He refused. The audience now began to take sides, confusion mounted and violence predictably broke out. In partisan fashion, *United Irishman* claimed all the trouble had been caused by Harrington, who had angrily thrown a chair into the audience.[49] Redmond later tried to play down the incident by saying that the disturbance would have been 'nipped in the bud, were it not that the people naturally shrank from using force to remove Mrs Maud Gonne MacBride and some other ladies'.[50] Seamus MacManus eventually picked Maud off the platform, afraid she would be hurt by one of the chairs being hurled at it. The last words Maud remembered hearing were 'Don't you dare touch her!' and 'We want no king!'[51] By this time the fight had spread to the audience, most of whom hastily left before the police arrived, leaving Redmond to speak to a wrecked and almost empty hall. *The Irish Times* summed up the affair by identifying the committee as having been responsible for 'one of the most sensational incidents in the recent history of Irish politics'.[52] AE wrote to Yeats of the 'most gorgeous row Dublin has seen since Jubilee time',[53] while Maud's happy reflection was that Harrington had been removed from his difficulties as no one could now suggest asking him to leave Dublin.

The People's Protection Committee was delighted with this coup. As a result of the publicity that had been generated, they were now able to form a national council, with Edward Martyn as chairman and Maud as one of the honorary secretaries. From as far away as London, Manchester and Glasgow, people wrote in, asking to become members; Anna Parnell was one of the well-known names to telegraph support.[54] A series of meetings was launched to protest against any address being voted by Dublin corporation and by July, when the corporation finally met to vote upon the question, it had become doubtful as to whether or not the resolution could attract sufficient support. The margin was close, but the address was voted against by a majority of three. As the nationalists left the crowded council chambers where they had assembled to watch over the count, Maud was cheered with 'almost delirious enthusiasm' as she and Jenny Wyse Power left the building. For the first time since the Norman invasion, as Griffith jubilantly wrote, Dublin 'refuses recognition to a British monarch'.[55] Maud's memoirs may be inaccurate and exaggerated, but in this case contemporary accounts confirm her strategic intervention.

One method the National Council had used to alienate popular enthusiasm for the royal visit was the rather dubious tactic of posting up thousands of copies of the Coronation Oath, with its repudiation of the basic doctrines of Roman Catholicism. The Inghinidhe, although lacking the money to pay for them (Maud optimistically said their patron saint, St Brigid, would provide), posted up an additional 10,000 copies on every available surface, the day before the visit.[56] But Maud was never content simply to register a protest, there had to be a further method by which she could arouse the Dublin population to a more active realisation of the national humiliation involved in submitting to a royal visit. Her gesture was one of frustration, rather than a deliberate act of defiance; it could have been duplicated in many nationalist homes, but it was not. Through it she succeeded in capturing the imagination, giving added weight to the nationalist claim that the Irish people were no longer willing to acquiesce in their own subordination.

Pope Leo XIII had just died, but there could be no official mourning in Ireland because of the profusion of Union Jacks, erected to welcome the royal couple. Maud, arriving home tired and dispirited after the postering campaign, on impulse hung out a black petticoat on a broom handle, where it kept uneasy vigil with her neighbours' Union Jacks. The next morning, what became known as the 'Battle of Coulson Avenue' began. Two policemen and three detectives rushed into the garden to tear down the flag, despite Maud's protests. She immediately put up another and, along with Maire Quinn and 'Mrs Fitz', her housekeeper, defended the house against the efforts of the police and irate neighbours. Maire Quinn is supposed to have thrown a bottle at a neighbour perched on Maud's roof, who suffered a bumped head and a possible broken arm when he fell off. Maud harangued the police by telling them that no good Catholic Irishmen should want her to take down the flag while the Pope lay in state in Rome. As they understood only too well the political significance of her act, this sudden outburst of piety did not impress them.

Meanwhile, Dudley Digges, Maire Quinn's fiance, had left a note on the door of the Inghinidhe office, telling all members to go to Coulson Avenue. Helena Moloney, under the influence of hearing Maud speak at a public meeting, had just decided to join the group; she found the note instead and immediately rushed round to the house, where she was asked if she was a member. The awe-struck young woman shyly said yes, although she felt she was claiming too great an honour, 'to be a member of such a body was the greatest honour in the world'. The police raid was her 'baptism of fire'; she joined formally the following week.[57] But Helena was only one of scores of nationalists to arrive in defence of Maud's petticoat. Many of the men brought stout sticks with them, while a cordon of police formed across the avenue. The police finally decided they were outnumbered and withdrew, but a night garrison of nationalists remained in case of further attack. The flag stayed.[58] A few foreign correspondents, seeing the procession of people making their way to Maud's house, were highly intrigued and wandered along, desperate for some news to report on the king's visit. Their presence ensured that the skirmish received coverage in many newspapers.

Maire and Maud also travelled to Belfast to participate at a nationalist rally which was held at the same time as the king's visit to the north. An estimated 5,000 people went to the Falls Road to hear speeches and watch a hurling match. A Belfast branch of Inghinidhe had recently been formed and its president, a Miss O'Farrell, sat on the speakers' brake with the other women.[59]

But the main event organised by the Inghinidhe was again a treat for the children. This time it was decided to hold the treat on the same day as that arranged for children in Phoenix Park, so that 'all the Dublin children who are too proud and too patriotic to be bribed by 6d into acclaiming the symbol of their country's slavery' would be able to show 'the reptile Press of Dublin Castle' where their allegiance lay. The plan was for the children to assemble at 3 p.m. at Beresford Place and from there to march to Jones' Road park, where they would receive refreshments and watch entertainments.[60] However, they had only allowed themselves one week to organise the event and it really appeared to be more of a symbolic gesture than a desire to emulate their loudly acclaimed Patriotic Children's Treat. Their intentions had been modest enough from the start, but pouring rain on the day made sure that the treat would be subdued. Inghinidhe then asked the owner of the park if they could postpone the event until Sunday, in the hope that the weather might improve, but he suddenly confessed to sabbatarianism (which was of interest to those who went to his Sunday race meetings), so the treat took place in the rain, minus the procession from Beresford Place.

According to the figures in the *United Irishman*, an unlikely (given the conditions) 15,000 children attended, as opposed to a meagre 9,000 in Phoenix Park.[61] Despite the gloss placed upon events by Griffith, the event was not a great success. The annual report of the Inghinidhe admitted that as arrangements were 'unavoidably hurried' they were unable to collect sufficient money to cover their expenses, and had to make up the deficit from their own funds.[62]

Why, given that the king's visit had been known of for months, did the Inghinidhe leave all their plans until the last minute? Maud's absence from the group cannot be the reason because not only were there other women with sufficient experience to undertake the necessary work, but Maud herself had been back in Ireland for the past two-and-a-half months. The most reasonable explanation concerns the direction of energy during Inghinidhe's development. Three years earlier, women who had not been politically involved came together for one specific purpose: to plan a children's treat which by its magnitude would symbolise nationalist revulsion against Victoria—'the Famine Queen'. That event was also of crucial importance for women themselves as it demonstrated they had the ability to organise and it provided a justification for forming a permanent group. Since that time, the women of Inghinidhe had been ceaselessly active. Their organisation had recently become part of Cumann na nGaedheal, a loose federation of nationalist societies; Maire Quinn, their secretary, was a regular attender and had actually chaired some of the executive meetings. So, for the past year, because members were engaged on 'more serious work and could not spare much time for amusement'[63] they had spent less time generally on organising any entertainments. In other words, providing treats for children had now become a peripheral aspect of their work; they had forged a political organisation and one that refused to be confined to 'women's areas'. To have organised another mammoth treat would have been to put back the clock, whereas their intention now was to ensure that women were accepted as an integral part of the nationalist movement.

Inghinidhe na hEireann and Cumann na nGaedheal/Sinn Fein

The National Council was only one of the loosely organised coalitions to have arisen at this time. Cumann na nGaedheal had been formed in 1900 as a means of uniting small groups like the Celtic Literary Society and the Inghinidhe na hEireann. Its programme was very similar to that of the Inghinidhe and had in fact been drawn up by Griffith, Rooney and Maud, who had developed a great admiration for Griffith. Without her financial support (she gave him 25s a week) he would have been unable to devote his time to the production of *United Irishman*. It was small wonder that Griffith gave so much encouragement to the activities of the Inghinidhe; this rare power to dispense money undoubtedly gave Maud a certain political leverage.

In December 1902, Inghinidhe voted in favour of joining Cumann na nGaedheal, and at the fourth convention of Cumann na nGaedheal, held in November 1903, Maire Quinn and Mary Macken became two of the secretaries, while Maud retained her position as a vice-president.[64] From the outset, it was clear that the women were regarded as valuable members.

The process of unification continued over the next few years. In 1907 the Dungannon Clubs (formed by IRB members in the north and militantly separatist) and Cumann na nGaedheal joined together to form the Sinn Fein League. The name 'Sinn Fein' (Ourselves Alone) was in fact suggested by Maire Butler, a member of Inghinidhe. Finally, in September 1908, the Sinn Fein League and the National Council regrouped under the title of Sinn Fein—pledged to work peacefully, through the establishment of native Irish institutions, for the independence of Ireland.

From its earliest days, women were voted onto the executive of Sinn Fein, with members of Inghinidhe supplying the bulk of the recruits. From 1906 Jenny Wyse Power, Mary Macken and Miss M. Murphy were executive members of the National Council; Jenny Wyse Power rose rapidly up the executive ranks until, in 1911, she achieved the highest rank possible for a woman, given that men at that time were unlikely to vote for a female president, by becoming a vice-president. By which time she had been joined by Countess Markievicz and Sydney Gifford.[65]

Only in 1917 did Sinn Fein unequivocally become a republican organisation. Griffith's conception of Irish independence was not endorsed by republican separatists: he wanted a dual monarchy rather than the abolition of monarchical rule over Ireland. By a policy of passive resistance he hoped the Irish MPs would withdraw from Westminster and a 'Council of Three Hundred' would be established in Ireland to build up a national identity. There were many who would not subscribe to this. Mary MacSwiney, later to become one of the most uncompromising of the Cumann na mBan members, refused to join Sinn Fein because she, like her brother Terence, would not accept the 'King, Lords and Commons of Ireland'.[66]

Helena Moloney, who had by now become an extremely active member of the Inghinidhe, also would have nothing to do with the organisation. After Maire Quinn left Ireland with her husband Dudley Digges, Helena had taken over as secretary; she was now to become editor of their journal, *Bean na hEireann*. She explained why the women decided to produce their own paper:

> The *United Irishman*, starting as a physical force, separatist journal, had gradually changed its policy to one of reactionary social and dual-kingdom ideas... We wanted a paper to counter-act this. We wanted it to be a women's paper, advocating militancy, separatism and feminism.[67]

Bean na hEireann

Bean na hEireann (Woman of Ireland), was the first women's paper ever to be produced in Ireland. By the time of its appearance Inghinidhe na hEireann had been in existence for eight years and the women had made a name for themselves through their work with children, their dramatic productions and their anti-recruiting work. Yet few people were properly aware of the unique nature of this independent women's organisation. It was still linked to the plethora of groups existing on the advanced side of the nationalist spectrum and needed a paper in which to express views, not only on feminism, but also on its conception of nationalism.

Sydney Gifford (who had taken the *nom de plume* 'John Brennan', because she wanted to become a journalist and thought if she sounded like a strong Wexford farmer her views would command more respect) was one of a group of women asked to attend a meeting to discuss the possibility of bringing out a journal. Mrs Dryhurst, a Dublin journalist and mother-in-law of Robert Lynd, the well-known writer, was Sydney's contact for this initial meeting, which was also her first experience of the Inghinidhe. She felt overawed on entering the room, imagining the women would be like the heroines of 1798 she had seen illustrated in supplements to the *Freeman's Journal*. She discovered, not romantic heroines, but a group of women dressed plainly in Donegal tweed, discussing finance in a business-like manner.[68] Helena Moloney had invited Countess Markievicz to the meeting—her first encounter also with the Inghinidhe—and the countess burst dramatically into the room, wearing a velvet ball gown as she had come straight from a function in Dublin Castle—one of the last she was to attend. To Sydney's fascination, she immediately offered to sell a diamond ornament she was wearing, in order to raise funds. The offer was refused, as the Inghinidhe were understandably suspicious of this woman from the ascendancy class; an attitude which endeared them to the countess, who later told Helena Moloney that it was the first time she had not been 'kowtowed to'.[69] The other women at this meeting were Ella Young, Chrissie Doyle (another writer), May Day and Miss S. Varian. All joined a committee which worked hard over the next weeks to raise support for the venture. Appeals were made for funds, and each member of the group was asked to persuade her friends to donate 1s a month to pay the printer, which was the only expense as the contributors were not paid. It was to be a monthly journal, price 1d.

The first issue appeared in November 1908. Helena worked

almost without editorial assistance, but the journal received generous support from people like Griffith, Katharine Tynan (who wrote a serial for it), Roger Casement and AE. Due to Helena's growing involvement with the labour movement, *Bean na hEireann* quickly established itself as being in full sympathy with socialist ideas. Under the title 'A Worker' she wrote the labour notes as well as the editorials. Madeleine ffrench-Mullen, the daughter of Dr ffrench-Mullen of Tuam, later a co-founder with Kathleen Lynn of St Ultan's children's hospital and a member of the Irish Citizen Army, edited the children's column and Countess Markievicz contributed another regular feature, 'The Woman with the Garden', where she succeeded in transforming ostensibly practical gardening advice into humourous, if bloodthirsty, parodies of nationalist propaganda, 'A good nationalist should look upon slugs in the garden much in the same way as she looks on the English in Ireland.' Although primarily concerned with the activities of nationalists, the scope of the paper was extremely wide, with coverage extending as far as the Scandinavian women's struggle for equal rights.

An editorial comment declared their battle cry to be 'Freedom for Our Nation and the complete removal of all disabilities to our sex'.[70] National freedom and women's emancipation were indivisible, so both had to be fought for. This assertion of nationalist-feminist principles led to the almost complete separation of the Inghinidhe from any of the existing political currents: they were bitterly opposed to the Irish party, many members had strong criticisms of Sinn Fein's strategy, and constantly criticised the newly emergent suffrage movement for its tacit acceptance of British rule. While Inghinidhe may have been in agreement with some sections of the suffrage groups as to the end they mutually wanted, they totally disagreed over the methods to be used to achieve that goal. The women of Inghinidhe were impatient for results—their sympathies lay unreservedly with the physical force tradition of Irish republicanism, as the following statements admits. It places Inghinidhe na hEireann in close proximity to the shadowy Irish Republican Brotherhood, far apart from the dreams of people like Griffith: 'A "Moral Force" movement i.e. a movement that stops short of shedding blood, and therefore forbids you to make the last sacrifice—that of your life—cannot be taken very seriously, and must end in contempt and ridicule.'[71] Their constant exhortations to Irish men (sic) to 'recognise their duty', with its clear implication of some form of armed uprising, would eventually find sympathetic listeners. In the meantime, the Inghinidhe continued to argue against the policy of giving even critical support to the Irish party's efforts to persuade the British government to pass a Home Rule bill. Another three years were to pass before people like Pearse lost hope of Home Rule achieving anything substantial.

If the Inghinidhe rejected the parliamentary path and also rejected the suffragist insistence upon giving total priority to women's demands, how did they propose to represent women's interests?

An early editorial on the franchise issue (April 1909) clearly expressed their awareness of the vital importance of developing women's self-confidence. They saw their role as organising a women's movement 'on Sinn Fein lines', which would foster a spirit of self-reliance through encouraging women to take part in nationalist life. A strong, visible presence would ensure that when independence had finally been achieved, women would automatically be granted political rights, because they had already gained the only form of citizenship that really counted: membership of such organisations as the Gaelic League and Sinn Fein. The solution to both the national question and to women's oppression was, therefore, conveniently the same: greater representation of women within the existing nationalist organisations, which would strengthen the organisations and enhance women's status—a combination which would eventually result in the obtaining of independence through the self-activity of the people and not by an act of parliament. To accept enfranchisement by a 'hostile Parliament' would only be 'humiliating', undermining all the work that had been achieved by nationalist groups in developing a spirit of nationhood. It was an extremely purist position, particularly since most of the population welcomed the prospect of Britain passing a Home Rule bill, but it does indicate Inghinidhe's total opposition to constitutionalism, whether it affected women or the nation.

It was obviously not a view accepted by everyone.

Republicans like Mary MacSwiney, who was at this time a member of the Munster Women's Franchise League, not the Inghinidhe, argued for the necessity of the vote, regardless of the compromise that would entail. Mary reminded *Bean na hEireann* readers that Sinn Fein had, for the first time, put up a candidate in the Leitrim by-election of the year before (when they brought Anna Parnell over to speak for them, in an attempt to claim the Parnellite mantle for the Sinn Fein cause), yet women, because they did not possess the vote, were as irrelevant as 'the village omadawn or the children playing in the streets'.[72] It was a point that could hardly be denied (although Mary was to change her views after joining Cumann na mBan) and to counter it, correspondents were forced to paint a ludicrously rosy picture of the superior position of women in the nationalist movement, where they were 'treated on the whole with an equal seriousness and a greater courtesy than are men'. The lack of politically active women was blamed on the unwillingness of women to come forward.[73]

Such a denial of the all-too-obvious prejudices that kept the majority of women confined to the domestic sphere enraged the feminists and Hanna Sheehy Skeffington, co-founder in 1908 of the militant Irishwomen's Franchise League, wrote a scathing polemic in answer to those whose nationalism appeared to blind them to the realities of everyday life. Hanna reasonably pointed out that a person holding nationalist views was not automatically transformed into a new being, freed from all the cultural prejudices that had been inculcated from birth. Ireland was a conservative, rural-based society, heavily influenced by religion, where women suffered immense social and economic disadvantages and most people—in political organisations or outside them—reflected the views of that society. The role played by women in political organisations was therefore likely to conform to certain expectations about women's traditional concerns, and she proposed to analyse their participation in a more realistic manner.

The core of Hanna's argument against the nationalist dismissal of the suffrage campaign centred on this question of the nature of women's political participation. She agreed that women were prominent in the Gaelic movement, in the industrial revival and in Sinn Fein, but claimed that this was far from progressive as the nature of their work reinforced their domestic role. The Gaelic League's primary appeal was to the young to learn their native tongue, and women were important in this movement as mothers, in ensuring that their homes were as Irish as possible, and as teachers in schools and Gaelic League classes. In the industrial revival it was woman, the consumer, who was being urged to buy Irish products. Only in woman's capacity as 'mother and housewife, not as individual citizen', had these movements recognised her importance, and such pressures ensured that women would remain confined to those 'purely incidental avocations'. In a memorable phrase, Hanna asserted that in spite of 'theoretical equality, some Sinn Feiners have not yet rounded Cape Turk where women are concerned'. These criticisms applied with even greater force to the Irish party, which had 'steadily ignored Irishwomen' since the extinction of the Ladies' Land League—and in fact it was to be the votes of the Irish party in 1912 that would kill the Conciliation bill, aimed at giving limited suffrage rights to women with property.

Hanna's conclusion was that it was imperative for Irishwomen to organise on Sinn Fein principles: for women to organise separately, as women, and 'to refuse any longer to be the camp-followers and parasites of public life, dependent on caprice and expediency for recognition'. The suffragist view that the vote provided the 'keystone of citizenship' was therefore equally applicable to parliamentarians and Sinn Feiners, and without it, women would remain on the fringes of political life.[74] It was the clearest statement yet of the justification for building an autonomous women's movement.

The following month's issue produced the standard nationalist reply. This time it came from an anonymous 'Sinn Feiner', who argued that 'this English agitation' would not only not produce any benefit for Irishwomen, but would harm the national cause by creating an Ireland 'quiet and resigned under British rule'. Women were again exhorted to join the national movement as the only guarantee that their voice would be heard in a free Ireland.

Both points of view were clearly articulated. One arguing from a feminist perspective that women, as an oppressed group, were entitled to devote all their energies into obtaining the franchise, the major symbol of citizenship, no matter what political implications were involved—if women did not have the vote, the national question would be resolved without women being consulted. The other standpoint argued that the national issue was of such overwhelming importance that it could not be divorced from short-term political ends, and that the logical consequence of obtaining the vote from Westminster was acceptance of British domination. In short, although they agreed that they wanted freedom for women, they disagreed violently over the means to be used to achieve that end. As the suffrage campaign gathered momentum and women began to go to jail for their beliefs, the controversy became even more vehement, but by that stage, as we shall see, Inghinidhe na hEireann was in decline and took little interest in continuing the debate.

There were many contradictions in the Inghinidhe position and very often the degree of sympathy with the feminist cause depended upon the attitude of the individual writer. For example, at one stage in the argument with the suffragists, 'John Brennan' rather patronisingly suggested that the Irishwomen's Franchise League, as a group of educated women, could most benefit women and the nation by opening up an Irish school for girls, modelled on Pearse's school, St Enda's. If they did, she believed they would have the support of all nationalist groups in Ireland.[75] Such a suggestion reveals a basic lack of understanding of the feminist view. Their intention was, by militant campaigning, to persuade the people and the politicians of the legitimacy of their demand, not to curry favour through noble gestures and self-sacrifice. Running a school was a time-consuming occupation that would have absorbed all their energies and confirmed the conventional view of the nurturant instincts of women. 'John Brennan''s advice appears to indicate that some nationalist women also had a tendency to think in stereotypes, yet many of the articles featured by Bean na hEireann contradict this. For example, the conclusion of an article on the Scandinavian women's movement declared 'the women's movement is progressing everywhere and its triumph will mean the triumph of justice in a renewal of joy and beauty in the world'. Editorials deplored the 'early Victorian' views of the Dublin Gas Company for refusing to accept a woman as guarantor, and denounced as 'pernicious nonsense' the *Irish Homestead* for romanticising over the barefoot Irish cailin in her red petticoat and hooded cloak when the reality was that poverty determined what Irish girls wore, and not the desire to look picturesque. While the *Irish Homestead* condemned girls for leaving their country for America, *Bean na hEireann* angrily explained that the harsh life of the countryside drove people out of their farms and it was therefore outrageous that they, rather than their living conditions, should be castigated. Other articles highlighted the appalling working conditions of women, in particular factory workers and nurses—and many of these were written by 'John Brennan'.

Helena Moloney had become not only the editor of *Bean na hEireann*, but also the principal understudy for the exiled Maud, who was now rarely in Ireland. Although Helena wrote faithfully to her, keeping her informed of events, the continued absence of their president, combined with the other preoccupations of Helena, began to have detrimental effects upon the organisation. The editorial in the June 1910 issue of *Bean na hEireann* called for greater support, admitting that, so far, it had held little appeal for the 'average woman'. This summary of the journal's achievements was soberly couched, with none of the brash confidence that had characterised earlier appraisals:

> Indirectly we have benefited our sex, inasmuch as that the expression of militant nationalism by women must do much to command the respect of men and compel them to readjust their views on women as a possible force in the fight against foreign domination. We have done our best to deserve the continued support of nationalists. We ask them boldly to increase it, and we hope we shall not ask in vain.

But times had changed. Nationalists were no longer solely dependent on Griffith's moderate publications as another newspaper—*Irish Freedom*—owned and controlled by the Irish Republican Brotherhood, began publication that November, and there was now insufficient demand for the 'ladies' paper that all the young men read'. The last issue appeared in February 1911. An interesting postscript occurred in the March 1912 issue of *Irish Freedom*, when a notice appeared stating that publication would now be on the first rather than the fifteenth of the month, because *Bean na hEireann* had ceased publication. The two were obviously regarded as belonging to the same physical force tradition.

The king's visit 1911

The collapse of *Bean na hEireann* did not mean the end of the Inghinidhe; however, as a functioning organisation it existed more in newspaper columns than on the street. Activities attributed to them were essentially the product of a few individuals who had been conspicuous within the group, but who now devoted most of their time to such organisations as Sinn Fein. Dorothy Macardle indeed believed Inghinidhe became 'absorbed' into Sinn Fein,[76] and this does appear to have largely been the case. For example, Jenny Wyse Power dropped out of the executive of the Inghinidhe, becoming vice-president of Sinn Fein, and in her later review of women's role within the Irish nationalist movement omitted all reference to the work of the Inghinidhe.[77] *Sinn Fein* stopped reporting Inghinidhe meetings after 1910, and reports had been fairly sporadic for a long time before that. The meetings appear to have been wholly concerned with cultural activities—the children's choir, Irish dancing—but with far less success than before, as 'John Brennan' revealed in a talk which pleaded for 'more frivolity' in Irish-Ireland entertainments. Mrs Tuohy, who presided over the meeting, retorted with some acerbity that there would be no need for such a plea if people could dance properly, conjuring up a dreadful image of solemn young people, desperately concentrating upon the intricacies of the various steps as they dutifully attempted to revive the ancient culture.[78] It was no wonder they failed to attract new members.

Countess Markievicz, an executive member of both Sinn Fein and Inghinidhe, was far too restless and energetic to limit herself to Sinn Fein when more vigorous action was required. In some respects Inghinidhe became a convenient expedient for more militant women to resurrect when they felt that a particular occasion warranted it. This proved to be the case with the commotion surrounding the king's visit.

The new king, George V, was due to pay a courtesy visit to Ireland on 8 July. As soon as this was announced Sinn Fein invited representatives from all the nationalist groups to a conference to discuss the formation of a broadly based committee to organise a united opposition. Eight years previously the national council had been hurriedly formed for the purpose, but many more groups were now in existence and it was hoped that such a joint venture might lead to further co-operation amongst the nationalists. By March the cumbersomely titled United National Societies Committee was formed, consisting of delegates from Sinn Fein, the United Irish League, Ancient Order of Hibernians, and the Wolfe Tone Clubs. Jenny Wyse Power and Countess Markievicz had attended the inaugural meeting, but as members of Sinn Fein; Inghinidhe was not represented. It was, however, reported that Inghinidhe, together with the Socialist Party of Ireland, had held a public meeting in Foster Place, where Helena Moloney and James Connolly spoke against the presentation of an address of welcome.[79] Helena had been an admirer of Connolly's for years; in 1909 she had written to him in America to say that she wished he was in Ireland publishing his paper *The Harp*, as there was 'very, very great need for a workers' Journal in Ireland',[80] and it was obvious that she felt herself to be far more in tune with the socialism of the SPI than with the orthodox nationalism contained in the United National Societies Committee. Inghinidhe was no longer a united organisation but was rather a collection of individuals who from time to time invoked the name of the organisation.

Confirmation of the fact that Inghinidhe was no longer considered capable of mobilising large numbers of women is evident in the formation of a Nationalist Women's Committee, presided over by the tireless Jenny Wyse Power. In some ways this was a retrogressive move as it meant that women's political contribution was again compartmentalised, but there was a specific reason for the committee's existence, which was to propagandise against an address to the queen which was being organised 'from the women of Ireland'. Great anger was expressed at shop girls and other vulnerable groups being pressurised by employers into signing; the employers apparently fearing the loss of custom of upper-class women, who were expending much effort in distributing the address. The whole issue became a battle of numbers as committees were formed in other parts of the country, all with the same aim of exposing the methods used to force women to sign.[81] Eventually, 165,000 signatures were presented in an elaborate address of welcome[82] but the nationalists claimed their work to be victorious as this was a small proportion of Irish women. In fact, as one-quarter of the women in Cork signed, to give the breakdown of only one area, the committee does not seem to have been that successful; unless it was the case that every pro-unionist woman signed, and one equates the figures. But this was not the only contribution the women made to the counter-demonstrations.

From the beginning, a proportion of the women in the committee had tried to force the pace, to ensure that the nationalists would provide the strongest possible opposition to the royals. In April the women sent a suggestion to the United National Societies Committee, urging a public demonstration during the 'enforced' Bank Holiday that was being granted to celebrate the coronation. It turned into the largest nationalist demonstration since the days of the Land League, but some felt that this was not enough: there had to be public dissension when the king and queen actually arrived. Many of the dissidents were women. Countess Markievicz, recalling the occasion in later years, remembered Inghinidhe as being 'always in favour of the most extreme action possible', while people like Griffith, she scathingly remarked, were 'in great dread of a riot'. The nationalists eventually decided to stage a dignified protest against the visit by organising a simultaneous demonstration to Bodenstown in honour of Wolfe Tone; by this it was hoped to keep out of the way 'all the turbulent young men who might possibly make a disturbance'. But the turbulent young women wanted 'something more vigorous', regarding the policy of abstention as futile because those who would boycott the king would be numerically insignificant.[83] It is a fair deduction that the women were, like Markievicz herself, Inghinidhe members, which would explain why she claimed the following incidents to have been organised by the Inghinidhe when they were actually the work of the Nationalist Women's Committee. The personnel might have been the same, but there was still an important difference.

Dublin Corporation again refused to address the king, the pilgrimage to Bodenstown went off as planned, and the small group of women defiantly distributed their handbills along the route of the procession taken by the royal couple. Their resources were so limited that it was all they felt able to do, and their numbers were so small that they needed the help of the older Fianna Boys, who loyally supported Countess Markievicz, their president. She stood with a young man on the corner of Nassau Street and as the king passed they produced a black flag and began to distribute their handbills:

Nationalist Women's Association. Today another English Monarch visits England. When will Ireland regain the Legislature which is by everyone granted to be her mere right? Never! as long as Irish men and women stand in the streets of Dublin to cheer the King of England and crawl to those who oppress and rob them. God save Ireland.[84]

Markievicz thought the ensuing row 'very tame'. One old man started to hit her with the stick he had mounted his Union Jack on, but her back, she happily reported, was pretty stiff and the stick broke almost at once.[85]

Members of the Socialist Party of Ireland joined with the women in holding a meeting of protest. Markievicz again indulged her love of flamboyant gestures as she held up a Union Jack which had been taken from Leinster House (then the headquarters of the Royal Dublin Society), and attempted to set fire to it. As she struggled to burn the fire-resistant material, the police shouldered their way through the crowd to reclaim the flag. Those who had gathered around the countess thought she was about to be arrested and a tug of war developed as people seized her, and the police tried to get hold of the flag. She managed to keep hold of it and finally, by persuading a boy to bring her some paraffin, set the flag alight.

While all this excitement went on Helena Moloney, longing to do something militant herself, spotted an optician's sign displaying pictures of the king and queen. She threw a stone at the offending pictures and after a short chase was arrested. After refusing to pay a fine of 40s, she was sentenced to one month's imprisonment—the first woman to go to jail for a political act since the time of the Ladies' Land League. Ironically, it was Anna Parnell who paid her fine, as she wanted Helena out of jail to continue the work of editing her history of the Land League period.[86] Helena's first response was fury, although she automatically assumed a man must have been responsible, 'I am extremely sorry his kindness took this form, which is most distasteful and irritating to me, and was done against the wishes of myself and my friends.'[87]

James McArdle had been sentenced to one month for burning the Union Jack, even though Countess Markievicz testified in court that she had been the person responsible. William Carpenter received three months for distributing a Socialist Party leaflet which had violently denounced the king. On McArdle's release from jail, the two groups sponsored a demonstration to welcome him and Helena. When Helena rose to give her speech she began by paying tribute to the absent Carpenter, jailed for declaring George V to be descended from one of the worst scoundrels in Europe. She audaciously continued, 'I will go further than that. Not only was King George the descendant of a scoundrel, but he himself is one of the worst scoundrels in Europe.' As the police hurtled over to arrest her, Countess Markievicz immediately rushed to her friend's defence. *Irish Freedom* later jeered that 'they picked on the wrong pair' when they pounced on the two women.[88] Congratulations poured in and Maud Gonne telegrammed her pleasure. Sinn Fein believed their arrest to be a test case for freedom of speech in Ireland and they planned to contest the charges. It could have developed into a *cause célèbre*, and the government wisely decided simply to release the women by the expedient of a judge being found to dismiss the case. But the meeting and court case were widely publicised, with even the *Sligo Champion* giving full coverage, to the consternation of Markievicz's aristocratic family.[89]

In these overly dramatic, desperate attempts by the women to publicise their opposition to the king the most notable feature is their concern to generate a visible opposition, unlike the members of the United Nationalist Societies Committee.

Markievicz scornfully dismissed 'those who preferred the lime-light and laurels to be won by a fierce speech at a rebel's graveside to the possibility of getting a hammering from the police or being arrested'.[90] This was not the reason for the caution of the Irish Republican Brotherhood. Although possessing at most two thousand members, it had a long history of covert operations, of quietly infiltrating open organisations and securing control of key places; it was biding its time. The Easter Rising was a mere five years away. The IRB, as the self-declared custodians of the national conscience, launched the Rising in the name of the Irish people, but in 1911 the women of Inghinidhe na hEireann and the members of the Socialist Party of Ireland, excluded from revolutionary separatist counsels, used the only means available to them to rally the country around the national cause. It could also be said that both were motivated by the democratic desire to involve as many people as possible in political activity, as opposed to the exclusiveness inherent in processions to Bodenstown, which appealed only to the converted. For a variety of reasons, the remaining Inghinidhe members were to move away from the nationalists, giving their support to the small group of socialists associated with Liberty Hall.

School meals for children

Despite her prolonged absences from Ireland, Maud Gonne continued to write articles for *Bean na hEireann* the whole time it was produced. Her greatest concern was the appalling level of poverty in Dublin, which had led to the city having the worst infant mortality rate in Europe. An act had been passed in England in 1906, enabling local authorities to provide meals for school children, but despite the overwhelming need for such provision in Ireland, it had not been extended. In April 1910 *Bean na hEireann* announced that the Inghinidhe intended to inaugurate a scheme to feed children from one of the poorest areas of Dublin, but they denied any intention of this becoming a purely charitable gesture: their ultimate aim was to force the authorities to accept responsibility for the care of the children. Other societies were called upon to give every possible assistance. James Connolly gave his whole-hearted approval and the Irishwomen's Franchise League immediately offered their help. The influence of the IWFL can be seen in a further editorial in *Bean na hEireann* seven months later, when the laws and social systems 'arranged and controlled exclusively by men' were condemned for allowing children to exist in starvation. Women were urged to become active in the campaign.

Many of the church-controlled schools were suspicious of the motives of these notorious women and refused to have anything to do with them. Yet again, Maud's vast list of contacts was to prove invaluable. She was asked by Canon Kavanagh of St Audoen's to provide food for the children of his parish; the canon was an old friend, having spoken at the Children's Treat ten years earlier. Maud spent several weeks in Ireland that autumn and the first canteen was established in St Audoen's national school, where 250 children were served Irish stew by such women as Maud herself, Hanna Sheehy Skeffington, Countess Markievicz, Helena Moloney, Muriel, Grace and Sydney Gifford, Kathleen Clarke, Helen Laird and Madeleine ffrench-Mullen.[91] Their activities soon extended to the national schools in John's Lane, where another nationalist-minded priest—Father Thomas Keans—welcomed their services.

In an impassioned plea for help in an article entitled 'Responsibility', Maud wrote that this 'small uninfluential body' of women who were 'attempting in desperation to do what the state ought to do', had written to, or interviewed, all the Irish MPs with the object of getting the Provision of Meals Act extended to Ireland, without receiving any favourable response. The women were told they must wait for Home Rule while, as Maud anguished, the children died from starvation.[92]

In November 1912, Maud presided at a packed meeting in the Mansion House, where a resolution was passed stating that pending the extension of the act, the Dublin Corporation should make a grant to meet the immediate needs of the children. The meeting also called on all Irish MPs to get the act extended without waiting for Home Rule. *The Irish Worker*, in reporting this meeting, while full of admiration for Maud, had a gut reaction against the intervention of liberals, and poked fun at the 'nice, aimable folks' who attended.[93] The corporation agreed to strike its own rate for the purpose—but it was then advised by its lawyers that it could not do so without the appropriate legislation from Westminster. Once this attempt failed, it was accepted that British intervention would be necessary. Hanna drafted a bill, which Maud then presented to Stephen Gwynn, MP.[94] In September 1914, the act was finally extended to Ireland. The following month the Dublin Trades Council passed a vote of thanks to the women's committee and although it also gave them a grant to continue their work, there was no longer any need for this. The following month the Trades Council sponsored a conference of all organisations interested in the proper application of the act.[95]

In this campaign to have the necessary legislation extended to Ireland, the women of the IWFL were being entirely consistent; it was another aspect of their work of improving the position of women, by legislation if necessary, regardless of the political implications. However, Inghinidhe had defiantly stated only two years previously that they would never 'sacrifice principle to expediency as soon as the temptation occurs', and they would therefore never join an agitation to force a bill through the House of Commons.[96] Admittedly, the statement was concerned with the ethics of the suffrage question, but the necessity for 'uncompromising people' to take a stand on all matters of principle was clearly stated. This discrepancy between the political beliefs of the Inghinidhe and their practice over this issue clearly revolves around the powerful personality of Maud Gonne, the instigator of the scheme and the person most determined to continue the work. Maud was never a stickler for principle if doing so meant that the weak were left to suffer, which was the rationale behind her work with the Red Cross, nursing the wounded in France during the first world war. Helena Moloney, on the other hand, had great reservations about charity being used to alleviate appalling working conditions, and stated so in her column 'A Worker'. She was gently rebuked in an editorial which has all the hall-marks of Maud's prose style, 'Surely little children who have to work hard with their brains at school, have as much right to a meal, as a thirsty citizen who drinks from the public fountain.'[97] Neither did Maud attribute all responsibility for the situation to England, or to the indifference of the Irish MPs; it was for all members of the community, now that they had been made aware of the facts, to protest and work for change.

It's also significant that on each occasion when a spokes-woman was required to put forward the case for legislative change on the school meals question, either Maud or Hanna volunteered their services. It was Hanna who wrote to the Dublin Corporation to ask them to receive a delegation of women, and in her letter she named the prospective spokes-women to be herself, as the President of the IWFL, and Maud as the President of Inghinidhe na hEireann. Again, when it was learned that a special act of parliament would be required, it was Hanna who drafted it and Maud who presented it to Gwynn. So, despite the often mentioned co-operation between the two groups, it could be argued that the contact stemmed from the preoccupations of the leading figures, and was not regarded as particularly meaningful by the other members. The two groups did unite during the 1913 Lock-Out (the attempt by Dublin employers to starve the trade union movement into submission), which saw misery on such a grand scale that soup kitchens were set up in Liberty Hall, under the supervision of Countess Markievicz, and all the women, except for Maud, who was back in France where Sean was ill, joined in the enormous task. But that was a time of exceptional crisis, and it involved the type of self-activity favoured by the Inghinidhe.

The Irishwomen's Franchise League and the Inghinidhe

While Inghinidhe na hEireann had repeatedly made it plain that they did not support this 'English agitation' of votes for women, the more conservative Sinn Fein, perhaps paradoxically, was initially far more sympathetic. During an early debate on the question Jenny Wyse Power and Arthur Griffith had declared that Sinn Fein members could join the suffrage movement without violating their principles, while Countess Markievicz, speaking as an Inghinidhe member, called upon Irish women to 'glory in not having the right of British citizenship' and to join with the men in the collective task of making Ireland ungovern-able. The Sinn Fein members, in more sedate fashion, simply replied that they refused to condemn any group that awakened 'civic and national consciousness' in women.[98]

Sinn Fein's advocacy of passive resistance and the Inghinidhe (or the countess's) delight in militant action partly explains their different attitudes: the Inghinidhe were unable to sympathise with a movement that reeked of constitutionalism, despite the growing militancy of the IWFL. They were at least far more consistent than Sinn Fein, whose support was conditional on the women not rocking the nationalist boat.

By 1911, when the Home Rule issue began to dominate Irish politics and the suffragists threatened to destabilise the situation by their insistence that women were to be included within the Home Rule bill, Sinn Feinn decided that support for feminism had gone far enough. It was all very well awakening 'civic and national consciousness', but not to the extent of demanding women's rights before national rights. Two years later, when suffrage militancy was at its height and most of the IWFL women had served prison sentences for their fight to have women included within the Home Rule provisions, Griffith loftily declared Sinn Fein to be 'not particularly interested in the suffragette movement... until Ireland has some kind of government of its own—then, so far as our opinion will go, Irishwomen, if they desire the vote, shall have it'.[99]

But a vicious attack upon IWFL members by members of the Ancient Order of Hibernians who were stewarding a meeting addressed by Redmond, leader of the Irish party, and other acts of violence against feminists, led to an ill-concealed rift within the Sinn Fein ranks. Countess Markievicz had always disliked Griffith and remained within Sinn Fein because it admitted women as members, not because she had any strong convictions about its policies, but the much more orthodox Jenny Wyse Power, as synonymous with Sinn Fein as Griffith was, became increasingly outspoken about her disagreement with her president's anti-feminism. For his part, Griffith appears to have become steadily more irritable and less conciliatory. While not exactly excusing the assault upon the women, he nevertheless managed to place the blame upon them because, by forcing their way through the crowd, they gave 'ruffianism the opportunity' —and after all, everyone did think that the tiny group of 22 women was about to launch an attack upon the Mansion House![100]

Although Countess Markievicz could be relied upon to

speak at IWFL meetings—especially if there was going to be trouble, as she relished in the banter and skirmishes—she constantly reiterated her point that no Irishwomen should join a suffrage society that did not have the freedom of the nation as its first priority. And of course, by their very nature as suffrage groups, none of them had. Maud Gonne sent messages of support to the huge public meetings the suffragists organised to protest against the Cat and Mouse Act and the exclusion of women from the Home Rule bill, but, as an organisation, Inghinidhe was silent. Markievicz appears to have been the only publicly identified member of the group at this time, and she was as likely to be wearing the colours of one of the other numerous organisations to which she belonged. As a result of their experiences working in Liberty Hall during the Lock-Out, Inghinidhe members like Markievicz, Madeleine ffrench-Mullen and Helena Moloney now directed their energies into the labour movement, encouraged by Connolly's support.

He had taken over, in 1914, as the Transport Union organiser, following Larkin's departure to America, and was very anxious that the work of the Irish Women Workers' Union be expanded and employment, through a sewing co-operative, created for those who had lost their jobs because of their trade union membership. Helena Moloney had been in France with Maud, recuperating after an illness, and when she returned she agreed to take over as secretary of the women's union. Another Inghinidhe member—'John Brennan'—decided in 1914 that she wanted to spend some time in America. It was to be 1922 before she returned. Inghinidhe was gradually fading away.

The significance of Inghinidhe na hEireann

There had been remarkable changes to Irish political life in the 14 years since a small group of women came together to form Inghinidhe na hEireann. Then, nationalist groups had been disorganised, consisting of like-minded people without any central structure to bring some cohesion to the movement, and the Inghinidhe had contributed life and colour to the endless rounds of meetings and campaigns, imparting an enthusiasm and freshness which revitalised older, more jaded spirits and drew many more people into nationalist politics. Because of their intervention, it became common practice at all nationalist occasions for there to be a woman speaker. If this was tokenism, it was certainly a vast improvement over the time when Maud Gonne was only allowed to attend a nationalist soirée on sufferance. Had Inghinidhe not existed, a whole generation of women would never have developed the self-confidence which eventually enabled them to hold their own in organisations composed of both sexes. No matter what reservations might be expressed concerning some of their policies, their importance is that they rebelled against their exclusion and by their very existence opened up a whole world of new possibilities for women. Previously, although women were expected to be patriotic, that patriotism could only be expressed through acceptable forms which were inherently passive, like learning the language or supporting Irish manufacture. The formation of their own organisation gave the lie to this stereotyped notion of women's interests being focused exclusively around hearth and home.

However, the strong prejudices that continued to surround them undoubtedly had an influence which was less positive for women: their determination to win acceptance as political equals resulted in a greater stress upon the interests of the nation, and proportionately less upon their own interests as women. Although they were pledged to support each other, this was an individualistic recognition of women's particular disadvantages and not a commitment to support all women, or to campaign on their behalf. The intervention of the suffragists highlighted this omission, and while the nationalists' initial reaction to criticism tended to be defensive in their reasons for not supporting the suffrage cause, some, like Countess Markievicz, had no hesitation in attacking the single-minded nature of the suffrage campaign, while at the same time being one of the few to offer public support.

Broadly speaking, the attitude of Inghinidhe na hEireann can be summarised by saying that while they were fully aware of the realities of women's oppression and were dismissive of any idealisation of women's position in a traditionalist Irish culture, they saw their priority as the winning of political independence from Britain and the fight against women's oppression as secondary, to be tackled when the national revolution had been won. But they demanded absolute equality of treatment from their fellow nationalists, and were confident that in this way they were promoting a vision of how the sexes would relate in the new Ireland.

Countess Markievicz's speech on 'Women, Ideals and the Nation', although veering too much towards traditional nationalism for some Inghinidhe members, encapsulated the new positive image that they were evolving as a model for Irish women. Her conclusion was highly significant. While continuing to urge women to lead 'really Irish lives' by all the usual means, she added, 'And if in your day the call should come for your body to arm, do not shirk that either.'[101]

Those words were spoken in 1909. The following years heralded a new era and saw the rise of new organisations to meet the challenge of the times. Inghinidhe na hEireann was to dissolve, becoming a fragment of a new organisation—Cumann na mBan. Would it follow the tradition of Inghinidhe as an autonomous group willing to unite with others, but determining its own attitudes? Would it accept some of the criticisms of the suffragists and fight for women's needs to be accorded some priority? Or would the overwhelming militaristic concerns of the time swallow up all issues, apart from the all-important fight for Irish independence?

3. Cumann na mBan, 1914-16
The early years

The Ladies' Land League had given women the opportunity to develop and direct a policy of militant resistance to landlord power. For a brief period, they had been a vital part of the most broadly based mass movement Ireland had yet produced. Inghinidhe na hEireann, formed as a result of women's subsequent exclusion from all political groups, had battled to prove that a new generation of women could also be resolute fighters for Irish independence. Aspects of these two experiences were to synthesise in the formation of Cumann na mBan, which was neither to have the freedom of the Ladies' Land League nor the autonomy of the Inghinidhe. Women were to be given a role, but a role that was carefully defined and limited. While Cumann na mBan would be an integral part of the military challenge to British rule in Ireland, its status was deliberately circumscribed by its constitutional requirement to 'assist' the men in their fight for freedom. The history of Cumann na mBan is, above all, an account of the tensions generated by this subordination and of the repeated attempts by some women to establish a greater degree of autonomy for themselves.

The formation of the Irish Volunteers

Since Parnell's alliance with the Liberals, following the dissolution of the Ladies' Land League, the Irish MPs had concentrated their energies upon the frustrating task of forcing the Liberal Party to honour its commitment to Home Rule. But all the Home Rule bills passed by the Commons were then blocked by the House of Lords. Two events were eventually to overcome this deadlock: the result of the 1910 election, which left the minority Liberal government dependent on the support of the 84

Irish MPs; and the curtailment, the year after, of the House of Lords' veto as penalty for throwing out Lloyd George's budget. The Irish party had guaranteed its continued support for the Liberals on condition that a new Home Rule bill was introduced and now, with the obstacle of the Lords removed, came the certain prospect of Irish self-government within three years.

This straightforward progression was immediately challenged by the Ulster Unionists, who were adamantly opposed to any weakening of their links with Britain. Under the astute leadership of Sir Edward Carson and James Craig, Unionist resistance rapidly assumed the character of a popular crusade. By September 1912, 250,000 Ulster Protestants had pledged themselves by a Solemn League and Covenant to resist Home Rule by any means. The following year saw the formation of the Ulster Volunteer Force to defend the union through force of arms. The Larne gun-running of April 1914 netted 24,000 German guns and made any peaceful solution to the 'Irish Question' highly improbable.

This upsurge of militarism in the north was welcomed, on tactical grounds at least, by the militant conspirators of the Irish Republican Brotherhood, who realised that the threat of armed resistance could be used as a means of weaning a large section of the nationalist population away from parliamentarianism and to an acceptance of the inevitability of armed conflict. Faith in the Irish party and Liberal promises was no longer the answer, as recent events made plain.

On 25 November 1913, at the Rotunda Rink in Dublin, the nationalist challenge—the Irish Volunteers—was launched. One half of the 6,000 strong audience immediately signed up, amidst scenes of frenzied enthusiasm.

The provisional committee responsible for organising this meeting was a careful blend of the moderate and the militant. The driving force behind this initiative, the IRB, was perfectly content to remain, for the time being, in the background. Their intention was to create a mass movement with sufficient credibility to undermine the reputation of the Irish party, and they therefore welcomed recruits from all sections of the population and from all political persuasions. It was a strategy that feminists were to criticise heavily.

Unionist women had, as the *Times* correspondent remarked, made 'an almost greater appeal to one's imagination even than the men', as they raised funds and trained as despatch riders and nurses.[1] In fact,234,046 Ulster women had also signed a female counterpart to the Covenant. True, they were cast in a wholly subsidiary role, but great play was made of this mobilisation of a section of the Irishwomen who had never before undertaken any public role. The Irish Volunteers were now laying their claim to having incorporated the fullest expression of nationalist sympathies—did they intend to include women also?

A number of women had attended the inaugural meeting, their presence confined to a gallery 'specially set apart for them'. Through this separation, the work of female activists during the past decades was symbolically dismissed and women again relegated to the role of passive observers, excluded from any meaningful participation in political events. This exclusion apears even more insulting when one remembers that at that time a number of Irish suffragists were serving jail sentences because of their militant campaign for the vote. And only four months previously, every variety of nationalist had considered it a duty to support the Mansion House meeting organised by the suffragists in protest against the Cat and Mouse Act. On that occasion they had been full of condemnation for a government that refused to allow women their basic rights.[2]

At the Rotunda meeting, Padraic Pearse was the only person to mention that they were there to defend 'the rights common to Irish men and Irish women'[3] but this assurance still did not go far enough. As women's right to citizenship was not included within the provisions of the Home Rule bill, Irish feminists were demanding 'Home Rule for Irish women as well as Irish men'. Pearse's vague defence of their rights was therefore totally inadequate—what was required was an unequivocal assertion by the Volunteers that they intended to ensure women would be granted equal rights when Irish independence was achieved. Such an assurance was not forthcoming. The Rotunda meeting was intended as a reaffirmation of the heroic spirit of Irish manhood, as each speaker made abundantly plain. They were making an 'honest and manly stand'; all who were 'manly, liberty loving and patriotic' would rally to their lead; membership of the Irish Volunteers would help them to 'realise themselves as citizens and as men'. As the subsequent editorial of the *National Student* unwittingly commented, the meeting 'addressed itself to the manhood of Ireland'.[4] It would have been impossible for any woman to have participated in this collective beating of masculine chests.

Women, however, were not entirely forgotten. The manifesto of the Irish Volunteers, read out by Lawrence Kettle, mentioned that 'there will also be work for women to do', and Eoin MacNeill, in his presidential speech, made a reference to women which neatly managed to exclude them from full participation: 'There would be work to do for large numbers who could not be in the marching line. There would be work for the women.'

Later evidence confirms the impression that a delicate balance had to be struck between those who opposed any female participation and those who were more enlightened. As Mary Colum admitted, a number of women had made representations to the male leaders who, uncertain how to respond, decided to couch any references as obliquely as possible, in order not to alienate any potential supporters.[5]

But even those who did concede some role to women were utterly traditional in their assessment of women's capabilities— the fact that a precedent had already been established by the Ladies' Land League was ignored, even by those who were well aware of the work they had carried out. The IRB, keen to enlist everyone's services (and no doubt influenced by the urgings of their female relatives), did try to combat such conservatism. Their paper, *Irish Freedom*, carried an article by 'Southwoman' which reassured readers that there was 'nothing unwomanly in active patriotism', adding (rather inaccurately), that no one called Joan of Arc, Anne Devlin, Maud Gonne or the Ladies' Land League unwomanly.[6] While this was useful support, it was couched in such low-key tones that it seemed to be a rearguard argument against those who stubbornly continued to denounce as 'unseemly' the women who did undertake an active role, rather than being a positive statement of the right of women to full participation. Significantly, Maud Gonne, the individual, was mentioned, but not the organisation she founded—Inghinidhe na hEireann. The remaining Inghinidhe members must have been conscious of this omission. They had already been written out of history.

It was quite clear that some people refused to countenance the establishment of a women's organisation as part of the Volunteer movement. It was equally clear that no one contemplated allowing women to join on a similar basis to the men. The desire to preserve unity amongst the ranks meant that there was little ground for manoeuvre, especially in the presence of committee members like Michael Judge, of the Ancient Order of Hibernians. He had once suggested the use of 'slender, stinging riding whips' for any suffragist who dared to approach Prime Minister Asquith and he was continuing to insist, as late as March 1914, that:

> The movement was one in which there was no room for the ladies, there was yet no need for an ambulance corps, or any other corps, but in the course of a few months there would be uniforms and rifles would be wanted... and the ladies could form a society and then collect money for that, and put their hearts and souls into it. (cheers)[7]

Caitlin de Brun's article in April's *Irish Volunteer* was scarcely more encouraging as she cautiously concluded that there could be no more 'intense delight' for patriotic Irishwomen than making flags for the Volunteers. Heated discussions continued behind closed doors until the eventual formation, in April 1914, of Cumann na mBan (Irishwomen's Council).

The formation of Cumann na mBan

The inaugural meeting of Cumann na mBan was held on Thursday 5 April at 4 p.m.—a time hardly convenient for working women—in Wynne's Hotel, Dublin. The initial appeal of the organisers was not to the ordinary woman—the shop assistant, clerical worker, or mother with young children—but to those who would have time to devote to the establishment of the new organisation. In other words, women who did not need to work; women whose husbands or fathers were already involved with the Irish Volunteers. The executive was, for many years, able to hold its meetings in the afternoon without inconveniencing anyone, but after complaints had been written into the papers, meetings for the rank and file were held in the evening. It was one indication of the broadening appeal of the new group.

The meeting was presided over by Agnes O'Farrelly, MA (later to become one of the three female professors in the National University), a stalwart of the Gaelic League and a woman of traditional views. Her address explicitly ruled out the possibility of women taking a direct part in the defence of Ireland, except in a 'last extremity' and, more importantly, dismissed any suggestion that the organisation would enable women to discuss current political events. It was acceptable for the male organisation to enter into debate, but not for their female counterpart, in case this led to 'disunion'. The political arena was to be reserved for men, while women's role was to 'put Ireland first', by helping to arm the men. Agnes O'Farrelly's emphasis did not challenge prejudices but reinforced them. In her eyes, nationalist women were simply extending their domestic concerns to the public sphere: 'Each rifle we put in their hands will represent to us a bolt fastened behind the door of some Irish home to keep out the hostile stranger. Each cartridge will be a watchdog to fight for the sanctity of the hearth.'[8]

One hundred women attended the meeting, and they adopted a constitution which declared their aims to be:

1. To advance the cause of Irish liberty.
2. To organise Irishwomen in furtherance of this object.
3. To assist in arming and equipping a body of Irishmen for the defence of Ireland.
4. To form a fund for these purposes to be called the 'Defence of Ireland Fund'.

Other activities, to be learnt when and if required, were: first aid, drill and signalling, rifle practice and the organising of boy scouts. Only in 1933 were the Cailini—the girl scouts—formed by Cumann na mBan; a curious time-lag.

A provisional executive was elected, many of whom were relatives of leading figures in the Volunteers: Agnes MacNeill, Nancy O'Rahilly, Louise Gavan Duffy, Mrs Tuohy,

Mary Colum, Nurse McCoy, Elizabeth Bloxham, and Margaret Dobbs.

The suffrage paper, *The Irish Citizen*, reported that some women, refusing to work in this subsidiary capacity, had decided to form a volunteer corps of their own, with their own aims and without any accountability to the Volunteers.[9] No further reference was ever made to this scheme—it is more than likely that the rebels joined the Irish Citizen Army instead—but there was another, more reliable rumour, concerning Inghinidhe na hEireann and the reluctance of the few remaining members to give up their independent status by joining the new organisation. Not until May 1915 did Inghinidhe na hEireann finally decide to join forces with Cumann na mBan, and this decision was the result of a tactful compromise whereby the Inghinidhe became a branch of Cumann na mBan rather than suffer the indignity of wholescale incorporation. Countess Markievicz conducted the negotiations and enrolled an initial 30 members into the new branch. As the recruits also decided to accept the invitation of the central branch to attend first aid lectures in the rooms of the Irish Volunteers, an amicable settlement had clearly been agreed.[10] As Elizabeth Coxhead has commented, this merger was a pity because it deprived Irishwomen of an independent and highly creative organisation, but in the changed circumstances of the time, women wanted to be part of the mass movement, and that entailed some form of unity with the Volunteers.[11] Maire nic Shiubhlaigh was one Inghinidhe member who joined Cumann na mBan, and she recalled the work of the early days unenthusiastically:

> Essentially, Cumann na mBan was founded to help in establishing the Volunteers... Apart from frequent classes in First Aid, stretcher bearing and occasionally field signalling, a great deal of the time was given over to the gathering of funds in support of the rapid expansion of the Volunteer organisation.[12]

Feminist objections

Cumann na mBan's development was as rapid as that of the Volunteers—in many ways, the one was a shadow image of the other. For example, the four Dublin branches of Cumann na mBan were attached to the four Dublin battalions of the Volunteers. It was an ambiguously close relationship, and one that was to prove extremely controversial, but while many feminists held aloof hundreds of women were eager to join. In August 1914 there were 40 branches, by October there were 63 some having as many as 100 members. The provisional committee was a mixture of the older, more conservative women, and the young. Some were purely figureheads, like Agnes, the wife of Eoin MacNeill, chosen because their husbands were prominent in the Volunteers, while others were more like Mary Colum, wife of the poet Padraic Colum, whose autobiography reveals a spirited, independent woman, well aware of the disadvantages suffered by her sex.[13] She worked three days a week for Cumann na mBan, without payment. It was to be women like her who were to counter the feminist objections to Cumann na mBan because, unlike some of her associates, she understood the significance of their criticisms.

The Irishwomen's Franchise League was the closest in political sympathy to Cumann na mBan and also its most persistent critic. Most other suffrage groups remained silent on the national question in order to preserve unity amongst their members. Hanna Sheehy Skeffington, the most prominent figure within the IWFL, was also a member of the Socialist Party of Ireland, and a close associate of James Connolly. She and her husband Francis, as socialists, were in favour of Irish independence, but as pacifists refused to join the nationalist movement. Because both the IWFL and Cumann na mBan argued strongly for immediate Home Rule, they had a common perspective within which to disagree over strategy. Many Cumann na mBan members had also been leading suffragists, but in other organisations. Mary MacSwiney had been a member of the Munster Women's Franchise League (a fairly conservative mixture of nationalists and unionists), leaving in protest in 1914 as a result of their support for Britain in the first world war. Mary Hayden, another well-known nationalist figure, was a member of the Irishwomen's Suffrage and Local Government Association, the most respectable of the suffrage groups. But only the IWFL attempted to come to terms with the problems confronting feminists who also wanted to be part of the nationalist movement.

The IWFL believed the formation of Cumann na mBan to be a retrogressive step which had put back the movement for women's emancipation. As soon as the men had realised the necessity of having a subordinate organisation to do the necessary but tedious work of collecting funds, the women had eagerly responded, but without first extracting a public commitment from the Volunteers that the women would be politically equal to the men. The feminists argued that as the Volunteers could not operate effectively without the money that was being collected by the women, they had the opportunity of using this position of strength as a bargaining counter. In other words, the women should now refuse to work for the Volunteer movement *unless* the men specifically stated in their manifesto that they were fighting for the liberty of men *and* women, and that they put this commitment into practice by giving women places on the Volunteer executive. This advice was not acted upon. Members of Cumann na mBan reacted to the suggestion in various ways, but all echoed Helena Moloney's words that 'there can be no free women in an enslaved nation'. Their task was, as Mary MacSwiney stated, to prepare 'our women to fulfil worthily the responsibilities, which in a few years at farthest will develop upon them'.[14] They obviously believed their efforts would be sufficient proof of their desire for full citizenship when independence finally arrived. Rosamund Jacob was one of the few to agree with some of the criticisms of the IWFL, while maintaining a nationalist outlook. She felt that the leadership of Cumann na mBan would be 'much to blame' if they did not insist upon representation on the Volunteer executive, and she called for 'all possible pressure' to be brought to bear on them.[15] But there was no internal pressure and therefore no demands were made. The close family ties between the two nationalist organisations might have made any systematic pressurising too fraught with other tensions.

As Cumann na mBan would not tackle the Volunteers, the IWFL decided to do so. They had been on the offensive from the very beginning. The manifesto of the Volunteers pledged the organisation to 'secure and maintain the rights and liberties common to all the people of Ireland'; an ambiguity the feminists were determined to clarify because, in legal terms, a woman was not a person (person being defined as 'male person'). So what was the Volunteers' definition of 'people', they asked, was it the government's, or was it the suffragists'? Clarification was a long time in coming, but eventually Thomas MacDonagh, the director of training, whose wife Muriel was a member of the IWFL, assured the suffragists that 'by the words "people" and "nation" he for his part meant women as well as men'. He added that this statement had been applauded at the Volunteer convention and there had been no dissent.[16] It was regarded as feeble reassurance. *The Irish Citizen* remained unconvinced as to the sincerity of the Volunteer members: 'It is regrettable that they had not the courage to definitely state as much in their constitution, by adding the words "without distinction of sex" after "people" wherever it occurs.'[17] *The Irish Citizen* was right. Despite MacDonagh's sophistry, the Volunteers still had no position on the question of votes for women. They were determined to preserve a united front, no matter what compromises this entailed. Five months after this exchange, Francis Sheehy Skeffington, editor of *The Irish Citizen*, wrote an open letter to his close friend MacDonagh, in which all the feminist and pacifist objections to the policies of the Volunteers coalesced in his concluding question on the reason for women's exclusion: 'and when you have found and clearly expressed the reason why women cannot be asked to enrol in this movement, you will be close to the reactionary element in the movement itself.'[18]

Cumann na mBan activists, far from resenting this segregation, reacted furiously to any suggestion that they held an inferior position within the nationalist movement. Mary Colum, busily touring the country setting up new branches, made a spirited attack on such detractors, declaring Cumann na mBan to be: 'not the auxiliaries or the handmaidens or the campfollowers of the Volunteers—we are their allies. We are an independent body with our own executive and our own constitution.'[19] She predicted that such was the enthusiasm women felt for the organisation, that were the Volunteers to disintegrate, the women would have the strength to bring the whole movement back to life. She also insisted that Cumann na mBan was an integral part of the entire movement, because 'where the members of Cumann na mBan are the most numerous the spirit of the Volunteers is best.'

This was undoubtedly the case, the work performed by Cumann na mBan *was* essential, no one was denying that—an energetic squad of Cumann na mBan activists meant that the local Volunteers would have little difficulty in equipping themselves. Cumann na mBan members were generally the sisters, wives, and girlfriends of the Volunteers and whereas inside the home they washed, cooked and cleaned, outside the home they now sewed haversacks, learned first aid and raised money for their men. It was a division of labour that duplicated the differentiation of sex roles in the wider society and discouraged the expression of any alternative views.

The unorthodox Countess Markievicz, amicably separated from her Polish husband and with her daughter Maeve brought up by her mother, Lady Gore-Booth, was one of the few who could risk challenging convention, but not even the countess voiced her criticisms directly to the Volunteers. She reserved her most severe criticisms for IWFL meetings, when she would be speaking to an audience of the already converted:

> Today the women attached to national movements are there chiefly to collect funds for the men to spend. These Ladies' Auxiliaries demoralise women, set them up in separate camps, and deprive them of all initiative and independence... take up your responsibilities and be prepared to go your own way depending for safety on your own courage, your own truth, and your own common sense... The two brilliant classes of women who follow this higher ideal are Suffragettes and the Trades Union or Labour women. In them lies the hope of the future.[20]

It seems surprising that someone who was to become so closely identified with Cumann na mBan should display such negative feelings about the organisation. But Markievicz, although a member of the executive, did not become actively involved with Cumann na mBan until after the Easter Rising. Before that time her involvement was limited to occasional speeches at recruiting meetings. She had been elected honorary treasurer of the Irish Citizen Army, in recognition of her work for the Transport

Union during the 1913 Lock-Out, and she was a member of the women's section of the ICA, along with most of the former Inghinidhe members. There was far less sex segregation within the ICA: first aid lectures, for example, were given jointly to women and men by Dr Kathleen Lynn. This had the effect, Frank Robbins recalled, of binding the men and women much closer to each other.[21] Connolly's influence was also important in achieving a fair measure of acceptance of women as comrades-in-arms. When Helena Moloney took over the work of organising the Irish Women Workers' Union in 1915, she and Connolly established a sewing shop for some of the women who had lost their jobs during the Lock-Out, which forged even closer links between the women and men of Liberty Hall. While the majority of prominent women within the ICA were middle class—Nellie Gifford, Madeleine ffrench-Mullen, Kathleen Lynn—the rank and file mostly consisted of young women who had been dismissed from Jacob's factory for their membership of a trade union, and women like Rosie Hackett, who was a newspaper seller. Relations between the ICA and the Volunteers remained strained until Connolly's secret meeting with the Volunteer Military Council at the beginning of 1916, and Markievicz was the only person who belonged to both camps. It was an example of class collaboration for which Sean O'Casey unsuccessfully attempted to have her expelled. In the end, he resigned in protest.

The consolidation of Cumann na mBan

In December 1914, eight months after its inauguration, Cumann na mBan held its first convention. The hostile comments they had been subjected to had obviously been noted, at least on the level of organisational autonomy. Whereas the original statement of aims had simply said that Irishwomen would be organised to further the cause of Irish liberty, a revised version declared Cumann na mBan to be 'an independent body of Nationalist Irishwomen'. It was now also explicitly laid down that the direction of the branches would be carried out by the executive committee.[22] What remained unclear was whether or not Cumann na mBan would be able to take decisions on political issues that affected the wider movement. A later president, Eithne Coyle, drew a fine distinction between subordination and the possession of secondary status:

> We were more or less auxiliaries to the men, to the fighting men of the country. It wasn't a case of taking orders because we had our own executive and we made our own decisions, but if there were any jobs or anything to be done, the men—they didn't order us—but they asked us to help them, which we did.[23]

But it was not an equal partnership. Cumann na mBan had no control over how the money they collected would be spent, and when political controversies arose within the Volunteer movement, they felt unable to voice their own opinions. In later years they would have no such inhibitions, but at this stage their indeterminate position led to major repercussions.

Redmond, the leader of the Irish party, had no intention of allowing his position as nationalist leader to be undermined by the Irish Volunteers. On 25 June 1914, he wrote to the Volunteer executive demanding that 25 of his nominees be added to the existing committee. Under protest, they accepted the ultimatum. The IWFL immediately urged Cumann na mBan to declare their absolute opposition to this agreement, on the grounds that Redmond, by his declared hostility to women's suffrage (and his party's vote against suffrage bills presented in the House of Commons), had forfeited any right to have an organisation of women working on his behalf. At first, Cumann na mBan failed to reply to the feminist arguments, a silence that *The Irish Citizen* took as proof of the danger of assisting a movement in which one had no say. One week later, Rosamund Jacob wrote that she at least deplored 'the silent acquiescence of the executive'. Two more weeks were to pass before any member of the executive replied, and then Mary MacSwiney curtly attempted to put an end to the discussion by insisting that such a debate could not be carried on through the inappropriate medium of a suffrage newspaper. She did, however, imply a personal rejection of Redmond's leadership by adding that she did not believe he could hinder reforms even if he wanted to.[24] There was no response from any other members of the executive.

The inevitable split with Redmond eventually occurred in

October. On the outbreak of war he had unilaterally offered the British government the services of the Volunteers and he immediately began touring the countryside, urging men to enlist in the army. Holding suspect views on women's right to equality could be tolerated, but this was too much. The original Volunteer committee immediately repudiated Redmond and his nominees, and at an emergency convention on 25 October the Volunteer manifesto was reaffirmed and the movement pledged to resist all attempts at conscription. Some 170,000 left to form the National Volunteers (and most, including Sheehy Skeffington's brother-in-law, Thomas Kettle, joined the British army), while only 11,000 remained with the Irish Volunteers. They were a minority of the population, but—with the removal of the half-hearted and the opportunists—a minority determined to transform the organisation into a tightly knit military body capable of taking advantage of British involvement in the European war in order to pose the final challenge to British rule over Ireland.

Ten days after this repudiation, Cumann na mBan issued its own statement:

> We came into being to advance the cause of Irish liberty
> and to organise Irishwomen in furtherance of that object.
> We feel bound to make the pronouncement that to urge
> or encourage Irish Volunteers to enlist in the British
> Army cannot, under any circumstances, be regarded as
> consistent with the work we have set ourselves to do.[25]

The numbers involved in this decision were small: 88 to 23 yet taken in relation to the proportions of the male vote, it was an overwhelming rejection of the politics of compromise. A few members did leave at this stage, but it was claimed that hundreds more flocked to their ranks.[25] Certainly, from this point on, Cumann na mBan improved its organisation and extended its activities.

The split over Redmond heralded the final rupture between constitutional and revolutionary nationalists, but the vote taken by Cumann na mBan to reject Redmond is also significant because it revealed that few women who agreed with the Irish party ever joined Cumann na mBan. Women joining Cumann na mBan challenged a great many more cultural norms, given the deep-rooted conservatism of Irish society, than did men joining the Volunteers. Accordingly, while Irish party members were quite happy to pack the Volunteer movement with their supporters, they did not encourage their female relatives to become politically involved. With no opportunity for women to participate in parliament, the constitutional path held very little appeal for Cumann na mBan. Those who joined this new, mass-based organisation, came either from strongly nationalist families who supported this commitment, or else they had sufficient resources to be able to act without their families' approval.

Early activities

One effect of the rupture with Redmond was a lessening of support for the Volunteers. For the time being, church-door and house-to-house collections became impossible as few sympathised with the refusal to back the British war effort. But as fund-raising was one of the main functions of Cumann na mBan, they became forced to devise alternative ways of adding to their 'Defence of Ireland' fund (which had reached £500 by mid-May). Some branches organised flag days in their areas, but the most popular means of raising money was through the staging of *tableaux vivants* (living pictures), which were also a favourite form of entertainment with the suffragists—Countess Markievicz as Joan of Arc, Muriel MacDonagh as Queen Maeve and Sydney Gifford as Anne Devlin, all performing at an IWFL fete being the best-known example. Maire nic Shiubhlaigh had also given her support and considerable professional experience to these occasions, and she took a leading part in many of Cumann na mBan's concerts. At a typical evening's entertainment in Cork, a 'Grand Concert' was followed by a *tableau* of Erin and her daughters, and the Heroine of Ross.[27] Cork members were far more diligent than many other branches in organising these events, possibly because the Cork district contained a fair number of traditionally minded women, who were quite content in this role. Some of the other branches took advantage of the difficulties involved in fund-raising in order to concentrate their energies upon training. This, not surprisingly, was extremely popular with the younger women.

By October 1914, more than 60 branches had been formed and a permanent headquarters for the executive established. At the beginning of 1915, the executive appointed Florence McCarthy as organiser, with responsibility for improving communications between the executive and the branches. She immediately embarked upon a gruelling lecture tour around the countryside, encouraging women to set up Cumann na mBan companies in their towns and villages.[28] First aid, stretcher bearing and drill and signalling, were the areas of activities that the branches were instructed to concentrate upon, and from all accounts the training was rigorous.

First aid classes consisted of a series of lectures given by a doctor (Kathleen Lynn of the ICA, the sole female doctor with nationalist sympathies gave most of the Dublin classes), with an exam to be passed at the end of the course. Fiona Plunkett (whose brother Joseph, one of the leaders of the Rising, was to marry Grace Gifford before his execution) was able, because of her family's support, to devote all her time to the organisation of first aid squads. Her mother, Countess Plunkett, lent Cumann na mBan a hall in Hardwick Street, which was used for training sessions and meetings. With the help of a captain from the Volunteers, Fiona formed six units for the Dublin area, each of which was attached to a Volunteer battalion. Although all of this was regarded as fun and a welcome diversion from everyday life, it also had its serious side and none of the participants had any doubt as to the eventual outcome of all these preparations. In one of their first joint manoeuvres with the Volunteers, the Inghinidhe branch was 'lucky enough' to have three casualties to attend to.[29] One has the distinct impression that the women were impatient for full-scale rebellion.

Cumann na mBan had come a long way from the original image of a group of rather genteel women, earnestly collecting for the national cause. A militaristic fervour was sweeping through the organisation: by the end of 1915, detailed notes on training had been prepared. Each branch was divided into squads of six, one of which was devoted to signalling, while the others concentrated upon first aid and home nursing. A quasi-military structure was introduced, complete with squad commanders and section leaders, the most important duty of the latter being to perfect a system of rapid mobilisation of her section. But despite all this emphasis on structures and training, no directions were given as to whether or not members should learn how to shoot. Rifle practice had been listed as one of the suggested activities in the 1914 constitution, but only a few branches acted upon that suggestion.

The most proficient shots were the Belfast members, who organised regular open-air rifle practice—Sundays at 11 a.m.— occasionally going to Divis Mountain for longer-range practice. Nora Connolly was the principal organiser of the branch, and she was determined to ensure that women were given the same opportunities as men. In the same spirit, the Belfast branch of the Fianna (the nationalist boy scouts organisation established in 1909 by Countess Markievicz), had a few girls as members, because they refused to accept exclusion. It was always a controversial question within the Fianna. At its inaugural meeting, which was attended by the countess and Helena Moloney, one of the boys had attempted to have the two women excluded on the grounds that there was no place for women inside a physical force organisation. It was only after Bulmer Hobson, the Fianna vice-president, had explained whose idea setting up the organisation had been, and who was paying the rent for the hall, that the women were allowed to stay.[30]

Nora and her sister Ina's spirit delighted the countess. The three of them presented a motion to the Fianna Ard Fheis (annual conference) in 1912, arguing for the admittance of girls. Only after a heated debate was the motion carried, and only by a majority of one vote.[31] While the Connolly influence was a guarantee that Belfast Cumann na mBan would be different, the Inghinidhe branch was also keen on target practice, setting up a rifle range in their premises. Although another one was established in the Father Matthew Hall, it was obvious that this would always be a minority interest. So little attention was paid to this aspect of their work by most members that eventually the executive's instructions had to insist that although target practice was optional, everyone had to learn how to clean and load weapons. Members were assured that rifle practice was 'interesting' and, more ominously, revolvers were suggested as the most suitable weapons of self-defence for ambulance workers.[32]

Most shrank away from the implications of this advice, but up in Belfast the Cumann na mBan members felt confident enough about their abilities to challenge the local Volunteers to a handicapped shooting competition, where the 'friendly rivalry' between the two groups gave 'additional zest' to the match.[33] Winifred Carney, who would later be Connolly's secretary in the General Post Office during the Rising, came first in one of the competitions. During the Rising, some women of the ICA were armed for the purposes of self-defence and a few of the Cumann na mBan women who commandeered supplies were also provided with revolvers.

A minority of Cumann na mBan members appeared determined to ignore the rigid division of roles that had been erected between the male and female organisations, even though they had been made painfully aware of the fact that a distinction did exist, and that it would be maintained. The Connolly sisters had already experienced this at a very early stage, which perhaps explains the assertive nature of Belfast Cumann na mBan. On the weekend of the Howth gun-running (25 July 1914), when the nationalists landed 900 guns and 26,000 rounds of ammunition from the *Asgard*, sailed by Erskine Childers, his wife Molly, Mary Spring-Rice and Gordon Shepherd, Nora and Ina were camping with Countess Markievicz at her cottage in the Wicklow hills, along with a number of Fianna boys. Ina recalled what happened:

> They all disappeared on Sunday morning, saying they had been invited out and no girls were welcome. We were to pass the day as best as we could and they would be out in the evening to see us. This was most unusual; even Madame had not been asked.[34]

What they were doing was ensuring that the ammunition was kept away from the untrained and possibly over-enthusiastic Volunteers. Bulmer Hobson had deliberately organised the boys because of their greater discipline, as they had been in existence for a much longer period of time. But he did not inform Markievicz of his plans and Ina, although secretary to the Belfast sluagh (branch) of the Fianna—the Betsy Gray—was also ignored. The women were upset and angry and Ina was positive she knew the reason for their exclusion:

> When we heard that guns had been run in at Howth and
> us sitting pretty a few miles away, it nearly broke our
> hearts. How could we face up to Belfast and father and
> say we knew nothing and did less? It looked as if we were
> not to be trusted... 'Had I been a boy,' I said, 'I should
> not have been overlooked.'[35]

Cumann na mBan had helped to raise the money for these
guns and the women of the *Asgard* played an important part in
ensuring that they evaded the vigilance of the coastguards, who
were on the lookout for such an attempt, but only the Irish
Volunteers were to enjoy the glory of parading through the
Dublin streets, rifles resting triumphantly on their shoulders.

Although Nora and Ina had been excluded from all this excitement, they were now asked to smuggle some of the guns up
to Belfast. A Fianna member drove the car but they were to take
full responsibility, as he would deny everything if they were
stopped. The two young women welcomed this opportunity to
demonstrate their patriotism, and when they were told of the
dire consequences if they were caught, they considered their
earlier disappointment 'more than made up for'. The self-
sacrifice was an honour, so they sat on the guns for the entire
journey. Fortunately, they arrived safely.[36]

In August 1915, there finally occurred an event which
allowed Cumann na mBan to do more than accompanying the
Volunteers on manoeuvres, anxiously waiting for an injury to
present itself for their attention. It was the funeral of the old
Fenian O'Donovan Rossa, the occasion when Pearse gave his
famous oration in which he warned that 'Ireland unfree shall
never be at peace'. This was the biggest nationalist demonstration to be held before the Rising, and the arrangements had been
organised by a committee which included representatives from
all the nationalist organisations, including Cumann na mBan.
Many people commented on the sight of the large numbers of
uniformed women who marched to Glasnevin cemetery, although
the IWFL couldn't resist a little dig by claiming that the crowd
almost invariably hailed them as suffragettes, the presumption
being, as *The Irish Citizen* pointedly commented, 'that all

women who take part in public life in any way must be connected with the movement for votes for women'.[37]

There may have been some basis for the gibe then, but times were changing fast. After the events of April 1916, the Irish public would automatically assume that politically active women were members of Cumann na mBan. All other women's groups were virtually extinguished, with their former members either channelling their energies into organising women workers in the Irish Women Workers' Union, or else working (as Hanna Sheehy Skeffington was to do) as individuals within the growing nationalist movement.

The Easter Rising

The different ways in which the commandants of the various outposts of the Rising reacted to women's urgings to let them also take part was more an expression of individual feelings (or prejudices), than evidence of any clearly defined policy. Class differences between the Volunteers and the Irish Citizen Army may have been wide, but the majority shared traditional Catholic views on the appropriate roles for women. Therefore, although the Volunteers welcomed Cumann na mBan in an auxiliary capacity while the ICA proclaimed the equality of sexes within its ranks, what happened in practice, when the time for armed rebellion finally arrived, was a traditional division of labour between the sexes within the ICA, and a discernible reluctance by many Volunteers about having women involved at all. In most cases, the extent of women's participation depended entirely upon the tenacity of the individual.

Cumann na mBan branches had spent the previous week making up endless medical kits in preparation for a route march on Easter Sunday, which many suspected would signal the start of a general uprising. When MacNeill's order appeared in the papers, cancelling all parades and manoeuvres (a result of his panic over the arrest of Casement and the loss of the expected German guns) everything was thrown into disarray. The leadership decided to overrule MacNeill and hurriedly began despatching couriers around the countryside with new orders for the Volunteers, postponing events for one day, but no one mobilised the women who were left in a state of total bewilderment. Maire nic Shiubhlaigh decided to go round to the Ceannts, as not only was Aine married to Eamon, a member of the Military Council, but Aine herself was an executive member of Cumann na mBan, as was her sister, Lily O'Brennan. Aine told Maire to ignore the countermanding orders and to join them the following day.[38]

If it had not been for the invaluable work of carrying messages that was undertaken by women, the Rising would have been an even more confused venture than it was. Nora Connolly was the first to undertake a courier role. It had been decided, in order not to antagonise the unionists still further, that there would be no fighting in the north. Instead, northern nationalists were to rendezvous at Coalisland and from there to march to the west, linking up with Liam Mellows and his troops. Nora had decided, although entitled to join the ICA if she wished, to stay with Belfast Cumann na mBan over Easter, as the girls regarded her as a leader. She and five other members of the group had barely arrived in Coalisland when news of MacNeill's demobilisation order was received. The inference was that the Rising was to be confined to Dublin, but while Nora argued that there must be some mistake, many of the Volunteers were deciding whether to return home or go to Dublin. She realised the necessity of getting word about this chaotic state to the Military Council as soon as possible and so, with her sister Ina and other members of the group, headed off for Dublin. As Eilis ni Chorra, one of the party, reasoned, at least there would be action there. She was another Belfast woman to pride herself on being a 'crack shot'.[39]

Reaching Dublin at dawn on the Sunday, they rushed to Liberty Hall where the confusion was immediately related to Connolly. The other leaders, quickly summoned, began to improvise their final preparations in an effort to overcome the havoc caused by MacNeill. After being shown the Proclamation of the Republic to memorise as best they could, the girls were sent back north to inform them that the Rising had begun and they were to proceed as planned.[40]

Other women were also sent out—Maire Perolz to Cork, to make contact with Tomas MacCurtain, Eily O'Hanrahan to Enniscorthy, Nancy Wyse Power to Borris, and others to Dundalk, Tralee and Waterford—in a desperate attempt to mobilise the countryside. They were of course chosen because they had a greater chance of travelling freely than the men, but the anxious and disappointed women who carried out these often futile missions were taking risks, and they knew it.

At the start of the Rising few were aware of the contents of the Proclamation, which had been read out by Pearse from the steps of the General Post Office, headquarters of the Provisional Government of the Republic, and which, amongst other assurances, guaranteed equal rights and equal opportunities to all citizens. Connolly had insisted upon that pledge, informing Hanna Sheehy Skeffington, shortly before the Rising, that the signatories had agreed to its inclusion.[41] Hanna had also been chosen (without her knowledge) as one of the five members of a civil provisional government which would come into being if the Rising continued for any length of time.[42] The feminists had succeeded in establishing women's right to equality, but for a long time afterwards the battle would be continued by Cumann na mBan.

Considering the incredible confusion of orders and countermanding orders that proliferated on the eve of the Easter Rising, it's an indication of the women's determination to fight that so many did eventually take part. For them in particular, the first day was a day of chaos, of searching for outposts, asking to be allowed to join and, occasionally, of being turned away.

Maire nic Shiubhlaigh walked the streets of Dublin in a fruitless search for the Ceannts, who had gone on without her. She eventually made her way to the Sinn Fein headquarters where she met up with a group of women, all wandering around in the same state as herself. The six women finally decided to go to Jacob's biscuit factory because one of them had seen Thomas MacDonagh there and it was only three minutes' walk away. Maire knew MacDonagh well, but she had to use all her persuasive powers before she could convince him that the women had an essential role to perform.[43]

Other women found the experience of trying to join the insurgents even more frustrating. Eilis ni Rian, told to report for duty at 12 noon on the Monday, spent the whole day with other members of her branch, in full kit at Palmerston Place, wondering what was going on as they listened to the sound of intermittent firing. At 6 p.m. a despatch rider told them that their services would not be required and they were to go home. They felt they had no alternative but to obey orders. However, Eilis and her friend Emily impulsively decided to go to the GPO, volunteering for any work at all. The sentry suggested that they report to an outpost on the opposite side of O'Connell Street, which they did. To their great relief they were welcomed by the Volunteers. After spending one day acquiring and preparing food they were ordered to the Four Courts garrison, which was commanded by Edward Daly, brother of Kathleen Clarke.[44] It was not surprising that Cumann na mBan members were being sent to the Four Courts at this time—when women had first reported there for duty, Daly had advised them all to go home. Most had refused to accept this advice and simply offered their services elsewhere.[45] This situation was only resolved late on the Monday when two members of Cumann na mBan managed to reach the GPO and informed Pearse, Connolly and Clarke of the difficulties being experienced by women. A hasty mobilisation order was then sent out so that by the evening of the first day women were established in most of the major outposts.

However, there still remained one commandant who steadfastly refused to have any woman under his command—de Valera in Boland's Mill. It was an incident that was never forgotten. Joseph O'Connor, a member of de Valera's staff, felt obliged during the fiftieth anniversary celebration of the Rising to explain why they had been 'deprived of the assistance of Cumann na mBan'. He inaccurately attributed this to the fact that the men were 'over anxious' to reach their positions before 12 p.m. and in consequence missed the women arriving.[46] In 1937, during the Dail debate over his proposed constitution, de Valera bluntly admitted that he had told the women who came to the mill that he did not want them: 'I said we have anxieties of a certain kind here and I do not want to add to them at the moment by getting untrained women, women who were clearly untrained for soldiering—I did not want them as soldiers in any case.'[47] Hanna Sheehy Skeffington later swore that de Valera sheepishly admitted to her that he wished he had not acted in this high-handed way—but only because it had meant that some of his best men had had to spend time cooking.[48]

The role in which many of the women visualised themselves did little to threaten the ingrained conservatism of such men; if anything, it confirmed them in their male image of self-sacrificing visionary. At times there was almost a biblical undercurrent, as when Eilis ni Rian reverently took off Edward Daly's boots and socks, bathing his feet and giving him fresh socks with plenty of boracic powder. He said he felt very comfortable after it, she proudly related.[49]

About 90 women eventually took part in the Rising, 60 of whom were Cumann na mBan members, the rest belonging to the Irish Citizen Army. No member of Cumann na mBan took an active part in the fighting, their role being confined to the three areas of nursing, cooking and despatch carrying. Communication with the leaders in the GPO was maintained largely through the efforts of the women. Not only did they carry messages to and from headquarters to all the outposts, they also got through the British cordons to bring supplies of food and ammunition (hidden in their clothes), arranged for flour to be sent from Jacob's to the other garrisons and, as those on whom the responsibility for catering fell, actually held up vans, commandeering their contents.

The women of the Citizen Army Ambulance Corps had a far different experience from the frustrations suffered by Cumann na mBan. Their roles had been allotted well in advance and when they assembled together with the men on Easter Monday they were told by Connolly that they were now all members of the Irish Republican Army. Shortly before the main body marched off to join the Volunteers a small contingent of ten men and nine women, under the command of Sean Connolly, had left to launch an attack on Dublin Castle, symbol of British rule in Ireland. Helena Moloney, a close friend of Sean Connolly's from the time they'd both acted in the Abbey, was part of the group. The women were all given revolvers (Helena already had her own) for self-protection, but both women and men took part in the charge upon the gates of the castle. Failing in that, they eventually occupied the city hall, where the women immediately established themselves in one of the top rooms, as far removed from the firing as possible, organising places for the men to be fed and the wounded treated.[50]

At the same time, Countess Markievicz, now a lieutenant of ICA was driving with first aid supplies through the Dublin streets, accompanied by Kathleen Lynn, who was medical officer. Helena Moloney had sent an urgent request for medical assistance for Sean Connolly, hit by a sniper's bullet and badly wounded, so Dr Lynn rushed over to the city hall where she attended to the dying man. Late that evening the garrison was forced to surrender. As the doctor was the only officer present, she insisted upon following military procedure in taking the surrender herself, to the astonishment of their captors who were at first unsure as to whether their code of conduct would allow them to accept surrender from a woman.

While Dr Lynn went to the city hall, the countess continued the work of delivering medical supplies. When she arrived at Stephen's Green the hard-pressed Michael Mallin immediately appointed her as his second-in-command, explaining that MacNeill's calling off of the Volunteers had left him short of men.[51] At most the numbers at the Green totalled 138, of which 15 were women. This was so much less than the original plans calculated on that such actions as the occupation of the buildings around the Green had to be abandoned and the women who tended the commissariat and the medical station had to take a turn at patrol. The countess relished this unexpected opportunity to take an active part in the fighting—one of her duties was to tackle any sniper who was 'particularly objectionable', a task she performed with great efficiency, having trained for years for this moment. She was also a great success in commandeering vehicles for use as barricades. Passers-by were confronted by the awesome figure of the 48-year-old countess in full military uniform, revolver in hand, with her best hat with plumed feathers perched jauntily on her head. On seeing three young Cumann na mBan girls wandering around looking for their contingent, she cheerfully invited them to join the group. They agreed, once they had met the calm and capable Madeleine ffrench-Mullen, who was in the summer house supervising the first aid post. They much preferred to join her than the flamboyant countess.

Markievicz also persuaded Mallin to allow Margaret Skinnider a turn as sniper. Margaret, a school teacher, was a member of Glasgow Cumann na mBan but through her friendship with the countess had also become a member of the Irish Citizen Army. She had learned to shoot at a Glasgow rifle club and used to smuggle over easily hidden pieces of equipment, such as detonators, on her frequent trips to Ireland. She and Markievicz had gained considerable experience with explosives as they used to test dynamite out on the hills around Dublin.[52] Mallin reluctantly agreed to Margaret acting as sniper, but was very dubious about her plan for bombing the Shelbourne Hotel, which contained a group of British soldiers. He finally agreed to her schemes although, as she recalled, 'not at all willingly, for he did not want to let a woman run this sort of risk'. Her indignant reply was that as the Republican Proclamation stated women were now equal to men, 'women have the same right to risk their lives as the men'.[53] She was to be badly wounded on the Wednesday, while taking part on an attack upon a house situated behind the Russell Hotel on the Green. It was thought to be occupied by the British, who had to be dislodged before more aggressive action could be taken, but a sniper in the house opposite opened fire, killing 17-year-old Fred Ryan and hitting Margaret three times. The only other woman casualty was Margaretta Keogh of Cumann na mBan, who was killed in the South Dublin Union while rushing out to help a wounded Volunteer.[54]

Most of the women who wrote accounts of their activities eliminated any trace of heroism from their experiences. Louise Gavan Duffy's recollections of her time in the GPO are so prosaic that it is impossible to extract any drama from them. Her week was spent in the kitchen near the top of the building, and as she refused to go down the hall she was aware of none of the events that occurred. When the front of the building began to burn on the Thursday she took no notice as she was at the back, far away from the fire. She was to be part of the final evacuation force who were delegated to take the wounded to the Jervis Street Hospital on the Friday.[55]

Maire nic Shiubhlaigh's remarkably honest recollections convey a vivid impression of loneliness and fear as she and the other women at Jacob's factory spent their time cooking meals, forbidden in case of sniper fire to leave the confines of the ground floor:

Though calls could be heard from the upstairs rooms, the sound of footsteps, an occasional clatter as a rifle fell, there was an eeriness about the place; a feeling of being cut off from the outside world... Our isolation and occasional periods of inactivity were not pleasant. We heard many of the rumours that travelled around the building as the days passed and we had no means of telling whether they were true or not.[56]

Only in the few accounts by the ICA women is there any glimpse of the excitement and colour of those five hectic days. As it's unlikely that the women of Cumann na mBan were more self-effacing it seems likely that the differences stem from the varying levels of integration of the two groups of women. While some of the ICA women took an active part in the fighting and the rest were treated as equal members of their particular outpost, the Cumann na mBan women were isolated from the action and excluded from the deliberations of the Volunteers, their work a duplicate of their usual role, simply transferred to another setting. There was little drama attached to that and so, unemotionally, they got on with their work.

Surrender

Different attitudes towards women's participation were clearly visible when the time came for the various outposts to surrender. Most of the commandants considered the women to be Red Cross nurses, not combatants, and consequently not bound to surrender along with the men. Thomas MacDonagh, as we have seen one of the more progressive of the Volunteers, who took feminist criticisms seriously, had precisely this attitude. He had admitted to Maire nic Shiubhlaigh on her arrival at Jacob's that no provision had been made for women in his garrison, and only agreed to their presence after she had convinced him of their usefulness. Some wanted to remain so that they could take messages for relatives, only reluctantly consenting to leave after MacDonagh had said that the sight of girls being arrested might upset the men. It was this consideration that persuaded them.[57]

The one notable exception was the experience of the 26

women who had joined Eamon Ceannt's forces in the Marrow-bone Lane Distillery. Ceannt himself, although commandant of the area was stationed in the South Dublin Union, leaving Con Colbert as military leader of the post. Colbert had been one of the first boys to join Markievicz's Fianna, which perhaps made him more inclined to regard women as comrades. There was certainly a strong feeling of camaraderie within the post—so much so that they even planned for a victory ceilidh to be held on the Sunday, blissfully unaware of the defeat of the other insurgents. At the surrender, the 22 remaining women marched alongside the men. Rose MacNamara, the officer in charge of Cumann na mBan, presented herself to the British officer in charge, announcing that they were part of the garrison and were therefore surrendering with the others. They joined the rest of the Republicans in Richmond Barracks that night and were then taken to Kilmainham Jail, where they were detained for a week.[58]

Countess Markievicz of course surrendered as she had fought: with great panache. As she and Mallin led their forces out of the side door of the Royal College of Surgeons in order to surrender to Major Wheeler, she shook hands with her troops and kissed her revolver affectionately before handing it over. She and Mallin then marched at the head of their small group until they reached Richmond Barracks.[59]

Of the 34 women at the GPO headquarters, 20 had been persuaded to leave, after an embarrassingly heated debate on the Friday morning. Pearse had called them together to praise their 'bravery, heroism and devotion in the face of danger', and had then ordered them to leave. The response was outraged protests and a unanimous refusal. Only after Desmond Fitzgerald had intervened (because Pearse was hopeless when it came to talking to women), did they reluctantly agree to depart. It was also necessary to evacuate 16 wounded men, so that evening, escorted by Father Flanagan and Desmond Fitzgerald, another group of women slipped out of a side door with the wounded and gradually made their way to Jervis Street Hospital. Three women stayed behind. Winifred Carney, Connolly's devoted secretary, adamantly refused to leave. Armed with a Webley revolver and a typewriter, she had stayed by his side throughout the week, typing out despatches and messages to the troops. Two nurses from Cumann na mBan were needed to look after Connolly's fractured leg and Elizabeth O'Farrell and Julia Grenan of the Inghinidhe branch stayed behind for that purpose. On the Monday of the Rising both had been despatch carriers—Elizabeth to Galway, Julia to Dundalk—and now, a few days later, Elizabeth was chosen to carry the final notice of surrender. The exhausted and demoralised garrison had been forced to leave the blazing GPO and tunnel their way through to houses in Moore Street, where the leaders decided upon their next course of action. They were only too aware of the retaliation being meted out to the civilian population by the British forces and, on Saturday afternoon, they reluctantly came to the conclusion that further loss of life could only be prevented by the complete surrender of all forces. Elizabeth carried a white handkerchief to the nearest British barricade and, although very frightened, announced firmly that Commandant Pearse wished to treat with the Commanding-General.[60] She spent the rest of that day, and the Sunday, touring the various outposts, under military escort, delivering the signed messages of surrender from Pearse and Connolly to all the commandants.

The resolute figure of Elizabeth O'Farrell, impassively handing over these declarations of defeat, announced the end of this attempt to remove the British presence from Ireland. Hostile crowds now lined the streets to jeer at the dejected prisoners marching off to jail; 16 leaders were to be executed, and 1,800 interned. Amongst those arrested, there were 77 women—although only 5 were detained for any length of time. Brigid Foley and Maire Perolz were released that June, Nell Ryan during the autumn, while Winifred Carney and Helena Moloney remained in jail until Christmas Eve 1916. All the women were members of the Irish Citizen Army. Countess Markievicz, as an officer, was courtmartialled, her death sentence commuted to life imprisonment because of her sex. She and the other women in Kilmainham had a ghastly experience which seemed to them to be interminable, as they listened to the volley of shots killing those men they had known so well. When Eva Gore-Booth visited her sister and Constance heard of the death of Connolly, the last to be executed, she broke down and wept, her only desire being to die with her friends. Instead, she was sent to Aylesbury prison in England, treated as a criminal and isolated from all the other political prisoners.[61]

Aftermath

British response to the Rising had been swift and vindictive. But as the executions continued day after day, the mothers, wives, sisters and daughters of the dead men became even more determined to ensure that resistance would continue. Maud Gonne, whose estranged husband Major John MacBride was amongst those executed, was now free to return permanently to Ireland. She would soon be back. Kathleen Clarke, with three young children to care for, had lost her husband Tom, her brother Edward and, through shock and sorrow, the baby she had been carrying. She was a woman of exceptional courage, who had neither told her husband of her pregnancy in case it upset him, nor commented to others on the miscarriage other than to say that she hadn't known if it was a boy or a girl. She worked at the fund for the prisoners even when confined to bed; as she said, it saved her from going mad.[62] Grace Gifford married Joseph Plunkett in his cell the night before his execution, but the prison guards refused to allow them any time together. She was to receive no sympathy from her mother, who denounced her in a newspaper interview as a 'very headstrong and self-willed girl' and blamed her daughter's involvement upon the evil influence of Countess Markievicz.[63] But she had staunch allies in her sisters—Nellie had fought with the Irish Citizen Army in Stephen's Green, and Muriel was now the penniless widow of Thomas MacDonagh, left alone with two young children. Mac-Donagh's last statement was full of concern for his family's future, although he had no regret at the price he had to pay. As he appealed 'without shame' for financial assistance for his family he added 'my wife and I have given all for Ireland'.[64] His words were more prophetic than he realised because, in August 1917, Muriel was drowned.[65] Aine Ceannt had the invaluable support of her sister Lily, who had been with her brother-in-law in the South Dublin Union; both women were to devote their lives to the furtherance of the Republican cause. Her husband's last message to her said he hoped that she would 'freely accept the little attentions which in due time will be showered upon you. You will be—you are, the wife of one of the Leaders of the Revolution'.[66]

In 1917, Chrissie Doyle, a former Inghinidhe member and a member of Cumann na mBan, published *Women in Ancient and Modern Ireland*, which attempted to give due prominence to the historical contribution of women. Grace Gifford Plunkett designed the cover and Aine Ceannt wrote the preface. She was determined that women should not be the passive victims of 1916 as her husband depicted them, but would continue the struggle so that women too would gain their independence:

> In reading of Ireland's glorious past we find the women taking their rightful place in Arts, Literature, Legislation, and even in the making of War.
> The Irish woman of today is debarred from entering on many a sphere which she would desire.
> Are we competent to take our proper place in the New Ireland which is dawning for us?
> Let us see to it that we be worthy successors of Brigid, Maeve and Grainne Maol.[67]

Only an enormous effort of will and an overwhelming sense of political conviction could have sustained these women during this black time. None of them ever wavered. Armed rebellion had been crushed and Ireland left in a state of shock which gradually turned into bitter resentment of the British and grudging admiration for the defeated rebels. Only the women remained free to consolidate this new mood and generate a new movement; it all depended upon their energy and their commitment.

4. Cumann na mBan, 1916-21
Years of strength

After the Rising: reconstruction

The most immediate task concerning those who had not been jailed was the organisation of immediate aid for the dependants of those who had been either killed or imprisoned. Women and children had been left, bewildered and destitute, with no source of income and no one to turn to. Tom Clarke, realising the almost inevitable outcome of the Rising, had left the remaining £3,100 of the Irish Republican Brotherhood funds to Kathleen Clarke, which she now began to distribute. On the Tuesday after her husband's execution, she called a meeting to set up the Irish Volunteer Dependants' Fund. Kathleen was the obvious choice for president, while Aine Ceannt became vice-president. Other bereaved women came forward, some as figureheads, but most with a grim determination to reorganise the national movement as well as to give out relief. Also on the committee were Muriel MacDonagh; Kathleen's sister Madge (one of the indomitable Dalys of Limerick; another sister, Nora, had fought in the GPO); Sheila Humphreys, whose uncle, The O'Rahilly, had been killed during the Rising; Lila, sister of young Con Colbert; Eily, sister of a lesser-known leader, Michael O'Hanrahan, who had also been executed; and Margaret Pearse, the elderly mother of Patrick and Willie.[1] An Irish National Aid Association was also formed, composed of more respectable public figures and without any direct connection with the Rising. The two organisations eventually merged (once Kathleen had ensured that all parliamentarians had been removed) to become the Irish National Aid and Volunteer Dependants' Fund. By April 1917, £107,069 had been collected by this enlarged body.

Kathleen was as much the dedicated Republican as her husband; at their last meeting, in his death cell, she had upbraided him for having surrendered to the British. No personal matters were mentioned in this, their final conversation, which was solely concerned with the future course of the struggle, now to be carried on by women.

As the majority of the population had no idea why the Rising had taken place, their priority was to gain the support of the people. The insurgents had been heckled and abused by the Dublin crowds that had watched them being marched off to jail and although the heavy-handed imposition of martial law and the execution of the leaders had engendered an emotional anti-British response, much more was needed before a political movement could emerge. And this vital work of propaganda was largely undertaken by women. At a time when nationalist organisations were unable to operate, the adherence of the Irish people to Roman Catholicism was invaluable: masses in honour of the dead heroes were held in almost every parish, collections were taken up at church doors and there was a co-ordinated appeal for prayers on All Souls' Day in November. Innumerable meetings were also held to demand the release of the prisoners, most of whom had been interned without trial. Another important task was the winning of international allies to back Ireland's claim to be treated as a nation; an incomprehending world had to be informed of the aims of the Republican movement. As even men like Arthur Griffith (who had not supported the Rising) were in jail, it was again up to the women.

Min Ryan was immediately sent by Cumann na mBan as their first envoy to America. She stayed with Mary and Padraic Colum and was soon informing the vast Irish-American community of the situation in Ireland. Margaret Skinnider, Nellie Gifford and Nora Connolly were others who went over in the first few months after the Rising.[2] Although Nora maintained that she was going over to find work in order to provide for the penniless Connolly family, she soon found herself in the middle of a hectic lecture tour. It was the duty of the nationalist movement to provide for the dependants of the dead heroes, and their duty to spread the word.

One of the most important of these early propagandists was a woman who had not previously been associated with the nationalist cause, Hanna Sheehy Skeffington. Her husband Francis, Ireland's best-known pacifist, had been arrested during the Rising while he was trying to form a citizens' militia to prevent the looting of shops. He was then, while in custody in Portobello Barracks, brutally murdered, along with two other journalists, who had all witnessed acts of savagery by Captain Bowen-Colthurst, the man who arrested them. It was days before Hanna found out what had happened to her husband; days in which her house was looted, her maid arrested and held in custody for a week, and her sisters, Mary Kettle and Kathleen Cruise-O'Brien, threatened for attempting to discover what the military had done with Sheehy Skeffington. In an effort to bring her husband's murderers to trial, Hanna went over to America.[3] As a member of the Irishwomen's Franchise League she had polemicised against Cumann na mBan, denouncing their 'servility', but all the old differences were now swept aside for what was to become a united movement against British rule. Hanna spoke at over 250 meetings on Ireland's claim to independence, and she succeeded in interviewing President Wilson, giving Cumann na mBan its biggest coup yet:

> Sometime in January 1918, I received a mysterious paper (smuggled over, I cannot tell how, but certainly not 'passed by the censor') from Cumann na mBan in Ireland, with a message that I was to deliver the paper 'personally into the President's own hand'. It was a petition signed by Constance de Markievicz, President of Cumann na mBan, by Mrs Pearse, Mrs Wyse Power, Louise Gavan Duffy, Mrs Padraic Colum and others. It put forth the claim of Ireland for self-determination and appealed to President Wilson to include Ireland among the small nations for whose freedom America was fighting... I was the first Irish exile and the first to wear there the badge of the Irish Republic.[4]

By the time the first batch of prisoners were allowed home in December 1916 they had, to their great amazement, become heroes, their release being marked by the burning of bonfires on the hillsides and general celebration. The National Aid Fund now had the burden of coping with an influx of young men who, as a result of their participation in the Rising, had lost their jobs. Their return also meant that the work of political reorganisation could begin. A full-time organiser was needed, to take over from the volunteers who had been working tirelessly for almost a year. Kathleen Clarke interviewed Michael Collins, an Irish Republican Brotherhood member who had been part of the GPO garrison, and immediately decided that his administrative abilities, leadership potential and, above all, his slight resemblance to Sean MacDermott, her husband's closest friend, made him the ideal person.[5] In February 1917, Collins became the paid secretary of the Irish National Aid and Volunteer Dependants' Fund; he also, as a result of the information Kathleen now passed onto him, became the chief organiser for the IRB and in consequence one of the most powerful figures in the nationalist movement. As the ex-internees began to regroup and return to their respective organisations the movement reformed, with many more flocking to join. A mass movement was slowly emerging.

In sad contrast to this was the disarray of the Irish Citizen Army, bereft of Connolly's leadership and with the Transport Union displaying increasing hostility to the link between the army and the union. Despite this, the women of the ICA were determined that the first anniversary of the Rising should be remembered. Maire nic Shiubhlaigh's father Frank was a printer and he agreed to print replicas of the Proclamation, which members of the ICA then posted around the city, as near as possible to the garrisons of Easter Week. A streamer was placed in front of Liberty Hall—'James Connolly Murdered May 12 1916'—which the police insisted be removed. In defiance of this order, Helena Moloney made another streamer and she, along with half-a-dozen other women, rushed up to the roof of Liberty Hall where they barricaded themselves in.

By the time the police had broken down a door and shovelled their way through a pile of coal, half Dublin had been made aware of the fact that James Connolly had been remembered by his comrades.[6]

The remaining prisoners were released in June 1917. There had been two by-elections in which the militant nationalists had trounced the once impregnable Irish party, and the British government did not want the embarrassment of any more convicts being elected to parliament. Countess Markievicz arrived back in Dublin the evening after the men; for the past six months she had been the sole woman prisoner. Ella Young, once a member of Inghinidhe na hEireann and, exhilarated by the enthusiasm of the crowds, soon to join Cumann na mBan, watched the triumphal return as Markievicz was driven through the streets, a radiant figure upon a float piled high with enormous bouquets, a tricolour and small red flowers. It seemed as if all Dublin was there to greet her:

> the Countess entered Dublin in the midst of a long procession, with banner after banner and brass band after brass band; with riders on horseback; with running boys waving branches; with lumbering floats drawn by slow-footed good-natured Clydesdale horses; with trade-guilds carrying emblems; with public notabilities in uniform; with ragged urchins from the slums—a glad and multitudinous company, laughing, shouting, singing.[7]

It was a deceptive spontaneity because behind it was the single-minded unremitting toil of those who had not been imprisoned. As Cathal Brugha, Minister of Defence, later paid tribute in a speech made in the Dail, 'it was the women... who kept the spirit alive, who kept the flame alive and the flag flying.'[8]

Political reorganisation

Despite the initial efforts to draw together the various sections of the nationalist movement, political opposition to British rule remained fragmented and uncertain—a disarray which was compounded by the fact that the two leading figures no longer in jail, Count Plunkett and Arthur Griffith, had deep-rooted and potentially divisive political differences. Although there had been an armed rebellion, there was as yet no agreement on either the ultimate objective of the nationalists—limited independence or a fully fledged republic—and neither was there agreement on the most effective means of continuing the struggle. Plunkett insisted that the movement should now commit itself to republicanism, while Griffith's Sinn Fein still maintained the old programme of winning independence through passive resistance, and it still held on to the 'dual monarchy' idea. As it was imperative that some common agreement be reached Count Plunkett, the only elected representative of the nationalists after his Roscommon by-election victory (the first to be won), called a convention which would attempt to formulate an agreed national policy. This took place on 19 April 1917, at the Mansion House in Dublin.

The ill-concealed differences between Plunkett and Griffith almost led to disaster, but at the last moment a peace saving formula was agreed upon whereby the Sinn Fein groups retained their separate identities while agreeing to 'get into contact' with a new central committee (the Mansion House Committee) in Dublin. This committee had been elected before the end of the meeting, and was an even mixture of both opposing groups.[9] As great efforts at conciliation were being made to ensure that every possible cause of future friction was anticipated and dealt with, when Helena Moloney angrily objected to the absence of any woman on the committee, she was hastily added to the list, along with Countess Plunkett.[10]

Although the committee was to have several meetings over the next few months—its chief aim being that of organising the appeal to have Ireland's case heard at the peace conference after the war—the movement was still far from united. Plunkett had begun to organise 'Liberty Clubs' in opposition to Sinn Fein and there was a danger of a ruinous split developing. Eventually, after undisclosed negotiations, Sinn Fein and the Liberty Clubs merged in June 1917, with Sinn Fein retaining, for the time being, its monarchist constitution, and Griffith his presidency. A new executive was formed, however, allowing for the co-option of prominent prisoners as they were released from jail. All agreed that a convention to review the situation had to be held.

The Sinn Fein Convention of October 1917, held after the final release of prisoners, was the tenth to be staged by that organisation, but as it was now dominated by Volunteers, all the old policies were swept away and an utterly transformed body created. The Rising had been dubbed the 'Sinn Fein Rebellion' by observers at a loss for a convenient label to describe the action which had taken the world by surprise; disclaiming Sinn Fein at this stage would have revealed the extent of disunity that existed, when what was needed was a strong, self-confident movement, to which all could give allegiance. The death of Thomas Ashe after forcible feeding (while on hunger strike for political status), in the month before the convention took place, had reinforced hostility to British rule. A crowd of 30,000, many armed and in uniform, had followed his coffin in defiance of martial law, and there was a grim determination that the flame of resistance would never again be extinguished, no matter what the cost. Reflecting this new spirit, Griffith decided not to contest the presidency and de Valera, the only commandant of the Rising not to have been executed (because he had been able to claim American citizenship), was the unanimous choice. The aims of Sinn Fein were redefined in terms broad enough to be acceptable to all:

> Sinn Fein aims at securing the international recognition
> of Ireland as an independent Irish Republic. Having
> achieved that status the Irish people may by Referendum
> freely choose their own form of government.[11]

Freedom was the primary goal. Any political decisions would come later. It was perhaps the only possible formula at the time, but its ambiguity was to have fatal repercussions during the Treaty debates.

During discussion on the new constitution both Kathleen Lynn and Jenny Wyse Power spoke strongly on the question of women's equality. Their motion was supported by Sean T. O'Kelly, who backed them by recalling the ancient traditions of Gaelic Ireland: 'any Irish man who could oppose women's claim for equality would be acting in an unIrish spirit.' Faced with this argument, the motion was carried unanimously. It was agreed that the final clause of the constitution should read: 'That the equality of men and women in this organisation be emphasised in all speeches and pamphlets.'[12]

On paper at least, this was a breakthrough for the women's movement in Ireland because for the first time women's right to equal status had received specific mention in the policy statement of a nationalist organisation. Rosamund Jacob, as Sinn Fein delegate from Waterford, was also successful in ensuring a tacit commitment to women's suffrage. As a result of her intervention it was agreed that any machinery set up to secure the views of the Irish people on the constitutional future 'would be adjusted to include the women of the country'.[13]

Included on the new 24 member executive were four women —Countess Markievicz, Kathleen Lynn, Kathleen Clarke and Grace Plunkett. Grace Plunkett was never particularly interested in political affairs, although she had a high reputation as a political cartoonist and satirist, but the other women, with years of political experience behind them, were determined to be far more than mere token figures. *The Irish Citizen*, now edited by Louie Bennett, welcomed these developments, but regretted the scarcity of women delegates. She did not, however, point out how familiar those few women were—the younger women who were now flocking to join Cumann na mBan had not yet made their voices heard in the wider movement.

Cumann na mBan held its own convention in the autumn of 1917. Countess Markievicz was again confirmed as president and four vice-presidents were elected. They were all women bereaved by the Rising: Nancy O'Rahilly (who was born Nancy Browne, an American woman from Philadelphia), Margaret Pearse, Aine Ceannt and Kathleen Clarke. Fiona Plunkett, the youngest daughter of Count and Countess Plunkett, was joint-secretary with Jenny Wyse Power's daughter Nancy. Jenny herself was elected treasurer, along with Min Ryan. Other executive members were Mabel Fitzgerald (whose husband Desmond was a leading Volunteer; they eventually parented Garrett, present leader of Fine Gael), Louise Gavan Duffy, Lily O'Brennan, Leslie Price, Madge Daly, Mary MacSwiney, and the O'Rahillys' daughter. Winifred Carney was elected Belfast delegate, although she had no previous connection with Cumann na mBan.

The 1916 Proclamation had been in advance of Cumann na mBan policy, with its guarantee of equal rights and opportunities for all citizens, and Cumann na mBan was forced to take note. For the first time, their policy statement contained a clause which related directly to women, as the members pledged themselves to 'follow the policy of the Republican Proclamation by seeing that women take up their proper position in the life of the nation'. There was also a clear indication that Cumann na mBan no longer regarded itself simply as an adjunct to the Volunteers: the first section of the revised policy for 1917-18 declared that all funds collected were to be devoted 'to the arming and equipping of the men *and women* of Ireland.'[14] The influence of the new recruits was becoming apparent.

Sinn Fein's commitment to women's suffrage, irrespective of the legal position as determined at Westminster, was never put to the test because, in February 1918, women aged over 30 were given the vote. Cumann na mBan rushed into print. No longer was the question of whether or not women held a vote irrelevant to national needs, it was now a crucial instrument in the battle for legal sovereignity: 'Generations of Irishwomen have longed to possess the weapon which has now been put into your hands... Ireland demands this service of you; to ignore that demand would be treason.'[15] This traditionalist response ignored the fact that the winning of the vote was a tremendous victory for *women*; a victory which had been won after a struggle lasting, in its militant phase, for over ten years; a fight for which many women served time in jail. Women were now to use their vote to free Ireland. They were simply to vote for whichever candidate Sinn Fein might put forward and nothing was said on what kind of free Ireland they wanted, or how a free Ireland could benefit women.

The fight against conscription

Before any election was called there was a more immediate problem to be faced: the threat of conscription. Although only men were in danger of being forced into the army, women were to be the blunt instruments in achieving that end. Conscription had already been introduced in Britain, but not yet extended to Ireland, for fear of provoking a violent reaction. But Britain desperately needed more soldiers in the final push against the Germans and the government began to recalculate the risks. Many loyalist employers had already co-operated by sacking their workers, an act which served two ends: men were forced through lack of alternative employment into the army and women, a cheaper source of labour, could be installed in their place. In the spring of 1917 a government decree institutionalised this practice by barring employers from filling vacant positions with men between the ages of 16 and 62, which the Irish dubbed 'economic conscription', and an impressive campaign, supported not only by trade unionists and nationalists, but also by church leaders and members of public bodies, was organised in opposition. The support of women was obviously crucial because with it, the government's stratagem could not be successfully implemented.

On 23 April 1918, the Irish Trades Union Congress organised a one-day general strike, which was effective throughout Ireland, apart from unionist Belfast. Cumann na mBan organised a flag day, the flags bearing the inscription 'Women won't blackleg', and the Irish Women Workers' Union demonstrated in support. Men and women marched to the city hall in Dublin and to central buildings in other towns to sign pledges of resistance. There was a special women's pledge, which Cumann na mBan maintained in their policy for 1918-19:

> Because the enforcement of Conscription on any people without their consent is tyranny, we are resolved to resist the conscription of Irishmen.
> We will not fill the places of men deprived of their work through enforced military service.
> We will do all in our power to help the families of men who suffer through refusing enforced military service.[16]

The women's slogan was one which was remembered for a long time, proof of their wholehearted support for the cause. Unfortunately, many were to take it to mean that because Ireland was never to have a situation of full employment, women would always concede the right of men to work, without demanding their equal right.

The prospect of imminent conscription had served as the potent unifying force the nationalists had craved. An overwhelming challenge to British policy had been staged and the government quickly gave its answer to the resistance by arresting all known leaders. To achieve this, the fiction of the 'German Plot' was conjured up, according to which, Irish Republicans were in a treasonable conspiracy with Germany to achieve Britain's downfall. On 17 May, 73 Sinn Feiners were arrested and deported, and more arrests were made in succeeding days. Kathleen Clarke, Maud Gonne and Countess Markievicz were amongst those rounded up and despatched to England. While the women were detained in Holloway Jail they were joined by Hanna Sheehy Skeffington, who had been arrested while making her way home from America. The former suffragist immediately went on hunger strike, a familiar tactic to her, and won her release in a few days. Outrage was felt at the vindictive jailing of Kathleen Clarke; even Tim Healy, Irish party MP and future Governor General, declared 'It should have been enough for them to shoot her husband and her brother, without depriving her children of their mother.'[17] Conditions of imprisonment were made worse by the fact that the detainees were required to sign an undertaking not to discuss politics with their visitors. As they refused, they were unable to see family or friends. The countess, well-used to the rigors of prison life, accepted this with equanimity, 'It's a nuisance, but unavoidable; and one is not looking for a bed of roses!' but she worried about Kathleen, fretting for her children, whose ill health became a cause of serious concern. She wrote to her sister of Kathleen's 'hero's soul' and the fact that, despite all her privations, she remained firm and uncomplaining.[18] Kathleen, as resolute as ever, became impatient with the fuss being made of her by Markievicz, and on one occasion rounded upon her by snapping 'Little and inoffensive I may be, but my charge sheet is the same as yours'. After that, she said, Markievicz 'shut up'.[19] Maud Gonne, never very strong, was released to a London nursing home in October, but Kathleen remained a prisoner until the following February when, after nine months incarceration, she too was finally freed. Countess Markievicz was again amongst the last to be released. Only in March 1919 did the government eventually clear the jails of the hundreds of Irish prisoners.

Once again, the welfare of prisoners and propaganda on their behalf became the main task of those still at liberty. Cumann na mBan formed two committees, one to look after parcels being sent to the prisoners, the other to collect information as to the prisoners' location and treatment. The former committee soon ceased operations as a result of a letter from the jailed de Valera, who urged them to campaign instead on the necessity of retaining in Ireland sufficient food for the people: 'Conscription is not quite dead yet. England wants the Irish harvest gathered in. A winter campaign might suit the Irish expeditionary force. Cumann na mBan will have its hands full.'[20]

Although Sinn Fein and the Volunteers also supported the Republican Prisoners Dependants' Fund, the spate of arrests had resulted in all the work falling on the shoulders of Cumann na mBan, as those still free went underground. Michael Collins and Cathal Brugha in particular went to great pains to avoid arrest in order to continue their work of perfecting the nationalist war machine: Brugha concentrated upon building up the army, while Collins organised what was to become a highly effective intelligence network. Indeed, one of the unforeseen consequences of the 'German Plot' arrests was that it enabled the militarists to gain control of the nationalist movement. The women's more public work was further hampered by a proclamation on 4 July which proscribed all nationalist organisations, meetings and demonstrations, and imposed heavy censorship upon newspapers. By the end of 1918, more than 500 arrests had been made but Cumann na mBan branches continued to work as normally as possible, although two Drumcondra branch members were jailed for one month for distributing leaflets, and many members were fined for such offences as selling flags without permits.

The Cumann na mBan Convention of 1918

Both Cumann na mBan and the Volunteers had held conventions in 1917. The Volunteer Convention had been held under cover of the Sinn Fein Ard-Fheis. As almost all Volunteer delegates had a dual mandate and effective control was in the hands of the same people in both organisations, co-ordination of policy was greatly simplified. Increasing repression made it impossible for the Volunteers to hold any conventions after 1917 and when Dail Eireann, the Irish parliament, came into existence, in January 1919, and established a Ministry of Defence, the Volunteer executive became redundant. Their allegiance was to the Dail, as they were now the Army of the Irish Republic, and they came under the authority of the Minister of Defence, Cathal Brugha.

For Cumann na mBan, the situation was far different. If the women did not decide their own policies they would be without any voice, as Sinn Fein was by no means as synonymous with Cumann na mBan as it was with the Volunteers. And the Ministry of Defence, when it came into being, would not be particularly concerned with the role of the women.

In September 1918, despite proscription, Cumann na mBan again held an annual convention. Once again, their president was in jail. During the past year, members had undertaken a vigorous recruiting drive, which had resulted in a vast increase from 100 branches in 1917, to 600 the following year. Alice Cashel had been appointed full-time organiser in February 1918 and she had toured the north-east in a determined but hopeless attempt to win Ulster over to republicanism. Mimi Plunkett (sister to Fiona) had toured Cork, Lily O'Brennan had gone to Longford and Wicklow, Aine Ceannt to Tralee, Jenny Wyse Power to Kells, Louise Gavan Duffy to South Armagh, Leslie Price to Cork, and Min Ryan to Wexford and Waterford. It was an impressive campaign, especially given the circumstances. They had proven themselves consistent and effective fighters and agitators and with so many male leaders behind bars and others unable to appear publicly they were, yet again, almost the sole visible proof of nationalist militancy. Was there any necessity for continuing to act as loyal aides, or had the altered situation, coupled with women's greater political experience, created a mood whereby Cumann na mBan felt capable of undertaking a more interventionist role?[21]

The conference decisions clearly revealed a desire on the part of Cumann na mBan to become the military equals of the Volunteers, rather than their handmaidens. The beginning of this process was evident in 1917, when policy was altered so that funds were to be devoted to the arming and equipping of both men and women, but the women had remained pledged only to 'assist' the men. Now this was significantly altered so that they were to 'develop the suggested military activities in conjunction with the Irish Volunteers'. The inference was plain, but the male view was not always in harmony with the women's intentions.

From the complaints reported to the executive, friction between Volunteers and Cumann na mBan members was a common occurrence. Miss Matthews (Dundalk) gave an instance of a dispute caused by a Volunteer interfering in the appointment of Cumann na mBan officers which was now resolved by a policy agreement that elections were 'purely a branch matter in which outsiders could have no say'. It seems incredible that an independent organisation should feel forced to make this obvious point, but the conference report conveys a strong impression that certain Volunteers, considering Cumann na mBan to be nothing more than a servicing agent for their requirements, felt they had a right to direct their internal affairs. So much resentment was expressed that executive members had to step in to prevent too much criticism of the men, reminding delegates that as their own military activities were meaningless apart from the Volunteers, they must be organised in such a way as to fit in with this work. Relations were not entirely eased by the agreement to work 'in conjunction with' the men, because the military activities of Cumann na mBan clearly remained supportive and therefore of necessity under the direction of the Volunteers, and some members were pressing hard for a greater degree of autonomy. It was obviously an on-going dispute, borne out by the fact that the executive had already the previous February issued a circular to all branches, directing branch officers to put themselves under the orders of the local Volunteer officer for the purposes of military organisation. The executive had also requested the Dublin branches to help arm and equip the Dublin brigade of the Volunteers and £296 had been collected in less than three weeks —evidence that they still at least supported the Volunteers as an armed organisation. Their disagreement centred on the lack of respect they were shown.[22]

Cumann na mBan undoubtedly attached a far greater degree of importance to military struggle than to political issues. All their policy changes suggest a realisation that Ireland would have to resume armed resistance before England would grant self-determination. Their primary loyalty was to the Volunteers and not to Sinn Fein, an identification which was strengthened by the fact that many local Sinn Fein clubs were attempting to divert women away from joining Sinn Fein and into Cumann na mBan, which they regarded as a more appropriate forum for women.[23] Cumann na mBan's dismissal of Sinn Fein was evident in members' annoyance that the work they had put into by-election campaigns had given people the impression that their branches were Sinn Fein women's clubs. Militant women regarded Sinn Fein as the moderate wing of the nationalist movement and were digging their heels in to avoid any incorporation into what they perceived as the constitutional path. Unwittingly, many men were in agreement with them, but from an entirely different perspective. One consequence of this joint antipathy to women becoming involved in Sinn Fein was that most women confined their activities to their own organisation and, as Sinn Fein became the public voice of the nationalist people, it remained what it had always been—a predominantly male voice. Women lacked the political finesse of those who had much more experience of entering political organisations in order to gain control—with the disadvantages of their sex, it would have been difficult for them to have had much leverage anyway—but this instinctive dislike of the manipulations of politicians (duplicated on the Volunteer side by many who considered themselves purely as soldiers), resulted in the continued relegation of women to the political sidelines.

One other conference decision was to have important future consequences. A delegate from Camlough, County Armagh, proposed and was seconded by Lily O'Brennan, that Cumann na mBan publish a weekly paper for women. *The Irish Citizen* still continued production, although now only on a monthly basis, but it reflected Louie Bennett's preoccupations and devoted most of its coverage to the development of trade unionism amongst women and was not a forum for nationalist women, although it did report their activities. A paper devoted specifically to the work of Cumann na mBan would have been an invaluable aid in establishing an authentic voice for nationalist women, but it was felt to be an impracticable undertaking in the light of the wartime shortage of paper and almost total censorship. An alternative solution was agreed—branches would get a column for women into their local papers once a month.

In theory, the prospect of establishing a paper was only postponed, but in practice, Cumann na mBan was never to have its own paper, a lack which seriously hindered their ability to define clear, cohesive policies. Local contributions understandably tended to concentrate upon the work performed by specific branches and more general discussions of political affairs were rarely attempted. The Belfast delegates proposed the formation of study circles to deal with social issues, so that women would be able to participate intelligently in government. This was agreed, and so was an addition to the resolution—that the executive issue pamphlets on social subjects, which would be read at branch meetings. Three pamphlets were issued, on such topics as *Why Ireland is Poor*, an analysis of English laws affecting Irish industrial development, but there is no trace of an intended fourth title.[24] Presumably the pace of events led to more emphasis being placed upon other activities. Most branches continued to rely on lectures given at irregular intervals by leading members. The fact that northern members were the most vocal in pressing for political education is significant: they came from hostile areas where overt action was almost impossible, and partly for that reason were keen for their branches to have work which was unrelated to military affairs.

Dail Eireann

For the first two years after the Rising, the nationalist objective had been to establish a mass movement against British rule. That phase was almost at an end. When the British government called an election, Irish nationalists were presented with the opportunity they had been waiting for: to construct a viable alternative to the British political machine.

The first world war finally came to an end in November 1918 and, on 25 November, the British parliament was dissolved and an election date set for 14 December. Although the Home Rule Act was still on the statute book, due to be implemented as soon as the war was over, Lloyd George shrank from the consequences because the intractable problem of Ulster remained. Sinn Fein, flushed with the success of its by-election campaigns, decided upon a vigorous contest which would show the world that the majority of Irish people wanted immediate independence. Their election manifesto was unequivocal:

Sinn Fein gives Ireland the opportunity of vindicating her honour and pursuing with renewed confidence the path of national salvation by rallying to the flag of the Irish Republic.[25]

Labour decided to abstain from the contest in order to allow a unified response to the demand for self-determination. Cumann na mBan urged Sinn Fein to put forward women candidates and received an indecisive reply: the issue would depend on whether or not it would be according to law.[26] This hypocritical concern to be law-abiding must have evoked cynical laughter from the women, in any case, it completely contradicted the decision of the 1917 Ard-Fheis. It was also a spurious argument, as the Representation of the People Act had been passed in February and women aged over 30 were able to stand for parliament. Two women were finally nominated—Countess Markievicz for St Patrick's division in Dublin, and Winifred Carney for the Victoria division of Belfast. Winifred, a committed socialist, disliked the lack of any class perspective in the Sinn Fein platform and insisted upon having her own electoral programme, which called for a workers' republic. She had been nominated for one of the most unpromising wards and few Sinn Feiners were at all enthusiastic about campaigning for a female socialist. The paltry 395 votes she received confirmed her hostility to the reorganised nationalist movement and thereafter she confined her energies to working for the Transport Union in Belfast, becoming a member of the Northern Ireland Labour Party in the 1920s.[27]

From Holloway Jail Markievicz sent the Irishwomen's Franchise League an election address bursting with excitement:

One reason I'ld love to win is that we could make St Patrick's a rallying ground for women and a splendid centre for constructive work by women. I am full of schemes and ideas. Remember me to all my friends in the IWFL.[28]

The election was an historic occasion for the IWFL: not only were they able to vote, but they also had a woman to vote for, and a woman who, despite all their differences, had always come to their defence when they most needed it. The IWFL and Cumann na mBan united in common sisterhood and joyfully threw themselves into the task of making sure that the first woman MP would be elected. With the exception of a few well-known women, like Hanna Sheehy Skeffington, who had sufficient confidence to speak at outdoor rallies, most concentrated upon the tedious background work. The South County Dublin branch of Cumann na mBan described their election work as providing clerical assistance, delivering leaflets, canvassing, providing meals and serving them on election day to workers in polling booths. Similar work was performed for other Sinn Fein candidates.[29] As so many men were still in jail, women's participation was vital. But not all feminists were as eager to support Markievicz; for them, feminism did not transcend other political considerations. For example, Anna Haslam, the elderly founder of the Irishwomen's Suffrage and Local Government Association, which had been in existence for almost 40 years, backed the Conservatives; Hanna's sister, Mary Kettle, backed her dead husband Tom's former party—the Irish party—along with Mary Hayden, who, although a close colleague of Pearse in the Gaelic League, and a former suffragist, had not approved of the Rising.[30]

The result was a landslide for Sinn Fein, which won 73 out of 105 seats. The Unionists won 26, all but 3 in the north-east of the country. The Irish Women Workers' Union was also delighted by the success of Markievicz, who had supported them since they were first formed: 'We rejoice that the first woman elected to Parliament in Ireland is one to whom the workers can always confidently look to uphold their rights and just claims.'[31] Although 15 women had stood as candidates in Britain, none of them were successful.

Sinn Fein had no intention of entering the British parliament. Neither were they proposing simply to abstain in protest. A majority of the people had declared their support for the Sinn Fein programme and so, in defiance of Westminster, an Irish parliament was convened—Dail Eireann—which the British of course refused to recognise. Invitations were sent out to all the newly elected Irish MPs, but, predictably enough, the only favourable response came from the Sinn Fein members.

On 21 January 1919, presided over by Cathal Brugha, the first Dail assembled in the Mansion House. It was a dramatic moment. When the roll of names was called, the response on 36 occasions was '*Fe ghlas ag Gallaibh*' ('imprisoned by the foreign enemy'). Although the Dail was a symbol of resistance, rather than a legislative assembly, it quickly revealed itself as a sober, non-revolutionary body. The Democratic Programme, read out at this inaugural meeting, and hailed as proof of the radical nature of Irish Republicanism, was, as a result of the insistence of Collins and the IRB, a much watered-down version of the original draft of Thomas Johnson, the Labour Party leader. Because of this, the Dail did not pledge itself to work for the elimination of class society and the establishment of workers' control, but only to 'improve the conditions under which the working classes live and labour'.[32] As the nationalist historian Alice Stopford Green approvingly remarked, 'There was nothing revolutionary in the Dail except that it transferred from the English to the Irish the control of the daily life and the destinies of the people of this island.'[33]

It was March before the prisoners were released and the second session of the Dail held. On this occasion, all the Sinn Fein deputies were present and a cabinet selected. De Valera was elected president, and Countess Markievicz became Minister of Labour. Apart from Alexandra Kollontai in the Soviet Union, she was the first woman to enter government.

Dail meetings continued until September, when the Dail was declared an illegal assembly by the British. All other nationalist organisations were also suppressed. After that date, only a few private sessions, held in secret, were possible, and the cabinet met 'on the run'.

Coinciding with the first meeting of the Dail and certainly not authorised by it, Volunteers from Tipperary had, on 21 January, ambushed a group of workers carrying explosives for the Soloheadbeg quarry. During the ambush two armed policemen were killed. It was the first time that Volunteers had engaged in a physical attack since the Rising and the action heralded the beginning of the War of Independence. As Dan Breen, one of the ambushers later explained, it was a deliberate undertaking borne of frustration as they believed that 'this business of getting in and out of jail was leading us nowhere'. He and his comrades were determined to prevent the Volunteers becoming 'merely a political adjunct' to Sinn Fein.[34] After that challenge, those who had been impatiently training for over a year didn't hesistate as they too went on the offensive. In response, the round of arrests started again. Only in 1921 did the Dail accept full responsibility for all IRA actions. In June, Countess Markievicz was sentenced to four months for supposedly talking sedition at a meeting in Cork; she had been free for only three months.

Armed police suppressed the Annual Convention of Cumann na mBan, which was due to be held in the Mansion House on 19 October. The delegates were undeterred and the convention was held in secret elsewhere. An additional policy for 1919-20 was issued, urging women to 'carry out the decrees of Dail Eireann and to assist in its scheme of National Reconstruction'.[35] Although the bulk of the money collected for the Dail came from America, Irishwomen devoted much time and energy to this new fund-raising effort.

Women were invited to stand for local govenment in the elections of January and June 1920. Maire Comerford, a Cumann na mBan member since 1917, at this time secretary to Alice Stopford Green, candidly explained the reason:

> The job fell to them mainly because it was difficult at the time for any courageous or public-spirited man to perform the duties of office. Hundreds of women had a brief experience of public life for the same reason in other places.[36]

'Hundreds' is an over-optimistic assessment, yet 43 women were returned to borough and district councils after the January elections. But Countess Markievicz held a much more pessimistic view of the situation, writing to her sister Eva of the difficulties in getting women to stand for municipal election, even though it was part of Sinn Fein's policy, because of repression, to run women. 'I could not get any woman to stand in either of the wards of St Patrick's.'[37]

As a result of the election, 29 of the 33 county councils and 172 rural district councils gained Sinn Fein majorities and pledged their allegiance to the Dail. Ernie O'Malley, Officer-in-Charge of the Second Southern Division of the Irish Republican Army (as the Volunteers were now known), reckoned that it was more dangerous to be a member of a public body, whose identities were publicly known, than it was to be a member of the IRA.[38] His assessment was perfectly accurate. After all, it was as Lord Mayor of Cork, rather than as commandant of the First Cork Brigade of the IRA, that Terence MacSwiney was arrested, and he himself had been inaugurated mayor because of the murder of the previous incumbent. And in one night in March 1921, George Clancy, the Lord Mayor of Limerick, and former mayor, Michael O'Callaghan, were both shot dead by armed men who had burst into their homes. While no woman suffered the same fate, they were subjected to the intimidatory effects of countless raids and ransacking of houses. Maria Curran, who chaired Arklow Urban District Council from the parlour behind her shop, underwent weekly raids upon her house before it was eventually looted and wrecked. Several women served jail sentences because of their political work. Alice Cashel, Cumann na mBan organiser and now Vice-Chairman (sic) of Galway County Council, received a six-month sentence in February 1921; Anita McMahon, Chairman of Westport Board of Guardians, also received a sentence of six months, for the possession of documents. Many other women suffered because of their relatives' activities: Mrs Brennan of County Clare, whose three sons were all involved in local government, had her house and barn burnt to the ground.[39]

In extending their policy of supplanting the British institutional presence in Ireland the Sinn Fein executive had, in February 1919, recommended to the Dail that Republican courts of justice be set up. On 29 June 1920, the Dail decreed the institution of national arbitration courts, a move partly prompted by the fact that there was intense agitation on the land question, with cattle drives and land seizures taking place in many areas. In order to obtain the necessary funding to establish this legal machinery, Republican Bonds were issued and a vast fund-raising campaign launched. However, a clause in the Dail decree setting up the courts of justice, which stated that once the Republic had been won, there would be justice for 'all those who have suffered wrong in the past through the power and operation of England's unjust law', was omitted at the request of Arthur Griffith. There was, therefore, no commitment to future land redistribution. [40] The Dail even went so far as to criticise the land seizures for diverting energies from the national struggle.

On paper at least, there now emerged a multi-layered system of parish courts, district courts, three-yearly sessions of district courts presided over by a circuit judge, plus a supreme court. Kevin O'Shiel was appointed Judicial Commissioner, answerable only to the Dail, of a Land Settlement Commission, so removing the land question from local pressures, while the arbitration courts continued to deal with civil and criminal matters. Many landowners, anxious for some legal authority, accepted the legitimacy of the Republican courts, despite their dislike of Sinn Fein.

The first session of a land court was held in Ballinrobe, County Mayo. It decided in favour of the owner. R.M. Fox believed that those operating the courts were 'inclined to listen to the flattery of the landlords who told them how fair they were when they sent the landless poor away with empty hands'. [41] It was fair comment. O'Shiel later confirmed that in the Ballinrobe case, the unsuccessful claimant's womenfolk immediately resumed forcible occupation of the disputed property, but 'caved in after a week'. [42] But Conor Maguire, a justice in south Mayo, gave a significantly different account of events, substantiating reports of the militancy of the small farmers and peasants. In order to crush the resistance, the IRA police seized the sons of the most defiant, and held them until the women gave in. [43]

The courts were far from being instruments of social revolution; the process of transferring power from British hands into those of an emerging Irish elite had begun. But the populist character of these courts has been a potent myth within Republicanism, and a myth which was given added colour by people like Countess Markievicz, who claimed that the justices were all elected in accordance with the

> old Gaelic custom... irrespective of sex or age, because those who knew them believed that each one would be just and that each one would have the courage to carry on the work, in spite of the perils attached to it. [44]

At best, this could only have applied to the lower courts, and although the Home Affairs Ministry of the Dail had accepted a form of appointment by local bodies, trade unions, Sinn Fein, Volunteers and clergy, 'Women eligible' was only tacked on at the end and Cumann na mBan was not mentioned at all.

Solicitors who supported Sinn Fein agreed to preside over the courts and Maguire said that except for the absence of judicial robes, 'the courts were carried on exactly as were our opposite numbers of the established legal system'.[45] This adherence to the traditional legal code must have been daunting for those without such a training. Aine Ceannt said that on her first appearance as arbitrator at a labour court in Clare, when she was conducted to the high chair in the Rural District Chambers she had her 'heart in [her] mouth'. Each side had solicitors and when she asked what the procedure was, they bowed politely and said 'Whatever Madam decides.' Aine Heron was another woman active in the Republican courts. Maire Comerford, who described her as a 'brave, splendid woman', explained that as Aine had a large, growing family, the work suited her 'because she could do it while the children were at school'. Aine Ceannt and Aine Heron sometimes sat together as justices for the Rathmines-Pembroke area, and on one occasion had their decision overruled. A money lender, who was also proprietor of a grocery shop, had brought a case against a number of women who had borrowed money to buy food from his shop and failed to repay him. The two justices calculated that he was getting 800 per cent interest on his investment and they dismissed the case, announcing that they wanted the system of money lending discouraged. But Austin Stack, the Minister of Home Affairs, refused to accept this verdict, telling them that their duty was to uphold the law and not to condone departures from it. Aine Heron appears to have been a person of compassion and spirit, who refused to be overwhelmed by the rigmarole of court etiquette. On another occasion she angrily told a barrister who was aggressively cross-examining a witness that she would not allow brow-beating, adding 'You must be fair, this is not a British court.'

Maire Comerford gives another example, this time concerning her good friend, the Honourable Albinia Broderick, sister of the Earl of Middleton, leader of the southern Unionists, who at the age of 47 was able, following her father's death, to train as a nurse. She later built a hospital in County Kerry, in restitution for her family's past expropriation of land, gaelicised her name to Gobnait ni Bruadair and became the most orthodox and unyielding of nationalists. In 1920 she was elected on to Kerry County Council, becoming one of the reserve chairpersons, and as a result came into conflict with the edicts of the Dail, at one stage briefly resigning from the council in protest at a decision to close down, as an economy measure, all the workhouses except one in each county. Maire described her anguish at the conflict between her instincts as a nurse, and her devotion to the Republican cause. After fighting for compromise, she eventually submitted.[46]

One wonders if many of the female judges experienced this conflict between their innate sense of justice and the harsh reality of the situation they were confronted with, which they had no power to alter. Although women's participation in public affairs was far-ranging, a product of exceptional circumstances, the important political decisions remained in the hands of the male administrators and politicians, while policing the courts and guarding the prisoners was the work of the IRA.

The intensification of the military campaign and the British response

The Soloheadbeg ambush had indeed launched the next stage in the war. This time, the Republicans concentrated their energies upon guerilla actions in the countryside, where support was strongest and shelter and aid could be relied upon, and where their relative lack of numbers and equipment could be compensated for by their superior knowledge of the terrain. The Royal Irish Constabulary was incapable of containing this renewed onslaught, so the British despatched a new force—the Black and Tans—of paid mercenaries which arrived in Ireland on 25 March 1920.

The Black and Tans and their later reinforcements, the Auxiliaries, resorted to wholesale destruction of property and indiscriminate murder in an effort to terrorise the population into surrender. Commercial premises were burnt to the ground and unemployment assumed catastrophic proportions. In 1920 alone, 203 people, including 6 women, 12 children, 10 old men and 2 priests, were listed by the Dail Publicity Department as having been killed by British forces outside of the casualties of combat. In one notorious case, a woman called Ellen Quinn was shot dead while sitting on her garden wall, a child in her arms. Over 4,000 arrests were made and 98 towns at least partially sacked and burnt.[47] Those who suffered the worst were those who remained at home. The *Interim Report* of the American Commission on Conditions in Ireland proclaimed 'the sanctity of the family home is violated' by the 48,474 raids which were carried out on homes during that one year. After the sacking of the towns of Cork and Balbriggan, where the infirm, the aged, the women and the children were forced to live in fields for days, the Commission concluded that being 'on the run' was not confined to those actively engaged in the fighting; all sections of the nationalist population were being made to suffer the consequences of resistance. Mary MacSwiney, in her evidence to the commission, described the situation in Cork, where:

> The shops were not allowed to be opened and the Black and Tans stood there and refused point blank to allow the women and children to get the food that was waiting for them... and the fourth day they allowed certain women to buy milk and bread—and nothing else.[48]

Ellen Wilkinson, a representative of the British branch of the Women's International League of Peace and Freedom, described what she had witnessed while on a fact-finding mission:

> the men come in the middle of the night, and the women are driven from their beds without any clothing other than a coat; they are run out in the middle of the night and the house is burned.[49]

Many of the witnesses to the commission gave evidence of the symbolic humiliation suffered by women suspected of involvement in Republican affairs: when their homes were raided, they had their hair cut off. During this period of terror, Cumann na mBan stopped all meetings and lectures. Uniforms were hidden away as their appearance would have meant immediate arrest, and the formal organisation collapsed. At the same time, more and more women were becoming involved in hiding fugitive IRA men and ministering to the growing band of flying columns —small groups of IRA volunteers detached from the regular brigades, permanently on the run, conducting raids and attacks upon the British forces, then melting back into the countryside. Without Cumann na mBan's support, their existence would have been infinitely less endurable. Tom Barry, who led a famous flying column totalling, in March 1921, 104 men, said that 500 women helped the West Cork IRA. Women who were 'sisters, relatives or friends' and not, he added sourly, 'women politicians, holding debating classes or propounding political theories'. The most unglamorous and gruelling of tasks fell upon these women's shoulders:

> They were indispensable to the Army, nursing the wounded and sick, carrying dispatches, scouting, acting as Intelligence agents, arranging billets, raising funds, knitting, washing, cooking for the active service men and burying our dead... On bicycles, those members of Cumann na mBan carried dispatches long distances day or night, and on occasions the quick delivery of those saved the lives of volunteers. Their work, particularly in Government concerns, as Intelligence agents, was vital to the well-being of the IRA... At times, members of Cumann na mBan scouted 'wanted' men on their journeys, and ran many risks to ensure their safety. They raised large sums of money for the Army, and without their hard work, amounting to drudgery, members of the IRA would often have lacked clean clothes or have gone hungry.[50]

It was a list which could be duplicated for every area where the IRA operated. Other prominent commandants later paid similar tribute to their local Cumann na mBan.

Ernie O'Malley, enmeshed in the problems of organising the Second Southern Division of the IRA, was much less enthusiastic in his reaction to the women he encountered on his travels—although grateful for the food and shelter they provided.

While he wanted only to get the taste of blood out of his mouth, to have the time to read a book, he felt they 'glorified the fighting'. His response to those women who regretted that they could not also fight was to wish they could, so that they would 'see the other side of the medal'. Women, in his opinion, were more bitter than men: 'if one had enough work to do, there was not time for spleen'.[51] Precisely. O'Malley was unable to comprehend the daily lives of such women, caught up in war, yet condemned to wait anxiously for news of their menfolk. As men were driven from their homes in order to avoid arrest, the women didn't even have the solace of writing and receiving letters. Only occasionally was word sent that their husbands or boyfriends were alive and well. Muriel MacSwiney, the young widow of Terence, who had died on 25 October 1920 after a hunger strike lasting 74 days, had been unable during their brief marriage to live at home because of the constant raids and was only able to arrange fleeting meetings with her husband. The two would meet after dark some place outside the city. With great pathos she said 'The only meal I could have him for was breakfast, and that on rare occasions. I hardly ever saw my husband at all, to tell the truth.'[52]

While younger women did the essential work of scouting out locations before IRA operations, conveying Volunteers from one safe place to another and cycling around the countryside with messages, the older women—those with families to care for and farms and businesses to look after—provided safe houses, food and medical help. Eithne Coyle, without any trace of irony, described married women as being 'able to work from the home'.[53]

Relatively few women were imprisoned during these years, certainly no more than 50, an insignificant number compared to the 4,000 men in jail. It was a reflection on the nature of their work and the difficulties involved in getting evidence of their involvement—many women were held on suspicion, without definite charges being placed. In April 1921, 26 women were in jail.[54] Countess Markievicz had received a further sentence, this time two years' hard labour, on the spurious charge of having organised her boy scout troop, the Fianna, in 1909. She caustically commented to her sister that she was amazed to see

Baden Powell made a baronet for starting his boy scouts in England. One of her main concerns was again the plight of the women who struggled to look after their families while the war raged around them:

> This last year many babies were born, whose fathers were on the run. It's awfully hard on the mothers. Curfew too, is terrible, for you can't get a doctor. However, the women are as brave as brave, and though they suffer terribly both mentally and physically, they put on a brave face and you'ld never guess.[55]

Aileen Keogh, matron of Father Sweetman's Wexford school, Mount St Benedict (where all the 1916 widows sent their sons), had received two years' hard labour for the possession of an incendiary device; Linda Kearns, captured in Sligo while driving a car full of Volunteers and guns, had received ten years; Maire Rigney was serving nine months for possessions of arms; Ada English was also serving nine months, for possessing Cumann na mBan literature; 14-year-old Mary Bowles had a five-year sentence for having tried to save from capture a machine gun.[56]

Margaret Buckley later wrote about some of the women in Mountjoy Prison with her: two old sisters from Ballinalee, aged 70 and 80, and three young girls arrested because they were weeding turnips in a field when a lorry load of Black and Tans were blown up. They received life sentences.[57] Eithne Coyle was given one year for the possession of Cumann na mBan documents and the plan of a barracks. She had been working in Roscommon, ostensibly for the Gaelic League, but in reality as courier for the IRA. As she cycled around the countryside she would note troop movements and reconnoitre likely-looking targets. At her eventual trial the prosecutor stated she had escaped detection for so long because she was a woman.[58]

Resistance to the British presence continued in the jails. On 5 April 1920, 60 men in Mountjoy, who were being held without charge, went on hunger strike and on the 12 April the labour movement called for a general strike in their support. Louie Bennett, speaking for the Irish Women Workers' Union, affirmed that 'there was not a single case in which the workers objected to refuse to work'.[59] After three days of strike action, and when the prisoners were on the tenth day of hunger strike, the government abruptly caved in and ordered their release. The prison issue was one where the government was particularly vulnerable and Republicans made every effort to draw world attention to prison conditions. At the end of 1919, leading women activists had launched an appeal to their 'sisters in other countries', urging them to demand the formation of an international committee of inquiry into the conditions under which Irish political prisoners were being detained. It was signed by Markievicz for Cumann na mBan, Hanna Sheehy Skeffington for the Irishwomen's Franchise League, Helena Moloney for the Irish Women Workers' Union, Louie Bennett for the Irishwomen's International League, Maud Gonne for Inghinidhe na hEireann, and Kathleen Lynn for the League of Women Delegates.[60] It was an impressive list, even if half the organisations existed only on paper, and it did have some impact, particularly in America, where women organised a lobby of Congress. The Transport Union also played an important role in hampering the ability of the British to wage war. For six months they boycotted all trains carrying armed men and refused to handle military goods, which meant that motor transport had to compensate for the lack of trains and soldiers worked in the docks instead of in combat.

Without the support of the people the small, badly equipped guerrilla army—now facing an immeasurably greater enemy —could never have survived. In the counties where the Republican forces were strongest, the civilian population suffered the worst, particularly when the policy of reprisals intensified. In December 1920, martial law was declared in Cork, Kerry, Tipperary and Limerick, and a proclamation issued by the British military authorities that any person in these counties convicted by the military court of such offences as possession of arms, wearing of uniform, or harbouring rebels, would be liable to death. As a result, almost every family in the province of Munster became potentially indictable. Martial law was later extended to Clare, Waterford, Kilkenny, and Wexford. Of course, Cumann na mBan, the IRA and Sinn Fein were all illegal organisations, having been proscribed at the end of 1919. But there was little attempt to adhere to the rule of law as arbitrary arrests, murders and destruction of houses and property reached horrendous proportions.

The scale of devastation was so immense that international aid was urgently needed. Following the publicity generated by the American Commissions's investigations into the situation, an American Committee for Relief in Ireland had been established, sending over shiploads of food and clothing, and Irish-Americans organised vast fund-raising operations throughout the country. To co-ordinate and distribute all these donations, the White Cross Fund was established towards the end of 1920. By August 1922, over £1,500,000 pounds had been contributed to the fund.

The executive of the White Cross was a deliberately wide cross-section of public figures: Cardinal Logue was president and Lawrence O'Neill, Lord Mayor of Dublin, was chairman; but the committee was again composed of the familiar names of Aine Ceannt, Hanna Sheehy Skeffington, Nancy O'Rahilly, Kathleen Clarke (now an alderman (sic) on the Dublin Corporation), Maud Gonne and Erskine Childers's wife, Molly.[61]

Maire Comerford was delighted to be loaned to the White Cross by Alice Stopford Green, her new role being to find out who was most in need of assistance. For a young woman in her early twenties, it was an exciting mission, much more interesting that her usual Cumann na mBan duties which she dismissed as 'routine'. As Maire said of her relative freedom as a single person:

> No home was burned over my head. No children in my care depended on income or wages lost which a soldier of Ireland, or a prisoner had ceased to earn, or which a worker lost with the destruction of creamery or factory. I was not one of the 10,000 victims of the Belfast pogroms. This left me available when the Irish White Cross was founded.[62]

Her first call was to Galway, to deliver a letter to Geraldine Plunkett Dillon (another daughter of the Count and Countess Plunkett). But she was followed from the station and as a result the house was raided and Geraldine arrested and taken to Galway Jail, where she joined Alice Cashel and Ada English.

Maire, after getting away safely, concluded that she was 'on the run' from Galway. She didn't linger.

White Cross relief, at the rate of 10s for each adult and 5s for each child per week, was organised through parish committees. Maire's task was to contact the parish priest in each area and find out from him the names of families most in need. She regarded it as an iniquitous system because many of the priests were hostile to the Republicans and therefore unsympathetic to the plight of those most destitute—because they were usually staunchly Republican. The experience haunted her:

> I have terrible recollection of women whose husbands were in jail or fighting and they would have a house full of kids and no income at all. And many of them were in the Republican tradition long enough to be at feud with the parish priest, to have been denounced off the altar... and there was no way of getting them help, except through the pp [parish priest].[63]

Despite their hardships and the threat of pauperism, Maire believed that they would never give in, because:

> It was in their blood and tradition to suffer in the causes of national, religious and personal freedom... Mothers would face anything if only we could together win our present battle. The thought that they were rearing the first generation of children who would live their lives out in a free country was enough to support us. There the issue lay.[64]

Her next assignment for the White Cross was a member of a three-person commission to Tipperary and North Cork, reporting on the extent of British destruction in these areas. Here she was joined by Meg Connery, a former member of the Irishwomen's Franchise League, who was now working for the Irish Women Workers' Union, and Robert Tweedy, an engineer.

There were many similar fact-finding expeditions at this time: there was the previously mentioned American Commission, the Women's International League for Peace and Freedom, and the British Labour Party also instituted its own Commission of Inquiry, which came over to Ireland in November 1920. The members of the last-named felt an 'atmosphere of sheer terrorism' pervading the country and they carefully documented a damning catalogue of destruction, brutality and murder. Their conclusions reaffirmed Labour Party policy: withdrawal of the British forces of occupation and the setting up of an Irish Constituent Assembly, to be elected by proportional representation. But although the report was invaluable in informing British public opinion, its recommendations were ignored by the government, which had already refused to institute an independent inquiry.[65]

Countess Markievicz had helped the members of the American Commission when they were over in Ireland; they, in their turn, had been appalled to discover that the countess was tailed everywhere she went. Maud Gonne and her friend Charlotte Despard performed the same service for the Labour Party inquiry. The two women braved the hazards of martial law conditions in order to tour Cork and the south-west, gathering at first hand evidence of the activities of the army and police. Charlotte, known internationally for her work in feminist and socialist movements, was President of the Women's Freedom League in Britain and a member of the Women's Peace Crusade. She had also been an unsuccessful Labour Party candidate in the 1918 election. Motivated by pacifist ideals, she had come to Ireland as guest of the Irishwomen's Franchise League in an attempt to mobilise feminists behind the Irish cause. She was also, and incongruously, the sister of Lord French, Viceroy of Ireland, and the man responsible for the introduction of the Black and Tans and the imposition of martial law. Maud later wrote to a friend of her amusement at 'the puzzled expressions on the faces of the officers and Black and Tans, who continually held up our car, when Mrs Despard said she was the Viceroy's sister'.[66] Maud's immediate response to what she witnessed was to write an article entitled 'Devastation', but she was unable to sell it.[67]

The truth of what was happening was slowly emerging, and in large part this was due to the ingenuity of the Republicans themselves. Despite censorship and constant raids the Dail had, in 1919, set up a publicity department, the chief aim of which was to counter British propaganda by means of a Republican news sheet which would, by systematically detailing events, refute claims that the British forces were merely preserving law and order. The first issue of the *Irish Bulletin* was produced on 11 November 1919 and sent to newspaper correspondents who appeared to be sympathetic to the nationalists. Its circulation and content rapidly increased. The *Bulletin* was issued five days a week and circulated by the publicity department; several MPs subscribed and used the information it contained to raise questions in the Commons. Dail envoys in New York, Paris and Rome ensured that it was also translated into French and Italian and widely distributed.

Robert Brennan was appointed director of the Sinn Fein press bureau and Desmond Fitzgerald became Minister of Publicity, responsible for the production of the *Irish Bulletin*. Frank Gallagher wrote most of the contents. There were also several women on the staff: Anna Fitzsimons, who had previously been Michael Collins's secretary, went through the daily press for suitable items to reprint and also compiled the 'Weekly Summary of Acts of Aggression Committed in Ireland by Military and Police of the Ursurping Government'; Sheila Murphy compiled the statistics; and Kathleen McKenna typed and duplicated the final copy.

Kathleen, who had secured her job through the help of Arthur Griffith, an old family friend, was overjoyed at the chance to be 'a soldier playing my humble part in my country's fight for freedom'. She was unduly modest. Although the men were responsible for the *Bulletin*'s content, the women's work was equally essential and all ran the risk of arrest and imprisonment. With constant street searches, the women were risking their freedom each day when they went off to carry such incriminating copy. After Bloody Sunday in November 1920 (when 14 British intelligence agents were shot on Collins's orders and the British retaliated by opening fire upon a crowd at a football match in Croke Park, killing 12 and wounding 60), neither Fitzgerald nor Gallagher was able to come to the office as cordons had been thrown up all over the city; the women were left for several days to produce and circulate the *Bulletin* on their own.

Their diligence was fully acknowledged by the British, who concentrated much of their energies on locating the whereabouts of the office of this seditious publication, whose contents were an acute source of embarrassment. Raids were frequent, with the staff only narrowly escaping, and the office moved constantly as they tried to find safe premises in which to store their equipment. It wasn't easy, as a typewriter, duplicator and tons of paper were an obvious pointer to the whereabouts of the underground propagandists. Kathleen McKenna remembered 12 different locations, mainly the homes of sympathetic women, like Mrs George Coffey who allowed her to 'prepare the *Bulletin* in the drawing room of her beautiful home'. They also spent ten days in the Brennan household, but had to leave as Una Brennan had three young children and the family was endangered by their presence.

After Fitzgerald was arrested in February 1921, having just left the office, Erskine Childers was appointed acting Director of Publicity. The content of the *Bulletin* was now further expanded by the inclusion of a weekly summary of the conduct of the war, compiled from reports sent in by the various commanding officers of the IRA units. Moira O'Beirne, Lily O'Brennan and Miss Ellis were appointed to work on this. During the Easter holidays of that year, the offices were eventually raided and all the equipment carted off. The British used the machinery and address list to send out bogus versions, which the Republicans were eventually able to prove were fakes. The counter-propaganda attempt back-fired as it was used as further proof of the perfidy of the British, but they continued to produce them until Collins ordered the Auxiliary headquarters (the home of the 'bogus *Bulletin*') to be blown up.

The last issue of the *Irish Bulletin* appeared during the euphoric days of the truce. The headline was 'Makers of the Republic' and beneath was the figure of 'The Dail Girl', wielding a cudgel in one hand and a revolver in the other. Further down the page was a tall, thin figure, 'The Mere President'. The women who had consistently provided the nationalists with their most invaluable weapon—propaganda—had been acknowledged.[68]

Truce

A better Government of Ireland Act had become law in
December 1920. In no sense was it a settlement of the issue, providing as it did for the establishment of two parliaments (one for
the 6 north-eastern counties and another for the remaining 26
counties), with an additional 42 Irish MPs for Westminster, and
the promise of an all-Ireland council. The subordinate parliaments were to have negligible powers in this remix of the old
Home Rule formula. The Ulster Unionists reluctantly accepted
the 6-county settlement, which was deliberately arranged to
carve out the maximum number of Protestants and minimum
number of Catholics, but Sinn Fein categorically rejected the
act. However, rather than ignore the proposed elections of May
1921 the Dail in effect conceded partition by declaring the
26-county elections to be elections to the Dail, and this time 124
Sinn Fein candidates were returned unopposed, to what became
known as the Second Dail. Instead of the lone figure of
Countess Markievicz as women's representative, there were now
5 other female deputies: Margaret Pearse, Kathleen Clarke, Ada
English, Mary MacSwiney and Kate O'Callaghan, the widow
of the murdered mayor of Limerick. Because of war conditions
(64 of the original 73 members of the Dail had been arrested and
6 others were in foreign countries), no formal meetings took
place until August 1922. In the north, the nationalist and Sinn
Fein candidates who were elected to the 6-county parliament
agreed to abstain, rather than accept partition.

Unrestrained repression had not had the intended effect.
Rather than coercing the Irish nation into submission, British
policy had created international sympathy for the right of
Ireland to self-determination and had turned many previously
unconverted into outright supporters of the nationalist movement. Even those not actively engaged in resistance seethed with
indignation at such a callous dismissal of human needs and
ruthless disregard for human rights. But sentiment alone could
not win the war. Apart from a chronic shortage of arms, IRA
activists hardly totalled more than 15,000 while the numbers
involved in Cumann na mBan have been estimated at around
3,000.[69] The British, on the other hand, had at least 40,000 fully

equipped police and soldiers. It was a stalemate with little prospect of resolution and, in the meantime, the bloodshed continued.

This appalling deadlock was finally broken by Lloyd George, capitulating to international pressure, who wrote to de Valera on 24 June 1921 proposing a conference to work out a peace formula. A truce between the British and Irish was finally agreed on 11 July. Although there was unrestrained joy at the cessation of violence, few were in any doubt that a truce did not imply a settlement. Armed struggle had been suspended, but whether or not this would be permanent would depend upon the outcome of negotiations, and no one knew what their conclusions would be.

The jailed members of the Dail were immediately released, but reconciliation did not extend to the other prisoners. According to Michael Collins, there were still 3,200 men interned and 40 women remained in jail.[70] However, some of the women decided not to wait for government permission before they left. Although the truce had been in operation for four months they had still not been released and, as Eithne Coyle said, were 'fed up' and always looking for a means of escape.[71] With the connivance of a friendly guard, contact was made with some local Volunteers and on Hallowe'en night a rope ladder was thrown over the wall of Mountjoy Jail; four of the inmates promptly grabbed it and climbed their way to freedom. Accompanying Eithne in this exploit were Linda Kearns, serving the longest sentence, Aileen Keogh, who still had a year to serve, and Mary Burke, a post office clerk from Kilfinane, who had been recently sentenced to two years for giving the IRA cypher wires from the military and police. Eithne was driven to the home of Dr McLaverty while the other three went to Dr Oliver St John Gogarty's. They then went to an IRA training camp in Carlow, where they laid low, doing the housekeeping, until the Treaty was signed.[72] Before Eithne went home to Donegal she was sheltered by Maud Gonne, where she was visited by Countess Markievicz who lent her £5, a kindness she never forgot.

The other prisoners were not released until the Treaty was signed. For the Volunteers and Cumann na mBan, the period of the truce was regarded as a welcome breathing space, not as the end of the war. They continued to train and to drill, in readiness for the time when their services might again be necessary. As the next Cumann na mBan Convention was to demonstrate, the war years had had a profound effect upon women. They were now experienced activists with a new maturity of understanding, confident of the importance of their work and determined to ensure that the war would be won on their terms. It had been, in every sense of the word, an ordeal by fire and they had come out of it not only alive, but fighting.

5. Cumann na mBan, 1921-23 Civil war

The 1921 convention

The Cumann na mBan Convention of October 1921 was the largest ever held. The organisation would never again be as strong. In attendance were 400 delegates, representing almost 800 branches. It was the first occasion since 1917 that the convention had not been suppressed, forced either to meet secretly, or unable to meet at all. But although it took place during the relatively elated atmosphere of the truce, no one felt in the mood for premature celebration. The women had been through too much during the past years to be able to shrug off their sombre memories of war, or to feel any real optimism about the outcome of the negotiations that were about to begin. It was, instead, a grim and determined event—and with good reason. No one could forget that one member of the executive—Eileen McGrane, Director of Propaganda—was still in jail, along with many other women. The Mountjoy escape had not yet occurred and a brief hunger strike was soon to be staged by the frustrated prisoners, as protest against their continued incarceration. And everyone was anxious about the fate of northern Catholics, where a vicious pogrom in June had resulted in 17 deaths and the expulsion of 150 Belfast Catholics from their homes.

Countess Markievicz, free to preside for the first time in four years, was full of praise for the work performed by the women of Cumann na mBan:

> Their courage, their capacity and above all their discretion, were praised to me. These girls did daring and brave things that nobody ever heard of from anyone... When the history of Ireland is to be written the name of

Cumann na mBan will be a name that will go down to
your children and your children's children, and as an
organisation will stand as a memorial to the Irish people
as a great organisation of the past.[1]

But she had no intention of allowing the organisation to rest
on its laurels or to disintegrate because of a mistaken impression
that the war had already been won. In a sobering reminder that
what had been accomplished had been due 'to the fighting
men and women of Ireland and no one else', she left her audience
under no illusions about what had still to be achieved. They were
instructed to:

go out and work as if the war was going to break out
next week... Action again I say is most important, as if
the enemy sees any weakening the whole thing is up.
When you go away from here, go and prepare yourselves
to do good work for Ireland in the way you have done it
in the past.[2]

By 1921 Cumann na mBan was a far different organisation
from the patriotic association that had been formed in 1914.
There had been gradual changes over the years as women began
to assert their own claims, a process which had been accelerated
as a result of the war. Not only was it a greatly enlarged
organisation, increasing eight-fold from its 100 branches in
1917, it had also achieved a maturity of purpose that enabled
members to intervene with much more confidence in the political
debates of the day.

The hazards of fighting a remorseless guerrilla war against
an enemy which was not only better equipped but also capable
of immediate and brutal retaliation had necessitated a complete
transformation of the internal structures of both the IRA and
Cumann na mBan. While the IRA was reorganised into divisions,
the Cumann na mBan executive restructured their own organisation, placing it on a military footing. This entailed dividing the
country into areas corresponding to IRA battalion areas, so that
each company of the IRA had a branch of Cumann na mBan attached to it, while the officers of the local Cumann na mBan
branches were grouped into district councils which corresponded

to IRA battalions. Military orders were to be passed from IRA officers to Cumann na mBan officers, who then gave orders to their members. So closely knit was this new structure that Cumann na mBan branches could only be formed if there was an IRA company not already catered for. In other words, Cumann na mBan's main function was to service the needs of the local Volunteers. It also meant that the strength of Cumann na mBan in any area depended upon the overall strength of the local IRA.[3]

To ensure the success of these arrangements, organisers and members of the executive had toured the countryside, meeting the commanding officer of each IRA unit, arranging for a corresponding company of Cumann na mBan to be formed, and explaining the procedure to the women. Mairin nic Daibeac, the secretary, reported this work to have been 'most strenuous and laborious', the strain impairing one organiser's health to such an extent that she was forced to give up the work. The women, it must be remembered, were touring areas under martial law, subject to constant surveillance and searches, where the possession of documents relating to Cumann na mBan carried the penalty of a prison sentence, where railways were often at a standstill, and where fear of Black and Tans reprisals, against women in particular, was enough to deter all but the most dedicated. The majority of those who undertook this work were women in their early twenties who had joined Cumann na mBan after 1916. Their results, as tabulated by Leslie Barry (formerly Leslie Price, and since 1920, married to Tom Barry, Officer-in-Charge of the West Cork flying column), were impressive: 375 branches and 57 district councils in Munster; 188 branches and 18 district councils in Leinster; 93 branches and 12 district councils in Ulster; 46 branches and 4 district councils in Connacht.

Cumann na mBan training camps had also been instituted, the first being held that August in Coolrain, north Tipperary. Officers spent six hours each day in classes on first aid, home nursing, drill, signalling, map reading, care of arms, and lectures on the constitution and organisation of Cumann na mBan. Local Cumann na mBan members attended to the domestic chores, leaving those in the camps free to devote all their time to training. Other camps were held in Cork and Kerry, and IRA officers were provided as instructors.

The 1918 convention had revealed several instances of friction between the IRA and Cumann na mBan, and the close liaison that had since developed appears to have exacerbated the already existing tensions. Markievicz felt it necessary, in her presidential address, to implore her members to 'avoid quarrelling and try to work everywhere together whenever you can', but at the same time many eloquent tributes were paid to Cumann na mBan by various commandants who recognised the importance of their work, and who regarded the women as comrades:

> In despatch carrying, scouting, and intelligence work, all of which are highly dangerous, they did far more than the soldiers. In addition to this the Flying Columns would have collapsed early this year were it not for the assistance of the women... When almost everyone deserted us during the Xmas panic those girls stood by us and at the height of the terror we found that the more dangerous the work the more willing they were to do it.[4]

> My only hope now, and I am expressing the sentiments of everyone who has served under me, is that you continue on in the future as you did in the past and that our officers and yours who know each other so well and who have worked so harmoniously together in the past, will always assist each other in the same spirit.[5]

Whether or not this was a majority view is impossible to tell.

The convention formally ratified the new structure which had had, of necessity to be instituted without full consultation of the members. The section of the constitution relating to organisation was amended to read: 'Cumann na mBan shall be organised into areas corresponding to IRA Battalion areas. Each Company of the IRA shall have a Branch or Squad of Cumann na mBan attached to it.'[6] The only flexibility in this arrangement was a proposal (which was passed), permitting squads of up to ten members to be formed if there were not enough members to constitute a fully fledged branch.

There was a co-ordinated attempt to get rid of such honorary figures as Margaret Pearse and Nancy O'Rahilly, who had been elected in 1917 as tribute to the bereavements they had suffered after the Rising. The only heroines the new generation of women believed in were those who merited that status because of their own achievements, rather than those of their male relatives. A number of motions requiring all executive members to undertake an active role were defeated, although a compromise amendment allowing for substitutes to take the place of executive members unable to perform their duties because of illness, imprisonment, or travel abroad was passed. It was perhaps a more tactful way of establishing control over the organisation. Even so, when it came to voting on motions proposed by branches, the attack was renewed without any attempt to disguise the impatience of the younger militants:

> That Honorary Members who have never been drilled, have never had First Aid or Signalling lessons, and are often difficult to get at even in an emergency be asked to resign if they cannot attend SOME of the Parades.

That blunt challenge by the Dun Laoghaire branch was defeated, but it is possible that it was voted against for purely tactical reasons. It was not an appropriate time arbitrarily to dismiss those names the public knew and revered, even though the need for such figureheads had long since passed.

A motion calling for Cumann na mBan to be run on strictly military lines, with Dublin having its own commandant, was also defeated, but a sequel to this, proposed by Maire Comerford and Fiona Plunkett, that the present scheme of organisation 'be perfected by the establishment of a regular military staff under the Directorship of a Chief Officer who shall appoint the staff from the best available material', and that this staff control all military activities and undertakings, was recommended back to the executive, instead of being voted upon. It was never implemented, but it has great significance in that two of the most active (and independent-minded) women were obviously impatient of the constrictions imposed by the branch structure. The system they proposed would have allowed a much greater degree of freedom to manoeuvre, and the possibility for independent action to be initiated by the most militant, without the need for the constant liaison with the IRA entailed by the current system.

It must have been a contentious issue, to all intents and purposes a declaration that Cumann na mBan reserved the right to decide for itself, if the situation allowed, what actions to take. A recommendation back to the executive preserved a delicate balance between the two groups—those content with their role, and those chafing at the limitations it placed upon them.

In response to continued pressure from the two women it was agreed that 'as a special qualification for military work Cumann na mBan members may be required to take a military oath'. In her memoirs, Maire Comerford explained why she put forward this motion. While organising Cumann na mBan branches in Leitrim the previous summer, John Mitchell, the officer-in-charge in the area, had expressed reservations in trusting 'these girls' with the secrets of the IRA. It seemed to him that women were recruited very easily into Cumann na mBan, while the men were carefully screened and had to take a pledge of secrecy. Maire brought this complaint back to Dublin, the outcome of which was a separate oath for Cumann na mBan: 'I pledge myself to support and de- fend to the best of my ability, the Irish Republic and to uphold the aims and objects of Cumann na mBan and the IRA.' Cumann na mBan never did have any trouble with informers and agents within the organisation, the most obvious explana- tion for this being that the majority came from staunchly Republican families and lived and worked in the area in which they had grown up. They were bound by close links to their com- munity and few of them would have had the male freedom to uproot themselves and start afresh some place else.

At no stage did any section of Cumann na mBan contemplate a merger between themselves and the men, whereby those who wished could be fully incorporated into the military structure of the overall organisation. There were good reasons why this was never proposed. It was not from any reluctance about adopting a full military role, because it was obvious a certain proportion of women were prepared to undertake this, and neither was it a legacy of earlier days, when Cumann na mBan declared its role to be simply that of assisting the Volunteers. Years of warfare in which women had done everything except actually take up arms had been lived through since that time. The absence of such a demand stemmed from their pride in Cumann na mBan and its achievements, and their confidence in their ability to continue and even expand the scope of their work. They were not envious of the freedom of the IRA—what many wanted was the opportunity to operate entirely autonomously, without the constant necessity for joint consultations. A realistic assessment underlay this calculation, the knowledge that in the short term at least, integration would have the effect of institutionalising the subordination of women instead of affirming their equal status. Token women might gain executive status, but the majority would remain in the lowest ranks, their numerical insignificance compounding their difficulties in voicing opinions. Cumann na mBan, as a separate organisation, was for many the means whereby Irishwomen could both make a valuable contribution to the military struggle against British rule in Ireland, and also express their feelings with regards to current political issues. Given the subordinate position of women in this highly traditional and intensely Catholic society, it was an achievement to have accomplished so much.

Cumann na mBan activists stressed time and again their conviction that they were not of inferior status, and that there were no restrictions preventing their own views from being put forward. Eithne Coyle was adamant on this point, although her personal experience was not necessarily the same as that of other, less strong-minded women:

> The men didn't order us. I mean, if they did, they might get a crack over the face—we got no orders, but we were asked—would you mind taking these guns to such and such a place, or would you get a safe house for us... we didn't mind because that was part of our programme.

When asked if Cumann na mBan was ever able successfully to persuade the men to co-operate with them, Eithne replied:

> We were always at them, and after them. Even up to the last, we were always making plans for certain things that we thought should be done. And they co-operated.[7]

Another telling indication of how far the organisation had progressed since 1918 was the unanimous agreement on the part of the delegates to the assertion that all citizens over the age of 18 had the right to a vote in any plebiscite or election 'in which the honour and fate of Ireland shall be at stake'. In resounding (and ominous) tones it was declared that a decision taken on any other basis 'would be unjust and its decisions not binding'.

So Cumann na mBan had issued its challenge: no longer would decisions be taken on their behalf. Young women and young men had willingly shouldered the burden of war, and they strongly believed that they had earned the right to be consulted on the terms of any peace settlement.

The convention ended with a moving tribute by Ada English in praise of the courage of the relatives of those who had died. It was also a tribute, by the organised women of Ireland, to their sisters suffering in isolation, struggling to maintain an everyday existence in the face of warfare and destitution:

> As an army of women we should express our appreciation of the extraordinary heroism exhibited by the women of Ireland, and particularly to the mothers—some of whom have seen their sons go out to die... Personally my admiration for the women of Ireland has increased enormously with the splendid stand they have taken in the sufferings they have endured.

The Treaty

Interned members of the Dail had been released on 6 August so that the Dail could meet to decide whether or not they agreed to the terms of Lloyd George's proposal for negotiations to end the war. On 16 August, the first meeting of the Second Dail took place. De Valera was once again elected President of the Irish Republic and Countess Markievicz reappointed Minister for Labour, but this time her position did not carry cabinet status. Both she and the labour movement were effectively demoted. When de Valera proposed a constitutional amendment to ratify the cabinet changes, Kate O'Callaghan strenuously opposed the motion. She regretted that the only woman member of cabinet would have no rank in the new arrangment, a sentiment which had the support of Mary MacSwiney, who warned of the precedent the move created. She would have been appalled if she had been able to look into the future: over 50 years were to elapse before the Irish government again had a woman in the cabinet. De Valera's motion, despite these objections, was carried.[8]

A lengthy exchange of correspondence between de Valera and Lloyd George had already begun and finally, at the end of September, an agreement was reached whereby five delegates from the Dail, invested with the powers of plenipotentiaries, would meet British representatives in London, the aim being to explore 'every possibility of settlement by personal discussion'. Arthur Griffith, Michael Collins, George Gavan Duffy, Robert Barton and Eamonn Duggan were the men appointed by the Dail. Collins agreed reluctantly, and many members of Cumann na mBan regretted the absence of a woman, in particular the formidable Mary MacSwiney, whom they considered would be a match for the wily Lloyd George. The course of Irish history might have been drastically altered by the inclusion of this unyielding Republican.

There has been much debate over the reasons for, and possible consequences of, de Valera's refusal to be part of the delegation. One probable explanation is a calculation on his part that the full goal of an Irish Republic would not be achieved through negotiation, and that he, as elected head of the as-yet unrecognised Republic, could not further degrade its status by putting his signature to a document which failed to grant complete independence. Whatever his motives, the outcome of the Treaty negotiations was undeniably a bitter blow to Republican aspirations.

On 6 December, under the ultimatum of Lloyd George's threat of 'immediate and terrible war', the five Irish plenipotentiaries, without consulting the cabinet, put their signatures to the 'Articles of Agreement for a Treaty between Great Britain and Ireland'. The Irish Republic no longer existed, even in name; instead, 26 of Ireland's counties were to be known as the Irish Free State, having the same constitutional status within the British Empire as Canada, Australia, New Zealand and South Africa. All members of the Irish parliament would be required to take an oath of allegiance to the Irish Free State and to the Crown. While a considerable degree of autonomy would be allowed in internal affairs, Britain would retain control of coastal defences.

The delegates had attempted to make the question of Ulster the principle around which to disagree over the terms they were forced to sign, but in this they were outmanoeuvred. Partition was accepted, the only proviso being, if Ulster insisted on remaining separate, the institution of a boundary commission to determine the exact geography of the 6-county state. The question of Ulster and the fate of nationalists in the north was almost forgotten as those opposed to the Treaty concentrated upon the unacceptability of the oath of allegiance—the symbol of enslavement—rather than on undertaking a detailed analysis of the type of society they hoped to construct. There were notable exceptions to this, but they were exceptions.

Debate over the Treaty began in the Dail on 14 December. The cabinet was deeply divided and the Dail reflected this division. Both sides invoked the names of the dead, the wishes of their constituents, the possible response of women, in a desperate attempt to sway the few who remained undecided, while some of those who rejected the Treaty cast aspersions on the integrity of the plenipotentiaries in a debate which became increasingly bitter and more personal in tone.

During the weeks of argument and counter-argument, the six women deputies remained unshakable in their opposition to the Treaty. The ghosts of dead sons, husbands and brothers haunted the Dail as their memories were used in justification of their stand, Muriel MacSwiney, widow of Terence, wrote to the Dail from Wiesbaden:

> I should not have thought myself important enough to have written to you anything at all if I did not represent one who is greater than any of us. I am absolutely certain that Terry would have said what I am saying, and would have refused.[9]

Her plea was difficult to refute as the MacSwineys had refused to join Sinn Fein until it had been reconstituted as a Republican organisation in 1917, but delegates without illustrious family members resented such claims—who, after all, would be bold enough publicly to proclaim rejection of the path Padraic Pearse would have chosen? And Margaret Pearse, elected, as she said of herself, 'so that the name of a Pearse would be in the first

Irish Parliament', was there to offer uncomfortable reminders of her son's death. As his mother, she could not vote for acceptance. But she also, knowing 'the hearts and sorrows of the wives of Ireland', enough believed that none of them wanted the Treaty. In her own right as well, she rejected it.

The united front presented by the women of the Dail gave great credence to their claim to represent the views of the majority of Irishwomen. The only comeback, on the part of those who supported the Treaty, was to discredit their testimony by raising doubts about their mental stability. It was a tactic that was resorted to on several occasions, most notably by Alec MacCabe of Sligo, who disingenuously felt that there might be some excuse for Mary MacSwiney because 'her mind and outlook were distorted by the terrible experience she has passed through.' Ada English immediately denounced such smear tactics as 'unworthy'. As she had 'no dead men' to be thrown in her teeth, she asserted her right to speak on behalf of other women. Kate O'Callaghan, in an early contribution to the debate, protested that when it was found the women deputies could not be canvassed, they were dismissed with the remark, 'Oh, naturally these women are very bitter.' Although she had seen her husband murdered in front of her, she stated firmly that 'no woman in this Dail is going to give her vote merely because she is warped by a deep personal loss', and she resented the implication that women were incapable of evaluating political issues, being motivated solely by emotion and by a stubborn determination to vote in the way they felt their menfolk would have wished. She reminded the Dail of the political background of the women deputies, and of the work they had engaged in, independently of their relatives. She was also enraged to be told that her husband had not been a Republican, and her vote should therefore be cast for the Treaty. 'The women of An Dail,' she announced, 'are women of character, and they will vote for principle, not for expediency.'

In a forceful speech, Kathleen Clarke recounted her last meeting with her husband in his death cell, and his final message that Ireland 'will never lie down again until she has gained absolute freedom... and though sorrow was in my heart, I gloried in him, and I have gloried in the men who have carried on the fight ever since.' She accepted the fact that the Treaty gave 'the biggest Home Rule Bill we have ever been offered', but that was not freedom. It left Ireland divided and in the Empire. She challenged the Dail to repudiate English force and swore 'there is not enough to force me, nor eloquence enough to influence me in the whole British Empire into taking that Oath, though I am only a frail scrap of humanity'.

Mary MacSwiney, in the course of innumerable lengthy interventions in the debate (she spoke, in all, for over 4½ hours, one speech alone lasting 2 hours and 40 minutes), spoke once of the ordeal of her brother on his fast to the death. She claimed that amongst his last words to her was the belief 'Thank God there will be no more compromises now,' but she refused to use the memory of her brother; it was her own political principles she defended. As war had achieved more than anyone could ever have believed she maintained that a continuation of the war was not only possible but necessary, if the British insisted on holding Ireland to the terms of the Treaty. She did not shrink from war and she resented those who declared that women knew nothing of the realities of war and the true condition of the IRA:

> You men that talk need not talk to us about war. It is the women who suffer, it is the women who suffer the most of the hardships that war brings. You can go out in the excitement of the fight and it brings its own honour and its own glory. We have to sit at home and work in more humble ways, we have to endure the agony, the sunshines, the torture of misery and the privations which war brings, the horror of nightly visitations to our houses and their consequences. It is easier for you than it is for us, but you will not find in Ireland a woman who has suffered who today will talk as the soldiers here today have talked, and I ask the Minister of Defence, if that is the type of soldier he has, in heaven's name send the women as your officers next time.

She was implacable in her belief that Irish women would stand up for principle, regardless of the consequences. In another impassioned speech, full of the most warmongering images, she declared:

> if [England] exterminates the men, the women will take
> their places, and if she exterminates the women, the
> children are rising fast; and if she exterminates the men,
> women and children of this generation, the blades of
> grass, dyed with their blood, will rise, like the dragon's
> teeth of old, into armed men and the fight will begin in
> the next generation.

Liam Mellowes and Countess Markievicz were the only participants in the debate to speak for working-class interests. Dressed in her green Cumann na mBan uniform the countess recalled Connolly's words. She stood not only on the principle that the Dail had pledged itself to the Republic, but for a workers' republic. As the representative of the working-class division of St Patrick's, she objected to this 'deliberate attempt to set up a privileged class' and she stood proudly by her beliefs. 'While Ireland is not free I remain a rebel, unconverted and inconvertible... I have seen the stars and I am not going to follow a flickering will o-the-wisp.'

The Dail adjourned for a Christmas recess—a break which helped the pro-Treaty faction considerably, as they were able to convince war-weary constituents of the advisability of ratification. In January, as the ten long sessions of debate painfully continued, passions mounted and exchanges between opponents became steadily more acrimonious. Insults were liberally traded, although in general the women retained a dignified aloofness. Kate O'Callaghan sadly felt she had lost any illusions she might have possessed during her brief time in public office, but Countess Markievicz was always in the thick of the fray, hurling back jibes as quickly as they were flung at her; her outspokenness had probably earned her more enemies than the other women (apart from Mary MacSwiney), and her aristocratic background was always a cause of controversy. At one stage she enraged Michael Collins by mockingly suggesting that he had designs on the Princess Mary and for that reason had signed the Treaty. Centuries of bitterness resurfaced as those who had been united for a decade in common cause now became completely estranged, glaring at each other across a distance which almost perceptibly widened as each day ground to its inconclusive end.

There was eventually no point in prolonging the agony; much as everyone dreaded it, a vote had to be taken. On 6 January, the Dail, by 64 votes to 57, ratified the Treaty. The old dreams were shattered irrevocably and an intolerable future stared bleakly in the face of each deputy. Many could not stomach the prospect and an immediate effort to find a mutually agreeable working arrangement for the future was proposed. As Collins and de Valera assured each other of their continuing personal regard and Collins suggested the formation of a joint committee, the voice of Mary MacSwiney ripped through the emotion-choked atmosphere. She refused to be swayed by the 'beautiful' speech of Collins and would have 'neither hand, act nor part in helping the Irish Free State to carry this nation of ours, this glorious nation that has been betrayed here tonight, into the British Empire'. The spell was broken. Normality restored, de Valera called for a meeting of all who opposed the Treaty; he then broke down in tears.

Cumann na mBan rejects the Treaty

The Treaty had now been ratified, but the constitutional status of the 26 counties remained confused and ambiguous. On 9 January, de Valera announced that he and his cabinet were resigning. Kathleen Clarke, seconded by Liam Mellowes, proposed his re-election as President of the Irish Republic. The motion was defeated, but only by two votes. Many of those who supported the Treaty maintained a high regard for their former president. Collins, seconded by Richard Mulcahy, now proposed that Griffith should form an executive. However, the Dail, elected to be the parliament of the Republic, could not automatically be transformed into the provisional government of Southern Ireland. Griffith therefore promised that he would keep the Republic in existence until an election decided whether or not the people wanted the Irish Free State. Amidst torrents of abuse, de Valera and his supporters walked out in protest against what they considered to be legalistic chicanery. In the calm which followed the removal of the opposition Griffith was elected president, Collins re-elected as Minister of Finance, and

Mulcahy replaced Brugha as Minister of Defence, with control over the IRA. But the anomalies remained. Mulcahy assured the anti-Treaty faction (who had now returned to the Dail) that the army would remain, for the time being, the Army of the Irish Republic. But would the army consent to control by Mulcahy?

On 14 January, the Parliament of Southern Ireland was convened by Griffith, acting now in his capacity as chairman of the Irish delegation. The anti-Treaty deputies ignored the invitation, but all the pro-Treatyites attended. Griffith was appointed chairman, and a provisional government elected—many now held dual ministries in the Dail and the provisional government, but it was the provisional government which carried out the arrangements for the formal transfer of power. The Dail was little more than a debating chamber and (for some) the symbol of Republican hopes.

The IRA was also badly split over the Treaty. While the majority of headquarters staff were pro-Treaty (including, of course, Mulcahy and Collins), many of the most influential commandants were anti-Treaty, and feared that the army might be used to 'disestablish the Republic'. On 11 January these officers requested the holding of a general army convention to renew the army's allegiance to the Republic and to arrange for the formation of an executive which would return the army to independent military control, rather than the authority of the Dail. On 26 March, the convention assembled, but as it had been prohibited by the Dail, only those in opposition to the Treaty attended. Mulcahy's position as Minister of Defence was rejected; from now on, an executive would be in control. A split became inevitable: those who supported the Treaty were being recruited into a Free State Army which, for those who rejected the Treaty, was in breach of Mulcahy's pledge to retain the army as the army of the Republic.

For its part, Cumann na mBan viewed the new alliance between the provisional government and the British with extreme suspicion. Maire Comerford recalled

> being one of a company of young women who looked very doubtfully at a poster which we had orders to paste up around the city. It was headed 'Saorstat Eireann'

> [Irish Free State] and we decided we did not like it. We
> wanted no change from 'Poblacht na hEireann' [Irish
> Republic], of the 1916 Proclamation.[10]

Once the Dail vote had been taken Cumann na mBan lost no
time in mobilising in protest. They held a demonstration outside
the Mansion House when the first meeting of the provisional
parliament took place. Their intention was to prevent press pictures being taken of members attending without also showing
pictures of their dissent and protest. It was an uncomfortable
experience for many of the delegates—some kept their eyes
averted, a few smiled apologetically—but they walked on.
Cumann na mBan decided to register a more definite protest, so
they began a series of raids on the tricolour whenever it appeared
on pro-Treaty platforms. For them, it symbolised the grossest of
betrayals. They also began a more concerted form of propaganda
work by issuing a newsletter with the rallying title of *Heads Up*.
The issue of 31 March 1922 was entitled 'The Banner of Independence', a self-explanatory title.[11]

Even during the Treaty debates Cumann na mBan had
resorted to outrageous stunts to demonstrate their feelings. One
of the more bizarre was recounted with humour by Maire Comerford. As they waited anxiously in their Dublin headquarters,
becoming more despondent about the possible outcome, they
decided to hoist the Union Jack over the building where the
debate was taking place, as a symbolic expression of what acceptance of the Treaty would entail. Stealing notepaper from the
Sinn Fein offices, they typed a request on Hanna Sheehy Skeffington's typewriter (with her consent), asking all shops for the
loan of their Union Jacks. But Mrs Cosgrave, wife of a pro-
Treaty minister, happened to be in the exclusive shop of Switzers,
and was told of what was happening. She of course immediately
reported the plot. Questions were asked in the Dail, but Hanna
Sheehy Skeffington refused to divulge who had used her
typewriter. It was, as Maire admitted, a silly escapade, proof of
the extent of their desperation.[12]

Cumann na mBan was to become the first national organisation to reject the Treaty. Following the decision of the Dail the
executive, by a majority of 24 votes to 2, had voted in favour of

a resolution proposed by Countess Markievicz: 'This executive of Cumann na mBan reaffirms their allegiance to the Irish Republic and therefore cannot support the Articles of Treaty signed in London.'[13]

This decision was immediately conveyed to all branches. Special arrangements for an emergency convention were made, so that the overall membership could decided upon the issue. A convention of Cumann na mBan was held in Dublin on 5 February where the following resolution, proposed by Mary MacSwiney, was overwhelmingly adopted:

(a) Reaffirming allegiance to the Republic and calling upon the Women of Ireland to support at the forthcoming elections only those candidates who stood true to the existing Republic proclaimed Easter Week, 1916.
(b) Asking the women to join in the re-imposition of the Belfast Boycott unless the prisoners in Northern Jails for political offences were at once released.[14]

The result was 419 in favour, with only 63 against. The loss of the dissidents was a serious blow to Cumann na mBan. They included some of the women who had been amongst the most dedicated members—Jenny Wyse Power, Louise Gavan Duffy (whose father George had been one of the plenipotentiaries), Mabel Fitzgerald (wife of Desmond, Minister of Propaganda), Mrs McCullough, Min Ryan (who was now the wife of Richard Mulcahy); Annie Blythe and Brigid O'Higgins, the wives of Ernest Blythe and Kevin O'Higgins, both Free State ministers, also took the pro-Treaty side. They were obviously all highly political women, and well able to determine their own attitudes towards the Treaty, but family loyalties must have played some part in their decision. Maire Comerford certainly believed that some had voted with great reluctance. 'Some were married to Free Staters. Mabel Fitzgerald crossed the bridge very reluctantly; we continued to meet over cups of coffee in Bewley's.'[15] With others, the split was irreparable. Sheila Humphreys, meeting Desmond Fitzgerald during the debates, tried to talk him round. They had had a close friendship and she felt intensely sad at the prospect of it coming to an end. He smiled lamely, but no agreement was possible.[16]

Once the Civil War had started, old friendships could not prevent arrest; in many instances, they were instrumental in securing arrest. In January 1923, Maire Comerford was involved in a plot to kidnap Cosgrave, Prime Minister of the Free State government, as hostage to prevent further execution of prisoners. Her first task was to inspect the 'safe house' that had been promised. The car broke down and she and her companion hailed a taxi. When it stopped, she discovered it to be already full and one of the passengers was Min Ryan. Both pretended not to recognise the other, but Min immediately went to the police and informed on their whereabouts. In consequence Maire was instantly arrested and sent to Mountjoy.[17] Not only did friendships disintegrate: whole families split apart. Min's sister Phyllis was married to Sean T. O'Kelly, a leading figure on the anti-Treaty side. It is doubtful if the sisters were ever again able to meet in friendship.

A woman's organisation in support of the Treaty was formed after the Cumann na mBan convention. It took the name Cumann na Saoirse (Society of Freedom). The members of the new body were almost all related to the members of the new government; it would seem that most of the wives rallied round their husbands' side, even those who had not previously been politically active, the most obvious example being the wife of Arthur Griffith. Mabel Fitzgerald does not appear on its lists, an indication perhaps that her heart was not in it. Other women, including the historian Alice Stopford Green (whose secretary Maire Comerford had been, until political events led to a parting of the ways) and Alice Spring Rice also joined the group. They clearly supported the Treaty, seeing in it a definite expression of their class interests, but there was another reason why they should have joined Cumann na Saoirse, while holding aloof from Cumann na mBan. Cumann na Saoirse was *not* another version of Cumann na mBan; it was not a militarily active organisation, prone to considering itself the guardian of the Republican conscience and prepared to use any means to further the cause. The organisation represented the aspirations of the emerging elite, and it looked with horror and distaste on the wild women of Cumann na mBan.[18]

The franchise debate

Women had made a significant contribution to the Treaty debate, both because of the uncompromising attitude of the six women deputies and also because they claimed, with some justification, to represent the views of Irish women. But the political direction women might take in any election was an unknown factor; after all, a section of Irish women had only been given the vote in 1918, and no one really knew how they would react. But those on the Treaty side, having had the experience of four-and-a-half hours of detailed analysis and vituperation from Mary MacSwiney, as well as the contributions of the other female deputies, obviously feared the worst. It was a fear that other anti-Treaty deputies helped to foster. Sean Etchingham from Wexford, well loved by both sides of the house, in his explanation of why he rejected the Treaty had described the views of his elderly mother:

> I may say that my mother, who is 84 years old, when the soldiers came to blow up her home and the home of my sister, what did she say to them? 'You may level every house in it but you won't kill the country', and I can't go back to her and say that I voted for this wretched thing.

If all Irish women resembled Mrs Etchingham, there was ample reason for refusing to concede any measure of franchise reform before the all-important election. The unequivocal stand taken by Cumann na mBan compounded the pro-Treaty side's hostility to the proposal to enfranchise all women over the age of 21.

It was Kate O'Callaghan who, at the 2 March meeting of the Dail, had raised the issue. After desperate attempts to prevent her motion being raised had been over-ruled she proposed that, in accordance with the pledge contained in the Republican Proclamation, women over 21 be given the vote. Those who supported the Treaty persisted in condemning the motion as an opportunistic attempt to jeopardise the Treaty. An Irishwomen's Franchise League deputation had already met, and been rebuffed, by Griffith when they asked for the compilation of a revised electoral register before any election took place. Griffith's answer was that, first, the Dail had no power to alter the franchise, second, that it would take at least eight months to alter the register, and, finally, Britain would refuse to recognise the validity of an election held under terms that differed from those already agreed and consequently the Treaty would be in jeopardy. To each objection Kate O'Callaghan made a detailed rejoinder. As someone who had, ten years earlier, been a member of a suffrage society, she denied her motion was a cynical calculation to discredit the Treaty. It was a proposal, in accordance with the spirit of the Proclamation, to remedy an injustice to Irishwomen who had fully participated in all the dangers of war. The Dail was the sovereign authority in Ireland and as such, had the power to alter the franchise; three months being the generally accepted time for the compilation of an electoral register. And finally, she said, if as Arthur Griffith predicted, 95 per cent of the women of Ireland were in favour of the Treaty, then to allow them to record their vote would strengthen, not weaken, the case for ratification.[19]

Griffith angrily dismissed these arguments. It was 'a trick on the Irish people', devised by those who sought to 'torpedo the Treaty'. He stood as a life-long supporter of women's suffrage and found it strange that only now, three years after the institution of the Dail, had such concern for women suddenly appeared. In his eyes the deputation of suffrage societies was sent (he hastily qualified this to 'most of them') 'not in enthusiasm for woman's suffrage, but in enthusiasm to destroy the Treaty'. He obviously viewed such veterans of the feminist movement as Hanna Sheehy Skeffington to be motivated more by Republican sentiments than by feminist principles. It was an ironic twist to the running battle the suffragists had been conducting for over a decade: in previous times they had been denounced as antinationalist by men like Griffith because of their attack upon the Home Rule bill when it was discovered women's franchise would not be included, but now they were dismissed as doctrinaire Republicans.

The suspicions fostered by the Treaty controversy had a distorting effect upon the minds of many, who could not see the inherent consistency of the feminist position and could only attribute malevolent intentions to all who questioned the stand taken by the supporters of the Treaty. In many ways the debate

over the franchise, firmly embedded as it was in the wider
political issue, was conducted on a more acrimonious scale than
the main debate. McGrath, the new Minister for Labour, sarcastically dismissed 'the women in men's clothing', only to be
angrily challenged by Countess Markievicz, who strongly objected
to his 'dastardly remark'. In a patently sincere speech she recalled
that her initial interest in woman's suffrage had given her a first
bite 'at the apple of freedom', a taste which led her to work also
for national and social freedom. As she rightly pointed out, it
had been impossible to raise the issue of women's enfranchisement during the height of war when the Dail was meeting in
secret and all business had to be attended to as quickly as possible,
for fear of raids. At that time only matters directly related to the
war effort could be dealt with. She also believed that it was this
experience of war, when women were 'dragged out of their shells
and made to take their place as citizens at the polling booths,
helping at the elections and helping the men on the run, that has
put this desire into the hearts of the young women'. She ended
her speech on a characteristically militant note:

> Our deputy here seems to think that Cumann na mBan
> would torpedo the Treaty. In the name of Cumann na
> mBan I thank him for his appreciation of their valour
> and strength and I can tell him that it will be up to them
> to do it whether they get the votes or not. Today, I
> would appeal here to the men of the IRA more than to
> any of the other men to see that justice is done to these
> young women and young girls who took a man's part in
> the Terror.

The debate continued. Cathal Brugha made his famous tribute
to the steadfastness of the women in maintaining the national
movement after its disintegration following Easter Week, and de
Valera spoke also, confining his remarks to the technicalities
surrounding electoral reform. It was as much as he could do. To
have suddenly emerged as a whole-hearted champion of women's
rights would have been the height of insincerity. And for some
who supported the Treaty, and who had genuinely favoured
women's enfranchisement in the past, it was galling to be placed
on the side of the devil, while others with far less progressive

views and a dubious record on the issue, suddenly emerged on the side of the angels.

Griffith wearily pledged that his government, after the election, would make provision for the full enfranchisement of women. Further than that he would not go. The current electoral register was hopelessly out of date, as everyone was forced to admit, but to revise it at this time would mean the inclusion of many young men who would, in all probability, reject the Treaty. It was not only the unknown dimension of the women that the pro-Treatyites would then have to contend with, and they were adamant in their view that the register was an adequate reflection of the voting population, minus the awkward problem of the women aged between 21 and 30. The vote was taken and Kate O'Callaghan's motion was defeated, on predictable lines, by 47 votes to 38. The names of the deputies who voted were not recorded but it would be fair to conclude that no one, regardless of their views on the issue, broke their respective party ranks.

Countess Markievicz, when writing to her sister while in jail during the Civil War, reaffirmed her conviction that this demand for the vote had been spontaneous. Women's 'humiliating' recognition of their political powerlessness had led to their declaration that 'if they are good enough to take part in the fight, they are good enough to vote'.[20] But minds warped with bitterness ignored the validity of this response, finding it more expedient to attribute responsibility to the unyielding women deputies rather than to admit any principle of justice was involved in the issue. The most vicious of these attacks came from P.S. O'Hegarty, writing at the end of the Civil War. In a short chapter entitled 'The Furies,' he concluded, 'The women were the implacable and irrational upholders of death and destruction... We know that with women in political power there would be no more peace.'[21]

Maybe it was a case of being wise after the event, because on occasions when men did not dare to act as visible upholders of the Republican ideal no one had had any scruples in handing over that duty to women. Thus, for the Bodenstown commemoration of the Wolfe Tone Anniversary of 1921, at a time when British forces occupied the city of Dublin, Michael Collins had given orders that Cumann na mBan members were to represent the Republican movement at the traditional wreath-laying ceremony. A taxi brought Elis ni Riain, captain of central branch Cumann na mBan, and her four section commanders— Fiona Plunkett, Maire Comerford, Emily Valentine and Margaret McElroy—to Bodenstown where, surrounded by British troops, the women laid the wreath.[22] Less than one year later such women found themselves facing the prospect of incorporation into a 'Free State' which denied them the rights of citizenship. The supposed 'irrationality' of women's intransigence has to be evaluated in this light.

The constitution of Cumann na mBan proudly affirmed their belief that in fighting for the establishment of an Irish Republic they had:

> regained for the women of Ireland the rights that belonged to them under the old Gaelic civilisation, where sex was no bar to citizenship, and where women were free to devote to the service of their country every talent and capacity with which they were endowed; which rights were stolen from them under English rule, but were guaranteed to them in the Republican Proclamation of Easter Week.[23]

Judged by this criterion, the Treaty settlement obviously fell far short of their aspirations for the future. As nothing less than the full implementation of the ideals enshrined within the Proclamation could be accepted, recognition of the Republic was inextricably linked with recognition of women's right to equality. The fight for both had to continue. Although the majority of those on the anti-Treaty side clung to an idealised vision of 'the Republic' without any clearly defined conception of the social and economic structures that would distinguish this Republic from the Free State, those within Cumann na mBan, while not fully articulating the basis of their political opposition, were conscious of their oppression as women and did have some awareness that this political and social oppression would not be alleviated by those who argued for acceptance of the Treaty. In this limited sense Cumann na mBan's rejection of the Treaty was at least partly based upon some feminist understanding of its implications.

Preludes to civil war

Despite O'Hegarty's accusations, the women of the Dail did take part in attempts to reach a political compromise. They had jointly written a letter to the pro-Treaty faction, imploring them to rethink their decision, arguing that it would be better to face Lloyd George's war together than to face war with each other,[24] and when a committee consisting of five members from each side was appointed by the Dail in a last desperate effort at reconciliation, it was Kathleen Clarke who chaired its proceedings.

In the meantime, the military men jostled for advantage as the IRA also began to fragment. Clashes between opposing sections of the army were frequent throughout February and March as arms and munitions were taken from one side by the other. When the British evacuated their barracks, formally handing them over to the local units of the IRA, the barracks also became part of this struggle for military advantage: some now had pro-Treaty garrisons while others were anti-Treaty. Although de Valera had asked the IRA officers to give the same co-operation to Mulcahy, the new Minister for Defence, as they had previously given to Brugha, those who opposed the Treaty demanded an army convention to discuss the altered political situation. Although the Dail agreed to this request, the Griffith cabinet refused, threatening penalties against any officer who attended. In response the Military Council, under Rory O'Connor, called a convention for 26 March. Held in defiance of the provisional government, this marked the break away of the Republican section of the army from control by the Dail. The new army executive was now the only body to which the anti-Treaty IRA owed allegiance. Liam Lynch was elected chief-of-staff and the army pledged itself to 'guard the honour and maintain the independence of the Irish Republic'.[25] On 13 April, the Four Courts complex was occupied and the military headquarters of the IRA established within its walls. Other buildings were also requisitioned. Fowler Hall, headquarters of the Orange Order, was taken over and used as a shelter for Catholics who had fled from the north. Bank and post office raids were organised (and receipts in the name of the Irish Republic scrupulously issued) to provide the necessary finances for these operations as the British government was now financing the provisional government; although Dail sovereignty continued to exist in theory, in practice the provisional government alone controlled the purse.

One significant aspect of the initial attempts by both de Valera and Mulcahy to reach some compromise with the anti-Treaty leaders of the IRA (Mulcahy had suggested holding a private meeting, knowing that Griffith would oppose any army convention) is the fact that it took the IRA longer than either the Dail or Cumann na mBan publicly to pronounce its views on the Treaty. And before that finally occurred, the dissident leaders were cajoled and pleaded with—an admission of the crucial importance of the military organisation in determining whether or not civil war would be the result of the political division. Cumann na mBan could meet and issue its statement on 5 February without the pro-Treaty leadership attempting any form of reconciliation because they were ultimately of little strategic importance. Their role was to assist the fighting men—and the political leaders' energies were engaged in ensuring that the men didn't begin fighting. As the role of the women was purely contingent, they could issue whatever statements they chose, the only reaction being the increasingly bitter remarks about women made during the Dail debates.

Republicans continued to argue against the holding of an election with an out-of-date register and to maintain that the proposed constitution of the new state be submitted to the people before the election. De Valera asked for a six-month postponement so that these arrangements could be made. But Griffith both refused to agree to these terms and refused to consult with representatives of the IRA executive. No agreement was reached in the negotiations of the Dail Committee under Kathleen Clarke, the sticking ground appearing to revolve around the question of the number of candidates to be allotted to the respective parties. Just when it appeared that war was the only means of resolving this impasse, a last minute electoral pact was agreed upon by Collins and de Valera in May, whereby there would be a national coalition panel for the Third Dail, the number of candidates being determined by the existing strength of each faction. A coalition government would then be formed.

This attempt to avoid a final confrontation was unacceptable to the British government, who condemned it as infringing the provisions of the Treaty. Neither would they accept the original constitution as drafted by the provisional government. The delay entailed in revising the constitution in accordance with British wishes meant that it was only published on 16 June—the day of the elections—to Republican protests that it was a deliberate attempt to prevent the people from fully considering the issues involved. No one in rural areas had any chance of seeing it before they voted. But by that time Collins had reneged on the electoral pact and the peace initiative was rapidly disintegrating.[26] Of the pro-Treaty panel, 58 won seats and 35 seats were won by the anti-Treaty section. For the first time Labour took part in an election, winning 17 seats. Farmers and independents won 7 seats each. Countess Markievicz, Margaret Pearse, Ada English and Kathleen Clarke were all defeated. The only women returned to the Third Dail were Mary MacSwiney in Cork and Kate O'Callaghan in Limerick, both areas with strong anti-Treaty support. But the Dail, due to assemble on 30 June, was aborted by the start of military action. The political manoeuvring had only succeeded in postponing war and now were to follow ten months of bloodshed and horror as former comrades faced each other across battle lines more bitter than anything experienced during the long years of struggle against British rule.

The collapse of resistance in Dublin

On 22 June, Fieldmarshall Sir Henry Wilson, chief architect of British military policy in Ireland, was assassinated in London by the IRA. Evidence points to the orders for this action as having emanated from Collins (in retaliation for the pogroms against Belfast Catholics) and not the anti-Treaty section of the IRA, but it provided the lever by which to remove the embarrassing presence of the Four Courts challenge. The British cabinet demanded that the occupation be brought to an immediate end or else they would consider the Treaty to have been, in Churchill's words, 'formally violated'.[27] Moves and counter-moves continued. Leo Henderson, Four Courts Director of the Belfast

Boycott, had been arrested by government troops; in retaliation, the Four Courts garrison kidnapped Ginger O'Connell, Deputy Chief-of-Staff of the National Army (as the pro-Treaty forces were now called). Everyone knew that an attack on the Four Courts was imminent—the kidnap of O'Connell merely provided the government with the pretext they had been looking for. On 22 June, the Four Courts was issued with an ultimatum to evacuate or be taken by force. There was no reply. By 4 a.m., on expiry of the deadline, heavy artillery which had been loaned by the British was being aimed at the 200 Republicans barricaded inside.

The garrison had already received support from Republicans outside. Dr Jim Ryan (previously a medical student with the GPO forces) had arrived with a group of Cumann na mBan women to establish a first aid post. There were many others who had slept only fitfully as they waited for this inevitable final confrontation. When Maire Comerford heard the artillery fire she raced out to her bicycle and cycled in to the Four Courts, to be given the task of maintaining links between the Four Courts headquarters and the Dublin Brigade. Under the command of Oscar Traynor the Dublin Republicans had ensconced themselves within various hotels along the east side of O'Connell Street. As armed men swarmed into the hotels and frightened visitors hastily packed their bags, snipers from both sides took possession of the roof tops. It was a hazardous undertaking, travelling along streets raked by gun fire, not knowing from which direction it came. Hand-to-hand encounters were also fought in the streets between the rival factions.[28]

News of the bombardment had galvanised Republicans into action. De Valera himself had reported for duty at the mobilisation centre of the Third Dublin Battalion. The initiative was now purely in military hands. Countess Markievicz, awakened by the sound of guns, made her way to the Sinn Fein headquarters in Suffolk Street, where she found members of Cumann na mBan and the IRA preparing to join various garrisons. She ended up in Moran's Hotel, where she characteristically insisted in taking her turn as a sniper.[29] The other women occupied the basement of the hotel where, as in Easter Week, they cooked and serviced a first aid centre. Annie Smithson, one of the garrison, remembered how impossible sleep was, because of the constant firing.[30] Nora Connolly and her husband had been sleeping in Margaret Skinnider's house when the boom of artillery woke them and sent them rushing into the city centre. Seamus was sent to the Gresham Hotel while Nora and her sister Ina took charge of a first aid post in Tara Hall—after first commandeering supplies from chemist shops.[31] Other Cumann na mBan women continued to brave direct fire as they brought despatches to the side gate of the Four Courts. One even brought in ammunition which had been given to her by a Free State soldier, such was the confusion of loyalties that existed. Madge Clifford, a Sinn Fein typist, was there as secretary, typing out proclamations intended to rally the people to the defence of the Republic. When Ernie O'Malley escaped after the fall of the Four Courts she continued, in heavy disguise, to report for work to his various hideouts.

In the middle of this chaos Maire Comerford continued to cycle around the numerous garrisons, trying to find out whether or not the Four Courts would receive support from the rest of the IRA. But Liam Lynch and his comrades had made the decision that each section of the IRA was to operate in its own area, and in accordance with this, returned south to continue the fight. Without their reinforcement it could only be a matter of time before the Dublin resistance was crushed.[32]

There were still a few people who, while rejecting the Treaty, were determined to prevent war. Maud Gonne was one. While in Paris she read of the shelling of the Four Courts; one wonders whether she realised that her son Sean was one of its occupants. Her immediate response was to leave for Dublin, where she met Laurence O'Neill, the Lord Mayor, who asked her to 'get together some of the women who are not afraid, and who want peace'. Together they would make 'a supreme attempt'. Maud had soon grouped together a formidable body of women. From the suffrage ranks came Charlotte Despard, Hanna Sheehy Skeffington, Meg Connery; from the labour movement; Louie Bennett, Maire Johnson, wife of the Labour Party leader, and Mary O'Connor of the Irish Women Workers' Union; from the nationalist side there was Agnes O'Farrelly and Rosamund Jacob. But while the delegation asked for firing to be suspended while they entered the Four Courts, news came of the surrender of the garrison after two-and-a-half days of constant bombardment. The peace committee changed its plans and divided into two delegations: one to meet Griffith, Collins and Cosgrave in government buildings, the other to see Oscar Traynor in the Hammam Hotel. In Maud's words, they 'claimed, as women, on whom the misery of civil war would fall, that we had a right to be heard'. They proposed an immediate cessation of hostilities until the first meeting of the Dail; until that time, all combatants were to return home, without fear of arrest. The Republicans agreed to the terms, although insisting that they held on to their arms, but Griffith refused to negotiate. He curtly told Maud, his close friend for so many years, 'We are now a government and we have to keep order.' They did not meet again, and the war continued.[33]

Before the surrender of the Four Courts, it was decided that the wounded and the women would be evacuated. Father Albert, one of two Franciscan monks with the garrison, handed Maire Comerford a Red Cross armband as evidence of her non-combatant status, but she angrily tore it off in symbolic identification with the military role of the men and marched out with the others. No one stopped her and, accompanied as always by her bicycle, she peddled her way over to the Hammam Hotel where she reported for duty. Traynor gave her brief instructions as to how to change gears and as soon as she had got the hang of that she took charge of an ambulance, driving around the various posts to see if there were any wounded.[34] She was not the only woman to drive a car under fire. When Ernie O'Malley met Tom Derrig from the Dublin Brigade a few days later he was told of the Cumann na mBan women who had 'practised gear changes up and down streets and back lanes until they felt themselves sufficiently skilled to act as despatch carriers.'[35]

The battle had now totally shifted to O'Connell Street, with the Republicans determined to hold on for as long as possible, in order to give the countryside time to mobilise. There were 70 men and 30 women occupying the block of buildings stretching from the Hammam to the Gresham[36] but when the bombardment of shells left the buildings engulfed by flames the entire area had to be evacuated. As in 1916, the women objected to being ordered to leave. They recited the Proclamation of Easter Week with its guarantee of equal rights and equal opportunities to all citizens and left with the greatest of reluctance after pleas from Cathal Brugha.[37] Brugha, with 16 others, remained behind to give cover to those who were now trying to escape from the Free State cordon. Linda Kearns, Kathleen Barry and Muriel MacSwiney were the three women who stayed with the men.[38] But while Brugha finally ordered the surrender of the rest of his garrison on the afternoon of 5 July (the women were immediately released after they came out), he refused to give himself up to the Free State. Rushing out of the building, gun in hand, he fell, mortally wounded. Linda Kearns, a trained nurse, held his severed artery between her fingers as he was driven to hospital. He died two days later. With Brugha's death ended the fighting in Dublin City. It had lasted eight days, leaving a large part of the centre in ruins, 300 wounded and 60 killed.[39]

On 9 July, Caitlin Brugha made a public request for the women of the Republican movement alone to act as chief mourners and guard of honour at her husband's funeral. No known members of the IRA were able to attend; those not in jail were once again 'on the run'. Her decision was a protest, she declared, against the 'immediate and terrible' civil war which had been made by the government upon Republicans. As the death toll mounted in the suceeding months the unenviable task of burying the dead with full military honours was undertaken by Cumann na mBan who, 'with eyes shut and faces screwed to one side, fired a volley over the graves with revolvers or automatics'.[40]

The north

A Belfast boycott had been spontaneously initiated by Republicans in 1920 as a means of forcing northern Unionists to reinstate Catholics expelled from their work. The boycott was later ratified by the First Dail and James MacDonagh placed in charge of operations. In each Dail debate he singled out the work of women for special praise. If it were not for their participation, there would be no Belfast boycott. By March 1921 there were 184 committees dotted around the country, by May there were 360.[41] It was work that the women could largely direct themselves, persuading shops not to stock goods manufactured in Belfast and issuing blacklists of firms handling Belfast goods: woman the consumer had become woman the activist. But although Collins had formally rescinded the boycott after meeting with Craig, Prime Minister of the Northern Ireland state, it had not been discontinued by the anti-Treaty IRA. The Four Courts garrison had commandeered goods from the north (boycott biscuits became their staple diet), and Volunteers obstructed railways, seizing goods from trains. After the murder of the five members of the McMahon family in Belfast in March 1922, Cumann na mBan issued a statement warning of retaliatory action if any more attacks on Catholics took place. Eithne Coyle considered the IRA to be 'quite indifferent' in enforcing the boycott and she decided upon individual action. She was in the Strabane area at this time and, armed with a revolver, she held up the evening train at Creeslough, removing all the Belfast newspapers and setting fire to them. For the next month she busily travelled up and down the railway line, sometimes with the help of other women, seizing goods in protest.[42] The boycott came to an abrupt end with the outbreak of civil war. The IRA was now fighting for its life and the position of northern Catholics could only be alleviated by the ending of partition anyway. The boycott, while it lasted, certainly harmed the northern economy—and Craig complained that it was even more effective after the Treaty—but it failed utterly in its objective of reinstating workers. It also reinforced the division between north and south, thus strengthening partition.

On hearing of the Four Courts attack, Eithne hurried back to Dublin, where she was given the task of carrying despatches between the First Northern and Third Western divisions of the IRA. It was a very small force of IRA men in the north who attempted to face British troops, police and 'B' Specials. The Cumann na mBan women who joined Charlie Daly's headquarters at Glenveigh Castle established First Aid posts along the border, transported arms and equipment and issued a news bulletin, but the odds against them were overwhelming. By autumn the campaign had collapsed. Daly was executed by the Free State in 1923. Eithne herself was arrested towards the end of September as she arrived by boat outside Donegal town. After spending six weeks at Rock barracks in Ballyshannon she demanded a transfer, only to be told that she had been doing a man's job and should be prepared to be treated like a man. After resorting to hunger strike she eventually ended up in Mountjoy —joining, amongst others, Sheila Humphreys and her mother and aunt, who had also been arrested recently.[43]

Sheila, together with other members of her branch, had been on her way to Donegal on the morning the Four Courts was shelled. Their task was to set up a field hospital because secret plans had been made for concerted action by both Republicans and Free Staters against northern Unionists. The fighting in Dublin changed all this, so the Civil War had the unintended repercussion of allowing Unionists to consolidate their power unchallenged. After finally reaching Ballybofey the women were sent back to Dublin, to be immediately taken to the Hammam Hotel by de Valera's secretary, Kathleen O'Connell.[44]

The guerrilla war

After the collapse of Dublin the fighting moved to the countryside. Anti-Treaty feeling was strongest in the most southern regions, which is where the IRA now found themselves being gradually pushed by their far better-equipped opponents. By August, the IRA had lost its strongholds in Limerick, Waterford and Cork and the leaders were in hiding in the mountains, forced back upon the guerrilla tactics of old. The Free State army was increased at a rate of 300 per day, with artillery and armoured cars imported from the British. In contrast, the IRA could only augment its supply of weapons by capturing them from Free State soldiers. Houses which had once given shelter to men on the run now closed their doors. In order to remain free the IRA had to break up into smaller and smaller units, which further reduced their capacity to fight effectively. The work of the women became even more vital for the small roving guerrilla bands struggling against the remorseless advance of the Free State.

Kathleen Clarke's sister Madge played an essential role in the Daly stronghold of Limerick, while one historian considers 'the brilliant and dominating young Miss MacSwiney', until her arrest, 'ran what was virtually Republican headquarters' in Cork.[45] Maire Comerford found the Republican army 'disintegrating like snow on a sunny day' as she continued to maintain links between the scattered groups. Sometimes she would return to a place only to find that the unit had vanished.[46] Ernie O'Malley, now assistant chief-of-staff with the responsibility of organising Ulster and Leinster, realised his most urgent task was to build an efficient communications system in order to bring some semblance of organisation to the command structure. The role of couriers was all-important because they were not staging hit-and-run ambushes but mounting a war which had to be handled on a nationally integrated scale. Sean Lemass became O'Malley's Director of Communications, helped by Cumann na mBan headquarters. It was dishearteningly slow work as large stretches of the communications route were in hostile territory and commands often existed only on paper. Special messengers were appointed to fill the gap, whose courage and dediction O'Malley praised. While in the Four Courts Rory O'Connor had remarked to him of the fearlessness of the women couriers, 'I suppose they really think we should have captured the guns by this,'[47] and now, desperate and outnumbered, in need of all the help in the world, O'Malley was finally able to appreciate the particular qualities of the women volunteers. Whereas once he had complained of their excessive zeal, he now admitted that in the Tan war they had never had 'sufficient status'. Only when their participation was needed as never before could women be truly considered comrades. They were 'loyal, willing and incorruptible comrades'; while the men were often 'supine, lethargic', the women were 'indefatigable, [putting] the men to shame by their individual zeal and initiative'.[48]

One of his most active couriers—Maire Comerford—was almost shot on her arrival one night at the Humphreys'. On hearing a knock after midnight, O'Malley was convinced Free State troops had come to arrest him and he prepared to shoot it out. Instead, Maire bounced into the room with a despatch from the north, laughing at his panic.[49] O'Malley managed to spend six weeks in the Humphreys' household, along with the widowed

Nell Humphreys, her sister Aine O'Rahilly, treasurer of Prisoners' Aid, daughter Sheila and son Dick. The house was so 'frankly Republican' that O'Malley reckoned it would never be suspected of harbouring him, even though Madge Clifford reported for work each day. But on 4 November, Free State troops surrounded the house while O'Malley lay sleeping in a concealed room. Sheila, in great excitement, woke him and when the soldiers searched the house he came out firing, accidentally wounding Aine O'Rahilly in the face. The troops, surprised by this opposition, ran out into the garden and the inmates of the house found themselves besieged. But despite the wounding of her sister and the certain prospect of their arrest, Mrs Humphreys remained utterly calm:

> The very presence of Mrs Humpreys seemed to banish rifle fire; one could sit down and drink tea slowly in such an atmosphere... Bullets seemed a minor matter in the amenities of this household; no one appeared to be disturbed by what was now happening, and an immediate future of storming parties was faced with resolute but utterly unemphasised courage.[50]

O'Malley was left free to make his decision to fight it out rather than accept capture. As he tried to cross the garden, believing it unfair to attract fire into the house, he was riddled with bullets and badly wounded. It has been suggested[51] that Sheila took part in the shooting, but neither she nor O'Malley make any mention of this. She was, however, one of the crack shots of the Ranelagh branch of Cumann na mBan and was certainly armed for some of her operations.

After the gun battle everyone in the house was arrested; when Aine recovered the following April she was removed from hospital to jail. Soldiers had also raided the home of the O'Rahillys that morning, arresting Madame O'Rahilly and Mary MacSwiney, who was staying there at the time. It seems likely that, with the fall of Cork, she had been forced to leave there and go 'on the run'.

Apart from sheltering wounded men, finding safe houses for the wounded and acting as couriers or secretaries, there was little that women in towns and cities could do, now that the war was concentrated in the mountainous regions of the countryside. But it was still important and dangerous work. Anything that required a visible presence was undertaken by women because no anti-Treaty man could appear in public as he could be identified all too easily by his former comrades. Many Cumann na mBan women found ingenious ways of evading military censorship, by painting walls and pavements with news of the war, accounts of ill-treatment of prisoners and general Republican slogans. Sheila Humphreys used to go off before dawn with other members of her branch, armed with paintbrushes. One morning they were all arrested while painting the walls of Trinity College, but later released. The irrepressible Sheila managed to bring back cartridges which she had stripped off the feed to the Vickers gun while she was inside the armoured car.[52]

Prison struggles

As the death toll mounted—both casualties of war and deliberate executions of prisoners—and the ever increasing numbers of prisoners found themselves herded together in overcrowded jails and internment camps, those not militarily active realised that an effective campaign of protest against the government's ill-treatment of its prisoners was essential. There were at least 12,000 people in jail, of whom 400 were women. Maud Gonne's son Sean and his future wife, Kid Bulfin, were both in jail and Maud found herself refused permission even to bring them food and clothes. Out of that helplessness came the Women's Prisoners' Defence League (WPDL), to which Madame Despard was elected president and Maud secretary. The only qualification for membership was a familial relationship to a prisoner and payment of a halfpence a week. 'The Mothers', as they were affectionately dubbed by their supporters, were to become an institution on the ruined streets of Dublin as they held their Sunday protest meetings in the rubble of O'Connell Street. Through the WPDL the conditions of prisoners were publicised, missing relatives traced, vigils mounted outside jail walls and the execution of prisoners marked by public protests. They were a decided embarrassment to the Free State government (now headed by Cosgrave since the death of Griffith in

August). As military defeat appeared more and more certain, the tireless activities of the WPDL became the most visible sign of opposition to the blatantly repressive policies of the Cosgrave regime. Michael Collins had been killed in an ambush on 22 August, the only person of stature who could have restrained a government whose most powerful weapon had become legalised terror. On 12 October, a proclamation announced that military courts would begin to function on the 15th. After that date any one who committed any act of war, carried arms or ammunition, faced death if captured. Its provisions were so all-embracing that women as well as men fell within its edict. Even before that O'Hegarty, military governor of Mountjoy, had warned prisoners that they would be treated as military captives and any resistance would render them liable to being shot. While the Labour Party members of the Dail asked in vain for an inquiry, Dublin City Council formed a committee to inquire into prison conditions, but the government refused permission for its members to enter the jails. In flagrant violation of the entire Republican tradition, the government refused to consider the prisoners as political.[53]

The executions began. Of the 82 men executed by the Free State, the most notorious cases were those of Erskine Childers, convicted of the possession of a small pistol which had been given to him by Michael Collins and shot while his appeal was still pending, and the shooting, on 8 December, of Liam Mellowes, Rory O'Connor, Joseph McKelvey and Richard Barrett—all officers of the Four Courts—whose 'crimes' had been committed before the October proclamation.

The protests of the WPDL continued. While others had attempted to reason with the government, the women challenged their actions on the streets. Their demonstrations were broken up, they were shot at and had hoses aimed upon them, but still they protested. In November, Maud Gonne and Charlotte Despard were speaking at a meeting in O'Connell Street, held to protest against the detention of Mary MacSwiney and to publicise the fact that she was on hunger strike, when a lorry load of pro-Treaty troops pulled up and opened fire upon the crowd. Fourteen people were wounded and hundreds hurt in the panicked stampede that followed.[54] Shortly after that Maud's house was ransacked by troops and the sole occupant, Dorothy

Macardle, another WPDL worker, was arrested. At the start of 1923, Maud too was arrested and held without charge in Kilmainham, joining such old friends as Dorothy Macardle, Grace Plunkett, Nora Connolly, Lily O'Brennan, Mary MacSwiney, Kate O'Callaghan and Nell Ryan.

The prisoners staged numerous protests against their appalling conditions. Those who had been most active while free proved themselves intransigent prisoners, constantly rebelling against their harsh treatment. The prison staff reacted by firing into cells, beating up prisoners and placing punitive restrictions upon them. In January, Maire Comerford and Eithne Coyle protested against the overcrowding by throwing the extra beds out of the cells. For this they received three months' hard labour and removal to the 'criminal' section of the jail. They went on hunger strike. While waving to their comrades in the exercise yard they were fired upon and Maire wounded in the leg. The tactic of hunger striking was resorted to continuously in the absence of any judicial mechanism for resolving grievances. *Eire*, the Republican newspaper printed in Glasgow to avoid military censorship, warned that a concerted campaign against Republican women was being waged by the Free State and the church. The pastoral letter of Cardinal Logue had singled out the women for condemnation and Kevin O'Higgins, Minister of Home Affairs, had contemptuously referred to 'hysterical young women who ought to be playing five-fingered exercises or helping their mother with the brasses', in an attempt to belittle their contribution to the conduct of the war.[55] It was feared that this campaign to alienate public sympathy from the female prisoners would leave them vulnerable to further attack. In retaliation, 91 women in Kilmainham went on hunger strike and after seven days won their demand to receive and send out letters, which had previously been denied to them. It was the fourth hunger strike conducted by women.

In October the Catholic Church excommunicated all Republicans who, the bishops stated, 'in the absence of any legitimate authority to justify it [were carrying on] a system of murder'. When the women attended Mass, the ordinary prisoners would receive communion while the others would be lambasted with the contents of the pastoral letter. If a woman attempted to have her confession heard she had first of all to accept the bishop's pronouncement. None of them would. A very few stopped practising but most shrugged philosophically. Eithne Coyle's attitude was probably the most common. In an argument with a priest, her retort to his contention that the bishops were always right was that they were hardly right when they burnt Joan of Arc. He was so angry he almost hit her.[56]

The 1923 commemoration of Easter Week that was held within the walls of Kilmainham was a potent reminder of the familial links between the male and female activists of the Republican movement. Most of the female relatives of the original leaders were now, seven years later, still fighting for the Republican ideal. In solemn procession the women marched to the place where the executions had taken place in 1916. In front were Nell Humphreys and Aine O'Rahilly, representing The O'Rahilly, shot by the British on Moore Street; Grace Plunkett, widow of Joseph, unfurled the Tricolour; Lily O'Brennan, now incarcerated in the same cell that had once held her brother-in-law, spoke on the life and death of Eamon Ceannt; Grace Plunkett then spoke about her husband and Nora Connolly concluded the ceremony by reading the Proclamation of the Republic and her father's last statement. Dorothy Macardle, in reporting the occasion aptly remarked, 'it was as if the voices of our dead leaders were speaking to us again.'[57]

While the ghosts of 1916 were momentarily brought back to life by those sorrowing women the brief ceremony has, for feminists, additional significance. As a commemoration of Easter Week it was of course appropriate that those most closely identified with its leaders should evoke their memories, particularly as they too were now in a similar position of apparent defeat. But in more symbolic terms, a strong impression is conveyed of women's role being solely one of bearing witness for the male representatives of the Republican movement rather than, on their own terms, incorporating that ideal into an autonomous vision. As the cult of martyrology has always been a powerful motivating force in Irish history and it has always been men who have paid the supreme penalty, this sacrifice of male lives for the national cause has obscured the continual yet less dramatic sacrifices made by women working for the same cause. It has also perpetuated an artificial distinction between man the leader and woman the auxiliary, not least in the consciousness of women themselves.

The ill-treatment of women prisoners reached an infamous climax during what became known as the North Dublin Union (NDU) riots, when women received such vicious beatings at the hands of Free State soldiers and guards that it seemed as if the government was hell-bent on providing women with their first martyrs. The cause of the riot was the refusal of women in Mountjoy and Kilmainham to accept being transferred to the NDU. Women in Mountjoy point-blank refused to budge, whereupon they found themselves beaten up and dragged downstairs. In Kilmainham, 81 women refused to allow themselves to be removed to the bleak former workhouse because of their concern over the condition of Mary MacSwiney and Kate O'Callaghan, both of whom were on their twenty-fifth day of hunger strike. A large number of women had already been transferred and the remainder understandably feared leaving the two women, weak and alone, to the mercy of their captors. Kate O'Callaghan was released at 10.20 that night, 30 April, and at midnight soldiers rushed up the top landing to the prisoners and began dragging them towards the iron staircase, where they were dragged down or, in some cases, thrown. The battle continued for five hours, by which time 70 women had been taken away. There appears to have been an element of sexual abuse in some of the attacks. Eileen Barry's clothes were dragged off her and she was 'treated very roughly', as Sorcha MacDermott, a London deportee, reported from Mountjoy. Sorcha herself was stripped of shoes, stockings and dress and beaten with her shoes by Cumann na Saoirse women. Rose Killeen, another of the 15 women deported from England and jailed by the Free State, had her dress cut off and found herself 'subjected to great indignities'. Mary MacSwiney was released the following afternoon, as a result of the events being made public.[58]

Some of the women in jail had the extra worry of their children's well-being, in some cases compounded by the fact that their husbands were also prisoners. Husbands and wives went to great lengths to communicate with each other when they found themselves in separate sections of the same jail. Margaret

Buckley, sharing a cell with Cecilia Gallagher, was touched and amused by her friend's efforts to reach the small window at the top of the cell so that she could shout a good morning to Frank as he emerged to do orderly duties, but other women found the strain too much. Noinin Cogley, a neighbour of Margaret Buckley's, whose husband was also in jail, fretted so much over her two children that her health broke down completely. After six months in Mountjoy she was released.[59]

Ceasefire

Outside the prisons and internment camps, the Republicans were suffering defeat after defeat. The most serious blow had come on 10 April with the death of IRA chief-of-staff Liam Lynch, the one man above all who had been determined to fight on, regardless of the overwhelming odds. With Lynch gone, a Republican ceasefire could not be delayed much longer. The pro-Treaty troops, scenting final victory, had saturated the last of the Republican retreats, capturing Austin Stack, Dan Breen and many other senior officers. De Valera, after meeting with what remained of the army executive, issued proposals for negotiation, which were peremptorily rejected by the government. There would be no terms, only unconditional surrender. Frank Aiken, the new chief-of-staff, finally issued orders to the remaining anti-Treaty troops to dump arms and cease fire on 24 May.

Cumann na mBan was not consulted in any of these negotiations, although they had previously made it plain that they considered they had a right to be involved. On 8 September 1922, Cumann na mBan had addressed a resolution to O'Malley (taking the precaution of also sending a copy to Mellows in Mountjoy) with the demand that, in the event of the army executive opening peace negotiations, Cumann na mBan should have representation. O'Mally however simply referred the matter to Lynch. Nothing came of this and the principle was never decided upon.[60] De Valera accompanied Aiken's ceasefire order with a message to his troops entitled 'Soldiers of the Republic, Legion of the Rearguard', which failed to make any mention of the contribution of the women. Men were exhorted to bear their sufferings 'in a manner worthy of men who were ready to give their lives for the cause'.[61] It's debatable whether he even realised the extent of women's sufferings.

Thousands more prisoners were added to the numbers already interned and the prison struggles intensified as those incarcerated bitterly resented their continued captivity. Maire Comerford, who had escaped from the NDU, was recaptured on 1 June and immediately went on hunger strike in protest at the government's insistence on continuing the war after the Republicans had laid down their arms. After 25 days she was released, carried out on a stretcher.[62] Maud Gonne had secured her own release by the same method and was back on the streets of Dublin, railing against the government's treatment of prisoners.

Confident that they were now inviolable, the government decided to hold an election on 27 August in order to win an unambiguous mandate for the Treaty. It was an extraordinary situation. Eighty-seven candidates—most of them in jail or on the run—stood on the Republican ticket, risking arrest each time they stood on an election platform. They had already been beaten into the ground and now the government was determined to hammer home, once and for all, the last nail in the coffin of Republican hopes. De Valera was arrested while speaking at an election meeting in Clare; it would be 11 months before he was free again. But despite the fact that they were harried and harassed wherever they appeared, and despite the fact that those in jail could not vote, the Republicans won 44 seats while the government won 63. The remaining 46 seats were won by Labour, Farmers and Independents. Mary MacSwiney was again returned for Cork, Markievicz regained her seat in Dublin South, Dr Kathleen Lynn was elected in Dublin North and Caitlin Brugha was returned at the head of the poll in Waterford. The only woman on the pro-Treaty side to be elected was Margaret Collins O'Driscoll—the sister of Michael Collins—in Dublin North. The election was notable for another reason in that it was the first occasion in which women between the ages of 21 and 30 could vote. Cosgrave, in announcing the new Constitution shortly before the election, had proclaimed 'The pledge of Arthur Griffith has been fulfilled,' but although it was far in advance of

Britain, for many women it was now too little too late.

The Civil War, at least as far as the Republicans were concerned, was over and a new Dail assembled, although many were unable to take their seats, even if they had wanted to. The government showed no sign of releasing the prisoners but instead continued to make new arrests. In August, Nora Connolly managed to secure a writ of habeas corpus on the grounds that her arrest had been unconstitutional, and judgement was given in her favour despite protests from state lawyers. On 20 November, Countess Markievicz was arrested while she and Hanna Sheehy Skeffington were collecting signatures on a petition calling for the release of the prisoners. At the time of her arrest a mass hunger strike was being conducted by the prisoners, in a desperate attempt to gain a general release. The protest had started on 13 October, when 424 men in Mountjoy refused food, to be followed by prisoners in other jails until a total of 9,000 men and women had joined in the hunger strike. Out of the original 340 women in the NDU, 225 still remained.

Although the hunger strike lasted a total of 41 days, by the thirtieth day only 400 men and 8 women continued to find the will power to go on. There were no recriminations from inside the jails; as Peadar O'Donnell, one of those who managed to stick it out to the end, wrote in his diary, 'The decision to go on hunger strike was made when none of us knew he had a stomach; now I have nothing else than a belly with needs that are ready to jump right through my mind.'[63] There was massive public support and even Cardinal Logue was concerned enough to express his hope that the prisoners would be released by Christmas. After two men had died, a decision was finally taken on 23 November to call off the strike rather than see morale disintegrate further. Those who had already come off were offered their freedom on condition they signed a form pledging loyalty to the state. Few would sign and the rule was changed to make it easier for prisoners to accept the conditions of their release. The one positive outcome of the hunger strike was the release of the 51 women hunger strikers. In December, all the women prisoners and many of the men were set free.[64] Sheila Humphreys was one of the women released after refusing food for 31 days. No joy was felt as, half alive, they stumbled out into the harsh reality of life in the Free State: 'We were flattened. We felt the Irish public had forgotten us. The tinted trappings of our fight were hanging like rags about us.'[65]

6. Cumann na mBan, 1924-40
The irreconcilables

Regrouping the opposition

The war was at last over, the women were free and the rest of the men were finally released in June 1924. The government, however, was determined to stick to a tough law-and-order policy and a Public Safety Act was brought in, allowing for the suspension of habeas corpus, an insurance policy against any active hostility. As the prisoners trickled out of the internment camps, their first thought was the reorganisation of their shattered forces. The IRA had dumped its arms but its members remained prepared to sit it out until another opportunity to strike a blow for the Republic arose. Many had nothing but their idealism to sustain them, with no jobs and no prospect of finding employment in a state slowly recovering from the devastation of a war that had cost £17 million. Republicans found themselves boycotted when they looked for work and because of the requirement of taking the oath of allegiance, would not work for the state. Teachers and doctors were unable to return to their professions—Hanna Sheehy Skeffington lost her job as a teacher of German in a Dublin technical college, and there were many others like her. Maire Comerford tried to set up a poultry farm in Wexford, eking out a meagre living on 5s a week and riding up to Dublin on her motor bike whenever she could scrape together the money. Due to her isolation, her links with Cumann na mBan gradually weakened. Eithne Coyle went to live with her sister who had a job and also kept a few boarders. Both lived frugally on her small income and Eithne found herself with all the time in the world to devote to Cumann na mBan activities, especially as she became an executive member for the first time in 1924. Any resources Republicans possessed were used in attempts to alleviate the appalling economic hardships suffered by so many. Maud Gonne and Charlotte Despard, for example, organised workshops in their home at Roebuck House where 15 Republican women and relatives of ex-prisoners made jam and learnt embroidery. Their profits were non-existent, the venture surviving through subsidies from what remained of the two women's private fortunes.[1]

The IRA was unable to hold a convention until 1925 (when it withdrew allegiance from the Second Dail on the grounds that it was unable to function as a government), but in April 1924, the Dublin branches of Cumann na mBan held a meeting to work out a scheme of reorganisation which it was hoped would soon be extended to all branches. It was an ambitious programme, particularly given the circumstances. The catastrophic defeat so recently suffered was barely alluded to in the presidential address of Countess Markievicz:

> No one knows when we may be attacked again or when we may see our chance to strike again. Peace is beautiful and we want peace; but we cannot shirk the fight if it is the only way to win.[2]

The countess still possessed the unerring instinct she had shown during the 1921 Convention to strike the right note in strengthening the resolve of her members and giving them hope that they would eventually triumph. On a more practical level, she also devoted a large part of her speech to a discussion of unemployment and urged everyone to make concrete suggestions on how work could be provided.

A programme of reorganisation was adopted: branches were to meet monthly, when military and physical drill would be given; special classes in first aid would be formed; officers' training classes would start once branch elections had taken place; fortnightly lectures by well-known speakers on historical, social and economic subjects would be given; a qualified choral mistress would form a choir; all members were urged to take up the study of the Irish language; and camogie and rounders teams would be formed and inter-branch matches played so that members from all over the country could get to know each other 'and a spirit of self reliance, comradeship and discipline' be fostered.

In their determination not to bow down to defeat they were premature. Many members were dropping by the wayside, either because of demoralisation, or the after-effects of imprisonment, which had undermined the health of many, or because of the claims of family life. For most, the necessity of earning a living became a primary consideration after the years of near-destitution. And a serious blow to morale was yet to come, with the defections to Fianna Fail.

Impatient with what he regarded as the now futile policy of abstention, which left few outlets for Republicans to challenge Cumann na nGaedheal now that the military challenge had been crushed, de Valera was searching for a means whereby deputies could enter the Dail without compromising their beliefs. Within Sinn Fein he began to argue that once the oath of allegiance was removed they could take their seats and begin the process of dismantling the Treaty arrangements. It was, to say the least, a controversial proposal that ran counter to the whole tradition of nationalist struggle. A Sinn Fein Ard Fheis was summoned for 9 March 1926 to consider the issue, the outcome of which was a split right down the middle of the organisation. Essentially, the division was over tactics rather than reflecting divergent political views as people on the left and right voted for de Valera and equally, people on the left and right voted against. Little of the debate was ever published, for fear of exacerbating the conflict as no one wanted the movement to disintegrate as a consequence of the dispute. De Valera resigned as president of Sinn Fein and he and his supporters left to form a new political party, Fianna Fail (Warriors of Fal).

Fianna Fail was publicly launched at the La Scala Theatre on 16 April, at a meeting presided over by Countess Markievicz who had had to resign from Cumann na mBan because her membership of Fianna Fail contravened the constitution of Cumann na mBan, which was pledged to work with the IRA. Sheila Humphreys said that it nearly broke their hearts to lose her. They hadn't wanted to accept her resignation which, under their constitution, they were compelled to do. They could not even bring themselves to arrange a presentation, because that would be to admit that she was no longer with them. Markievicz had never been an orthodox member of Cumann na mBan in the sense of devoting all her time and energies to the organisation —she was linked to too many groups to be able to do so—but she had been an inspirational force to the younger women, particularly those who had shared prison cells with her, and they loved her deeply. But no one would claim her loyalties for much longer: on 15 July 1927 she was dead, a result of complications following an operation for appendicitis.

Eithne Coyle was now the new president of Cumann na mBan, while Mary MacSwiney became vice-president. In a letter written to Maire Comerford in 1964, Eithne speculated upon the thorny question of whether Markievicz, had she lived, would have followed de Valera's example by taking the hated oath to enter the Dail. Many who knew her felt that she would have baulked at such a final surrender of her Republican principles, but Eithne believed, despite being assured by her when they were in Mountjoy Jail together that she would never take an oath of allegiance to an English monarch, that she would have taken her seat. 'Madam was no fool... she had more than average intelligence to realise all the implications involved' when she resigned from Cumann na mBan to join de Valera. But, as Eithne sadly concluded, 'Poor Madam it is not fair to talk about her when she is unable to defend herself.'[3]

The first executive of Fianna Fail contained a number of women: Margaret Pearse, Countess Markievicz, Kathleen Clarke, Dorothy Macardle, Linda Kearns and Hanna Sheehy Skeffington. Apart from Hanna, all the women remained staunch supporters of de Valera for the rest of their lives. The elderly Margaret Pearse rather pathetically believed de Valera to be the reincarnation of her son; her daughter, Margaret Mary Pearse, became a Fianna Fail TD in 1933 but was out of her depth in the Dail and doesn't appear to have contributed to any debates. In the 1927 elections Countess Markievicz was re-elected and Kathleen Clarke became a senator, serving for almost ten years. She later became Lord Mayor of Dublin. While always remaining a Republican, her greatest desire was the peaceful solution of the national question; more than most, she knew the personal tragedies that always accompanied war. In the early 1940s she was active in campaigning on behalf of political prisoners, her motivation humanitarian rather than party political. Hanna Sheehy Skeffington was a most incongruous figure within the Fianna Fail ranks, given her fierce opposition to de Valera's paternalistic attitudes towards women, and she didn't remain there for long. She later wrote a scorching criticism of de Valera's portrayal of Countess Markievicz as a philanthropist rather than a revolutionary, taking the opportunity as she did so to remind her readers of de Valera's refusal to allow women into Boland's Mill during the Easter Rising. In summing up the differences between Connolly and de Valera —one fighting for revolution, the other for evolution and constitutionalism—she isolated their divergent views on women in order to emphasise her point, 'To the one, woman was an equal, a comrade: to the other, a sheltered being, withdrawn to the domestic hearth, shrinking from public life.'[4] No, there was no way a feminist could belong to Fianna Fail.

In forming Fianna Fail de Valera and Dr Jim Ryan arranged a meeting with Cumann na mBan, seemingly confident that they would be easily won over to the new departure. As with all the other occasions when political differences had arisen within nationalist ranks, few of the women deviated from the strict guidelines laid down in their constitution and were annoyed to discover that de Valera had thought otherwise.[5] Their most prominent member had indeed defected, but most of the well-known activists remained loyal to Cumann na mBan. Mary MacSwiney admitted, however, that the 1926 Convention of Cumann na mBan was 'a greatly diminished' event as a result, although it is impossible to calculate how many members were lost.

Sinn Fein held another Ard Fheis in October 1926, but this time there were only 200 delegates. Possibly as a result of the drop in numbers, women were well represented on the new executive. Mary MacSwiney was vice-president while Caitlin Brugha, although not wanting to stand for office again, was prevailed upon to remain as secretary. Amongst the eight Dublin representatives were three women—Kathleen Lynn, Margaret Buckley, and Lily Coventry. Maire Comerford and Dulcibella Barton represented Leinster, while Kate O'Callaghan and Albinia Broderick (Gobnait ni Bhrudair) were two of the Munster representatives.[6]

It was an extraordinarily heterogeneous grouping. Madeleine ffrench-Mullen, a former member of the Irish Citizen Army, attempted to inject some social and economic awareness into the proceedings by proposing, along with Dr Lynn, that Sinn Fein support feeding schemes for school children, house-building programmes and improvements in education. She had been a member of Inghinidhe na hEireann when that group first aroused public interest in school meals but the impoverished and truncated rump of Sinn Fein could now do little but signify agreement without committing themselves to positive action. Maire Comerford, placed for the first time on the executive of what she admitted was 'a greatly weakened organisation', and one that 'gathered speed downhill',[7] felt unable to contribute much, desperate and penniless as she was on her lonely Wexford farm. That didn't prevent her from proposing a motion publicly to burn the Union Jack at a mass meeting in O'Connell Street if it was found on display on Armistice Day. The motion was carried. Since the Treaty settlement had ended hostilities against the British, southern Unionists had again begun to display Union Jacks from business premises to commemorate Armistice Day and Cumann na mBan were tireless in their efforts to ensure that such symbols of imperialism were removed. Regular riots accompanied each Armistice Day; the Republicans' attitude towards their enemies was most cogently expressed by Frank Ryan, speaking on Armistice eve in 1932 when he declared 'while we have fists, hands and boots to use, and guns if necessary, we will not allow free speech to traitors'.[8]

Less than one year after the formation of Fianna Fail, on 10 July 1927, Kevin O'Higgins, Minister of Justice and the man most hated by Republicans for his responsibility for the execution of prisoners, was shot dead outside his home. In reaction, the government rushed through three bills: a Public Safety Bill which curtailed the right to trial by jury, a bill to ensure that every candidate for election would, on nomination, swear to take the oath, and a bill proposing to amend the constitution to members of the Dail who had taken the oath. It was a direct challenge to Fianna Fail. If they did not enter the Dail to fight the proposals they would never be able to go in. De Valera took up the challenge by leading his deputies into the Dail where they signed the book containing the contentious oath. So some of the dissidents were back in the fold and by their presence conferred a greater degree of legitimacy to the Free State settlement. There was now a Republican opposition that accepted the parliamentary path. Only the speaker's casting vote saved the government's proposals and a general election was called for 15 September. Cumann na nGaedheal got back in, but with a reduced majority and Fianna Fail settled back on the benches to await their turn. Sinn Fein decided not to contest the election, now that prospective candidates had to take the oath, and principled abstentionism became almost the sole political strategy of this impotent group of intransigent Republicans, marooned from the mainstream of political events, clinging on to the fantasy that the surviving members of the Second Dail constituted the legitimate government of Ireland.

Continuing the struggle

While Sinn Fein languished and the IRA quietly reorganised, Cumann na mBan impatiently awaited the time when once again its members could take part in the struggle for independence. But in the meantime, the women were determined to keep sacred the memories of those who had died. When the Abbey staged Sean O'Casey's *The Plough and the Stars*, which dealt with the impact of the 1916 Rising upon the Dublin working class, outraged Republicans disrupted each performance of the play, which they felt belittled the men of 1916. It was too soon after the experience of war for them to assess objectively what O'Casey was trying to convey. Relatives of some of the men of 1916—Mrs Barrett, sister of Sean Connolly (who had died in the attempt to take Dublin Castle), Fiona Plunkett, Sheila Humphreys, Hanna Sheehy Skeffington, Maud Gonne—together with members of Cumann na mBan and the IRA all turned up to protest that 'their men didn't drink'. That, far more than the portrayal of Nora Clitheroe's rage at the men who went to fight for Ireland, was what enraged them. Their heroes were unblemished and their role was to bear witness to their sanctity. Maud Gonne later tackled O'Casey in a public debate arranged by Hanna Sheehy Skeffington. No agreement as to the role of the artist in society was reached and the embittered playwright, looking at Maud sitting beside Hanna saw 'not her who was beautiful, and had the walk of a queen, but the Poor Old Woman, whose voice was querulous, from whom came many words that were bitter, and but few kind'.[9] It was an incident that was later a cause for shame amongst many of its participants but their reaction was wholly explicable in terms of the raw nerves of the defeated, left with nothing but romantic memories of a glorious past.

But members of Cumann na mBan were doing more than simply protest. Maire Comerford had the bright idea of reminding jurors in cases where Republicans were being charged of their patriotic duty. In 1926, during one of her rare excursions to Dublin, she received a nine-month sentence for trying to influence a jury. Sheila Humphreys was arrested that December, on the eve of the Cumann na mBan Convention, which disrupted proceedings considerably as they had to forgo their secretary's report. In January 1927 Fiona Plunkett and Maeve Phelan were also arrested and sentenced to two months, on the charge of 'loitering with felonious intent near a judge's residence'.[10]

At first the jury campaign was very much an individualistic affair but Cumann na mBan was desperate for an organised campaign which would both give the members some scope and also help attract new recruits. In the hiatus that had followed the ending of hostilities there was little Republicans could do except to oppose the Cosgrave regime at every conceivable opportunity, and hope that this would be sufficient to keep alive the Republican ideal. It was a particularly difficult situation for Cumann na mBan because if the men were inactive there was little reason for their own continued existence. At the end of 1927 the Cumann na mBan executive, in exhorting members to attend the forthcoming convention, attacked the 'general apathy' which had arisen since the IRA first announced its ceasefire—in effect criticising the IRA for its 'strict adherence' to that policy—and announced that 'enough time has been wasted on a drift policy and it is up to our organisation to end it by embarking on a campaign to end British influences in this country.'[11]

The anti-juror campaign was now organised on a systematic basis as Cumann na mBan launched its first campaign of the post-Civil War period. Jurors' names were acquired through a contact at Green Street Courthouse in Dublin, and letters sent out to them, stating the reasons why the particular individual should not be found guilty.[12] 'Ghosts' was the name given to these leaflets and letters, the majority of which appear to have been written by Sheila Humphreys. The following gives an example of the ferocious style in which they were written:

> The enemies of Ireland are imprisoning the men and women who are carrying out the only practical programme to attain freedom. Unfortunately some of Dublin's degenerate and slavish citizens assist them in this work. Last month the following [12 names and addresses]... helped Carrigan and the infamous 'Judge' Sullivan to send the Irish patriot CON HEALY to penal servitude for five years. These men are traitors to their country. (Death would be their fate in any free country in the world.)
>
> —Issued by 'Ghosts'[13]

On 10 May 1928, Sheila Humphreys was arrested on the charge of wrongly influencing juries and of possessing illegal documents. Discovered in her home were 20,000 copies of 'Ghosts'. At her trial the jury disagreed and she spent nine months in jail before finally being found guilty. She was then released because of the amount of time she had already served.[14] That May, over 50 homes in Dublin alone were raided by a government quick to react to the slightest sign of disaffection. Sheila MacInerney, a member of Cumann na mBan and the manager of *Irish Freedom*, the semi-official newspaper of Sinn Fein which was owned by Albinia Broderick, was sentenced to six months for the possession of arms and illegal documents. Florence McCarthy was also given six months after a raid on Cumann na mBan headquarters, charged with conspiracy and the possession of treasonable documents. Mrs MacDermott and Evelyn Jackson, also of Cumann na mBan, were arrested at the end of February, charged with having distributed treasonable literature. In their case the jury failed to agree and they were remanded in custody.[15]

Cumann na mBan's attempt to destabilise the political consensus which was being so methodically constructed by Cumann na nGaedheal was having some success. Once again Republicans were being jailed, the Women's Prisoners' Defence League was reactivated and Cumann na mBan threw itself enthusiastically into its activities. There were more public meetings, and demonstrations outside the houses of judges. In July, the five imprisoned women went on hunger strike in protest over their treatment, held in solitary confinement and denied letters and visits. Fianna Fail called for an adjournment debate, demanding that Republican prisoners be accorded the status of political prisoners. De Valera pointed out that the Republican cabinet used to meet in the home of Sheila Humphreys during the Black and Tan war and 'nothing that this young girl is doing now is different from anything which was preached in that home by members of the Republican Cabinet, some of whom are now persecuting her'.[16] But there was a difference—Cumann na nGaedheal were now in power and their attitude was the same as that of governments everywhere. 'The food is there for them at any time they wish to take it,' Fitzgerald-Kenny curtly replied. After almost six days of hunger strike Mrs MacDermott collapsed and was released to hospital. The strike was called off and some concessions made. However, the government was determined to show no signs of leniency; when she recovered she was rearrested and, together with Eva Jackson, sentenced to 12 months for having pasted up handbills threatening the life of Judge James MacNeill.

The Cumann na mBan campaign was seriously undermining the willingness of juries to convict and their reluctance was intensified when the IRA threw its weight behind the campaign by shooting the foreman of a jury. In May 1929, the government retaliated by introducing the Juries' Protection Bill which provided for the total anonymity of jurors and allowed for conviction if nine out of the twelve agreed. It was back to the old days of harassment, raids, imprisonment and protests. Cumann na mBan headquarters were raided on a daily basis, its officers spending a great deal of time in the Bridewell. In Kerry, Albinia Broderick found herself subjected to the same treatment. Repression had its usual spin-off, as former members returned to their organisation, outraged at the rough tactics of the government. Cumann na mBan hoped that all their branches would soon return to their former strength, and cheekily expressed the hope that 'the enemy will be good enough to transfer its activities to other parts of Ireland, that we have the same good results'.[17] Despite their hopes, this resurgence remained a largely Dublin affair.

However, by 1930 Cumann na mBan's fortunes had revived sufficiently for it considerably to extend its activities. The publicity department was issuing 5,000 leaflets each month on Irish history, which were circulated to schools, their hope being eventually to gain access to each school in Ireland. The Easter Lily Commemoration which had been initiated by Cumann na mBan in 1926 grew in strength and now had committees dotted around the country, with Sinn Fein and IRA members giving full support and supplying delegates to a central committee. Only 1,000 Easter Lilies had been sold in 1929, in 1930 they hoped to dispose of 10,000 in a general collection, the proceeds to be distributed amongst the various organisations, all of which were still desperately short of funds. By the end of the year, the executive of Cumann na mBan felt strong enough to launch the campaign which had been spoken of for years but which had never, because of lack of resources and personnel, been systematically organised: a boycott of British goods.

Boycotting British goods

For some reason it was decided to begin with the promotion of Irish sweets, a calculation having been made that if Irish sweets alone were eaten, 3,200 more people would have jobs. One leaflet in their Irish Manufacture series ended with the doggerel 'every British sweet you eat deprives an Irish mouth of meat'. Persuasive appeals alone were not enough. Shopkeepers who did not comply were regarded as the enemy and treated accordingly. If all else failed, windows were smashed and the offending items removed, to be publicly burnt. Two separate leaflets, one for shopkeepers and one for the public, were distributed and public meetings held in various areas of Dublin, dealing with unemployment and emigration—the result, it was claimed, of not buying Irish products. The campaign, although initiated by Cumann na mBan, could not be carried out solely through the efforts of its members. The executive complained that nine out of ten members, when asked to join the boycott campaign begged to be excused, saying 'they were no good for arguing'. Members were sternly reprimanded for their inability to state a convincing case for buying Irish goods, and told to read the works of MacSwiney, Pearse, Lalor and Connolly.[18] Such blandishments were not enough to boost self-confidence. This lack of intellectual confidence amongst the rank and file, only now becoming apparent, was to recur continuously over the decade. It was one thing to brave danger in war, but quite another to articulate the rationale of orthodox Republicanism to an unconvinced general public. The confident, well-read and capable leaders of Cumann na mBan during this period were far in advance of their members, equally undaunted by physical repression or by the challenge of lecturing on such subjects as Lenin and the role of women in the Russian Revolution, which was the title of a talk given by Sheila Humphreys. This clearly discernible difference in the levels of ability within the organisation wasn't necessarily a reflection of differing class positions or educational opportunities—Eithne Coyle after all had grown up on a small Donegal farm, reared by a widowed mother—and it was probably a factor which had always been present but which before had remained concealed. The attempts of the executive to develop a wider range of activities for the various branches, who obstinately persisted in clinging to such traditional tasks as organising fundraising events for the IRA, brought this disparity into the open. Members were caustically reminded that they had 'a higher destiny to fulfil than to act as collecting boxes' but the problem was that not everyone welcomed the opportunity to extend their horizons beyond the restrictive framework that had for so long confined Republican women.

Because of these difficulties the boycott campaign and the Easter Lily Committee were extended to other Republican organisations. For example, the boycott committee was composed of members of the IRA, Sinn Fein and Cumann na mBan, meeting each week at Cumann na mBan headquarters. Dublin was divided into four parts with a director in charge of each section. Each sweet shop was visited and a black list compiled of those shopkeepers who refused to change their merchandise. The foot slogging was no doubt left to the women, while threatening the shopkeepers and speaking at meetings was mainly the work of the men. It was to be men from the IRA who later took over the direction of the campaign—Donal O'Donoghue became overall director.

In 1931, the March and April issues of *Workers' Voice* saw a heated debate between Cumann na mBan and the Revolutionary Workers' Group over the political justification for Cumann na mBan's 'buy Irish' campaign. While Sheila Humphreys, as Cumann na mBan director of publicity, insisted that her organisation had no intention of allying themselves with local capitalists but concerned themselves solely with the development of Irish industry and the material improvement of the Irish people, *Workers' Voice* pointed out that their lack of any class perspective had led them down the blind alley of consumption, ignoring the fact that the working class was exploited internationally, regardless of the nationality of the individual capitalist. As a consequence, they had failed to see the necessity of showing solidarity with workers who were fighting against capitalism —such as the laundry workers at Greenmount, or the 5,000 railway workers who had just been made redundant. While 'Cumann na mBan are blathering about sweets and buns', Irish capitalists continue to exploit workers and underpay them without any protest from Cumann na mBan who simply exhort people to buy Irish without fighting for the higher wages necessary for people to be able to do so. However, while this debate raged *Workers' Voice* constantly reiterated its high regard for Cumann na mBan and its belief that both groups agreed on the ultimate objective, that of the destruction of capitalism. Amidst the confusion of thought and inability to explain how Cumann na mBan differed from such reactionary groups as the Irish Industries' Purchasing League (supported by the property owners) was a radical kernel which was to develop further over the next few years. *Workers' Voice* was partly correct —there were some members of Cumann na mBan who would not have significant differences with their socialism, even if they retained a wariness about describing themselves as such—but there were other members who would probably have approved of the aims of the Irish Industries' Purchasing League.

Unless Republicans could divorce themselves from the highminded purists of the Second Dail and develop a political programme which could attract people to the Republican movement, the only serious challenge to the Cosgrave regime would come from inside the Dail, through Fianna Fail, who would reap the electoral benefits and be able to claim that it alone provided a credible Republican alternative. Only a programme of action that based itself firmly upon the needs of the workers and small farmers could mobilise enough support to break the link with imperialism and institute a workers' republic. Economic depression was becoming more acute, the emigration rate was rising, strikes against redundancies growing in strength and the campaign against the payment of land annuities to Britain gathering support, yet all that Republicans had to offer was the feeble cry of 'buy Irish', which in the circumstances was fairly pitiful.

The formation of Saor Eire—and the backlash

There were many within the IRA who understood this only too well and who were determined to push the IRA to the left, broadening it out beyond purely military concerns. In February 1931, the Army Convention met in the house of Roisin Walsh, chief librarian of Dublin City Library. Eithne Coyle was one of the women present. She vaguely recollected that the plan to launch Saor Eire (Free Ireland) as a radical movement based on the people was finally agreed during the meeting.[19] Despite the misgivings of some of the Army Council the new venture was quietly publicised to the Volunteers over the next few months. In the meantime Republicans were determined that regardless of government repression their growing strength would be publicly demonstrated.

The arrests were continuing and so was the denial of basic rights to those in jail. An 11-day hunger strike in Mountjoy was called off by the IRA in a move to force those on the outside to mobilise in support of the prisoners instead of leaving the challenge to the government to the prisoners themselves. In response, Cumann na mBan decided to show solidarity by organising a march to Mountjoy. Frank Ryan, editor of *An Phoblacht* and on the far left of the IRA, was one of those invited to speak. While he was in the middle of his address the police rushed the speakers' lorry, pulled off the four men on it and began baton-charging the demonstrators. A report in *Irish Freedom* described the 'magnificent behaviour' of the Cumann na mBan women, many of whom were experiencing their first baton charge:

> Not one single member broke the ranks, although the general public rushed through them at a terrific pace. Members stood their ground on the tram tracks, holding up all traffic, and finally marched back to Cathal Brugha Street where from the platform the thousands of people gathered there were told what had happened at Mountjoy.[20]

Ryan subsequently received a two-month jail sentence, so did two of the other male speakers.

The 1931 Wolfe Tone commemoration at Bodenstown was banned and all bus and train services cancelled. The two speakers, Mick Price and Sean Russell, were arrested the day before by a government determined to clamp down on Republican activity. Yet around 15,000 people managed to crowd into Bodenstown, leaving the Free State soldiers impotent. Fianna Fail had also decided to march and in protest Sinn Fein decided they could not be contaminated by participating in an event with the 'oath-bound'. Instead, the small group laid their wreath on the Friday, reciting a decade of the rosary as they did so. Cumann na mBan had no such scruples and took advantage of their superior Republican credentials by marching directly in front of the Fianna Fail contingent.[21]

On 26 September, Saor Eire was publicly launched at a meeting in the Iona Ballroom, Dublin, which was attended by 120 delegates. Sheila Humphreys was elected joint treasurer while the other women on the executive consisted of Helena Moloney, Sheila Dowling (who had been in jail during the Civil War and was now a member of Friends of Soviet Russia and organiser for the Irish Women Workers' Union) and May Laverty of Belfast, a Cumann na mBan organiser.[22] Eithne Coyle's future husband, Bernard O'Donnell, was involved but she held back, feeling that 'one out of the house was enough'.[23] It could also be that she was, as yet, unconvinced of the necessity for the formation of such a group. Sheila, on the other hand, embraced the new direction with enthusiasm:

> I used to feel that a lot of our activities were leading nowhere and the first time I felt that we could have some impact on the ordinary people and show them what freedom really meant was when I joined Saor Eire. We were, at last, doing something worthwhile.[24]

Members of Cumann na mBan entered Saor Eire as individuals; the organisation did not formally endorse the actions of those who joined. To have done so would have precipitated a disastrous internal crisis as many completely disapproved of this 'socialistic trend'. They lost no time in adding their voice to the chorus of disapproval which greeted the public unveiling of the Republicans' new hope. Speaking at a Sinn Fein meeting in Dublin, Mary MacSwiney forcefully declared her oppositon to the organisation because it 'sought to divide the people of Ireland on a class basis'.[25] Old-style nationalists could contenance any number of divisions over Republican principles, but regarded with abhorrence the 'artificial' division between economic classes.

Saor Eire was of course denounced by both church and state. Fitzgerald-Kenny condemned the IRA and Saor Eire as wanting to force 'by means of threats and crimes of violence, a republic of soviet nature on this society'[26] and the bishops wrote a joint pastoral letter which condemned Saor Eire by name and warned congregations of the dangers of radicalism. The 'Red smear' was successfully utilised to scare off recruits and to justify the suppression in October of 12 organisations, including the IRA, Saor Eire, Cumann na mBan, the Women's Prisoners' Defence League, the Revolutionary Workers' Group and Friends of Soviet Russia. For the first time ever, Sinn Fein was left off the list, a clear indication of its now limited appeal and reactionary character. Not only was every progressive organisation in the country proscribed and newspapers either censored or banned outright, but a Constitution amendment bill—Article 2A—was also introduced, which provided for military tribunals with the power to impose the death penalty. The church had declared no Catholic could belong to the IRA or to Saor Eire, and the government had banned them. Faced with this onslaught, Saor Eire collapsed, still-born, and its members braced themselves for what was to come.

IRA leaders went on the run. *An Phoblacht* ceased publication after four issues in a row were suppressed and Frank Ryan brought out a new paper—*Republican File*—composed simply of reports culled from other newspapers. Despite this precaution he was soon in jail and Hanna Sheehy Skeffington took over as editor. Sheila Humphreys' house was constantly raided and, on 2 November, she found herself summonsed on two charges of possessing documents relating to Saor Eire and Cumann na mBan. She didn't turn up for trial.[27] However, on 16 December, she, Maeve Phelan and Kathleen Merrigan—all executive members of Cumann na mBan—were arrested and brought before the military tribunal. It was an unruly occasion. Sheila declared she had 'great fun at it' and hoped, by forcing her prosecutors to read out the programme of Saor Eire, finally to get its contents reported. Although she was unsuccessful she did manage, when acknowledging her membership of Cumann na mBan and Saor Eire to say:

> I am charged with being a member of Cumann na mBan and I admit it. You are very foolish to try and suppress that organisation, for we thrive on suppression. I am also a member of Saor Eire, because I see in it the surest and most effective way of securing the only thing worth fighting for—the national, economic and political freedom of the country.[28]

Her sentence of 29 days imprisonment was dated back to her arrest and so she was immediately released. Maeve Phelan, charged with Cumann na mBan membership, received the same verdict while Kathleen Merrigan's charge of distributing Cumann na mBan documents was dismissed. The president of the court announced that the tribunal was not satisfied with the way in which the police had presented the women's cases. In other words, the blunt instrument of military tribunals which appeared to allow the police a free hand had rebounded upon them because of their crude determination to place troublemakers behind bars, regardless of legal niceties. And perhaps the president of the tribunal foresaw the political capital that could be made if women, who belonged to no military organisation, were condemned to jail by a military tribunal.

Other women suffered raids. Police tentacles stretched down to people like Madge Daly in Limerick, possibly to even up old scores from the Civil War days, but there were no mass arrests. The tactic adopted was to lock up the leaders and hope this would scare off the others. But the numbers of prisoners began to mount and in retaliation the Republican women stepped up their demonstrations. As the Women's Prisoners' Defence League had been banned, it reappeared under the name of the People's Rights Association. The stalwart 'Mothers' were by now an institution in Dublin, having held their weekly meetings without fail since 1922, shifting from one ruined site to another as O'Connell Street was rebuilt. They were determined to continue their protests and became more and more inventive in outwitting the law. When they were evicted from their offices and found it impossible legally to acquire premises elsewhere, the committee arranged to hold weekly meetings in Woolworth's cafe. When that became too well-known they alternated their tea parties by going to nearby Bewley's. The press flocked to speak with them and impromptu press conferences were held in the safety of the crowds that surrounded them.

On the first Sunday after the Coercion Act became law, huge crowds waited in O'Connell Street to see if the women would turn up and defy the act. At the usual time, a lorry-platform drove up bearing the inscription 'People's Rights Association'. As it was not on the list of banned organisations, the police had no alternative but to allow them to hold their meeting. When it was her turn to speak Helena Moloney, to tremendous applause, quoted Shakespeare, 'A rose by any other name would smell as sweet!' Each week saw a battle of wits, with the women determined to hold a meeting and the police determined to prevent them. A blanket proclamation soon forbade any meetings near O'Connell Street on Sundays, but the women always managed to contrive some kind of presence. On one occasion, Charlotte Despard, Helena Moloney and some of the other women held a poster parade in O'Connell Street to announce that because of trouble in Portlaoise Jail the usual meeting was being held outside the jail, and Maud Gonne and 'John Brennan' (who had returned from America in 1922, immediately to join her old mentor from the days of the Inghinnidhe) held the meeting in Portlaoise. On other occasions meetings were held in Dublin on the Saturday and in places like Dun Laoghaire, outside the city boundaries, on the Sunday. The main concern of the WPDL was to explain in detail the provisions of the Coercion Act—Article 2A. Maud felt that if they could focus attention on the sections of the act that forbade coroners' inquests upon the deaths of prisoners and enabled any policeman or soldier of officer's rank to arrest and charge without warrant and to search and detain anyone they chose, young girls included, that the public would be appalled and the Cosgrave government brought down 'in ignominy'. As the press was censored and meetings of banned organisations forbidden, it was only through the efforts of the People's Rights Association that such facts could be publicised.[29] Women's comparative immunity to imprisonment meant that, once again, they were the most visible sign of opposition. Their refusal to be intimidated into silence led Fitzgerald-Kenny, Minister of Justice (sic) to single out 'Mrs Despard and Mrs MacBride and those who were trying to bring in Soviet conditions... We are going to put people like these in prison, and if they persist, and if it is necessary, we are going to execute them.'[30] Such attacks on elderly women were unlikely further to endear the government to the people.

The *carte blanche* that Article 2A gave to the police to search women was a cause of concern for many women's organisations. Ruth Jacob, acting-secretary of the Women's International League for Peace and Freedom, wrote to all the newspapers informing them that her organisation had passed a resolution of protest against Article 2A and that they viewed with particular concern the 'moral danger' in which it placed women and girls who could, under its provisions, be searched and detained at will by any man in the police force.[31]

The invective rained upon women activists at this time had its origins in the anti-communist fervour sweeping through Europe. Politically motivated women were now a most sinister phenomenon; that they were out on the streets at all was sufficient proof of their Bolshevik sympathies. And many women were favourably disposed towards the Soviet Union, which appeared to be the one country in the world where women were not only granted complete equality but positively encouraged to take their rightful place in the construction of the new socialist society. In the summer of 1930, Charlotte Despard and Hanna Sheehy Skeffington had been for a six-week tour of Russia; Madame Despard was secretary of the Friends of Soviet Russia, and she, along with Hanna, Helena Moloney, Sheila Dowling and Kathleen Price gave numerous lectures on aspects of life in the USSR. On International Women's Day of 1931, the Irish section of Friends of Soviet Russia inaugurated a week-long celebration of 'Women's International Week', the purpose of which was to 'draw attention to the enslaved conditions of women in all parts of the capitalist world and to encourage women of those countries to take an active part in the struggle for freedom'.[32]

Although Cumann na mBan was not actively involved with the Friends of Soviet Russia many of its members were certainly interested in the role women had taken during the Revolution. But they were the most prominent women's organisation in Ireland and, as such, came in for a great deal of anti-communist abuse. A London newspaper, *The Sunday Graphic*, ran a scurrilous article entitled 'Irish Gunwomen Menace'. This product of a fevered imagination claimed that trigger-happy harpies—who practised in their drawing rooms—still nurtured bitterness over sufferings endured in the troubles ten years previously; their new path of action was to carry away numbers of impressionable young girls to form the nucleus of a revolutionary organisation 'ready to the hand of Moscow'.[33] The IRA visited Dublin newsagents and ordered them not to sell the edition containing the offensive article.

The IRA was beginning seriously to consider armed resistance as the only response left to this attempt by Cosgrave to crush all opposition while for its part the government, believing that they had defeated their opponents, felt complacent enough to call an early general election. The Dail was dissolved and an election date set for 16 February 1932. Peadar O'Donnell was making up the front page of *An Phoblacht* when he heard the news and he spontaneously decided, without consulting the Army Council, to headline the paper 'Put Cosgrave Out'.[34] While not endorsing Fianna Fail, the IRA agreed on pragmatic grounds that they would lend their support to the Fianna Fail election campaign as the only alternative to the continuance of Cumann na nGaedheal's reign of terror.

It was not just Republicans who wanted a change of government: there had been ten years of Cumann na nGaedheal rule, years of bloodshed, repression, unemployment and economic austerity which had recently culminated in the highly unpopular reduction of pensions, bar on married women teachers, and a reduction of salaries for those who worked in the public sector.

Hanna Sheehy Skeffington reprinted an article by 'Femina' from *Nationality*, which called on women to protest at the fact that there was only one woman in the Dail and so few women senators, by refusing to vote for any political party unless they put forward more female candidates—but it was a forlorn cry. The election was too important for abstentionism to be popular and the only two women returned were Cumann na nGaedheal members—Margaret Collins O'Driscoll and Mary Reynolds.[35] The result of the election was victory for Fianna Fail, which won 72 seats to Cumann na nGaedheal's 57.

Early days of Fianna Fail—Republicans reassess

The first act of the new government was to release the prisoners, who came out to a tumultuous welcome as 30,000 people packed in to College Green to greet them. In his speech of thanks, Frank Ryan praised the work of the men of the Dublin Brigade and the women of Cumann na mBan, singling out for special mention Hanna Sheehy Skeffington, who had kept his department going while he was in jail. The other speakers all mentioned Cumann na mBan. Thomas O'Dalaigh of Clann na Gael spoke of the women of Cumann na mBan who had 'stood behind the soldiers of Ireland in good days and in bad days'. Despite all their endeavours, their initiatives and their publicity-grabbing coups, Cumann na mBan was still perceived by many as standing, not shoulder to shoulder with their male comrades, but *behind* them. Only Hanna Sheehy Skeffington's speech redressed the balance as she recalled the last meeting to be held in College Green—on Armistice Day of the previous year—when 'a few women of the movement... faced the batons of the police and the sticks of the CID'. She reminded her audience that some of the women afterwards faced the tribunal and 'helped by their splendid and defiant attitude in no small way to break down that infamous machine'.[36]

This recognition of the independent activities of women and their centrality to the struggle against repression was left to the former suffrage leader to express. No other woman was invited on to the platform. Cumann na mBan members never spoke at these monster meetings—only when men were forced out of the public arena did women take their place on the platform. Mary MacSwiney, in her capacity as Sinn Fein executive member, was one of the few exceptions; her force of personality commanded such respect as to enable her to transcend the alleged limitations of her sex. Maud Gonne and Charlotte Despard were also exceptions, but of a different kind. As Maire Comerford said of Maud, she was a person of reactions, resenting injustice. She was a protester, but she didn't have the same relationship to the Republican tradition.[37] The women who personified that tradition—the women of Cumann na mBan—were still perceived in secondary terms and not considered important enough to warrant a place amongst the leaders of the Republican movement when the rare opportunity for mass celebration arose.

For the first time in ten years, there were no political prisoners in 26 counties of Ireland. The Women's Prisoners' Defence League announced it was disbanding, its aim accomplished. Within three months, they had regrouped. The election motto had been 'on to the Republic'; the demand now was for Fianna Fail to 'restore the Republic'. While Republicans waited to see what the Fianna Fail government would do, feverish reorganisation and recruitment began. Half-a-million Easter Lilies were distributed for the 1932 Anniversary, a sign of the changed times as many people formerly afraid to sport any symbol of Republican allegiance now willingly pinned on their lilies. Within Cumann na mBan the executive began another recruiting campaign, while making the political allegiance of the organisation unambiguously plain: until the Republic was established, members were ordered to give all possible assistance to the IRA and to encourage men to join up. They were also to give active assistance to Sinn Fein.[38] What remained as yet unexpressed was the political direction Cumann na mBan would take under the altered conditions of an avowedly Republican party now constituting the government of the Free State. The IRA was divided between those who wanted to launch another version of Saor Eire and those who insisted the IRA was a purely military organisation which would wait, for the time being, in the wings, drilling its members in case arms had to be taken up again. The obvious danger was that if a positive alternative to Fianna Fail policies was not offered, further impasse would eventually be reached and the recently revived Republican fortunes would once again be dissipated by unconnected actions and directionless stunts, to be followed by a new wave of repression as the relentless wheel of Irish history turned yet again in its familiar groove.

The immediate response of Cumann na mBan and some sections of the IRA was simply an extension of the old campaign of boycotting British goods. The national executive of the Boycott British League, under Donal O'Donoghue, together with such people as Sheila Humphreys and Mick Price met in October and announced that Bass Ale would be added to the hit list: 'No British ales. No British sweets or chocolates. No British goods of any sort. Shoulder to shoulder for a nation-wide Boycott of British goods. Fling back the challenge of the Robber Empire.'[39] It was hardly an impressive or particularly stirring call. A series of raids on Bass pubs and trucks, ceremonial pouring out of ale onto the streets, scuffles and the inevitable arrests now followed. Eithne Coyle was one of those forced to kick her heels in the Bridewell for a month. With hindsight, Sheila Humphreys admitted the futility of it all, and the terrible waste of time and energy.[40]

The one positive action of Cumann na mBan in that first year of Fianna Fail rule was the national flag day it organised in aid of the starving people of Belfast. The Outdoor Relief Movement had been organised in protest at the cutting of relief at a time when 25 per cent of the insured population of Belfast was out of work. The Unionists had responded in the only way they knew—by baton charges and guns—killing two men and wounding nineteen others. Cumann na mBan called for the active support of every man and woman who wished to see social justice in Ireland. It was a genuine show of solidarity with oppressed workers, coupled with a desire to applaud the unprecedented class unity of Protestants and Catholics. There was little that Cumann na mBan in the north could do, other than to show goodwill. The IRA in the north, many of its members on the dole and the Outdoor Relief schemes, had unofficially supported the Unemployed Workers' Movement, later giving military backing when the Royal Ulster Constabulary went on the offensive[41] but political direction came not from the Republicans, but from the small Revolutionary Workers' Group, later to become the Communist Party of Ireland. A leading member of the group was the young mill worker Betty Sinclair, a well-known communist militant until her death in 1981.

The Outdoor Relief Movement eventually collapsed as Unionists successfully replayed the Orange card and sectarian violence again haunted the poverty-ridden streets of Belfast.

In the wave of reaction that followed, all meetings were banned and Republicans rounded up and jailed. In January 1933, two members of Belfast Cumann na mBan—Sarah Grimley and Mary Donnelly—received two- and three-month jail sentences respectively, for posting up Republican literature in protest at the visit of the Prince of Wales.[42] Hanna Sheehy Skeffington, now assistant editor of *An Phoblacht*, also received a one-month jail sentence after defying an exclusion order barring her from the six counties. She had insisted on speaking at a meeting in Newry to demand the release of Republican prisoners and made a strong speech against partition, 'I would be ashamed of my own race, I would be ashamed of my own murdered husband if I admitted that I was an alien in Armagh, Down, Derry or any of the thirty-two counties.'[43] On her release from Armagh jail she was met in Dundalk by Eithne Coyle and the two travelled on to a vast meeting in College Green where the Republican left gave her a rousing welcome home.

It was Hanna who advised Madame Despard (whose Workers' College in Eccles Street had been wrecked and looted by Blueshirt fascists) of the possibilities of socialist agitation in the north, which she felt might provide a more congenial atmosphere for the communist-feminist than the nationalist ethos of southern political life. At the age of 90, this extraordinary woman gave away her Eccles Street house to the Friends of Soviet Russia, left Roebuck House, which she had shared with Maud Gonne, to her old friend, and moved to Belfast, spending the last years of her life trying to spread, while bloody riots spilled around her, her particular vision of a Christian-based communism. In her oration at Charlotte Despard's funeral in November 1939, which was attended by representatives from all the Republican and left groups, Maud Gonne summed up the life that been dedicated for over 60 years to feminism and socialism: 'Throughout her life she was like a white flame in the defence of prisoners and the oppressed.'[44]

Throughout this period Cumann na mBan continued to assess its role, analysing its history and making fresh efforts to come to terms with the changing political situation. In looking back over their unwavering commitment to Republicanism, undeflected by the split over the Treaty or the formation of Fianna Fail, they came to the conclusion that they had had 'a far clearer conception of what they were struggling for and a greater spirit of perseverance than the men', and they wondered why it was that an organisation which had contained over 1,200 branches in 1921 had not wielded more influence.[45] The most obvious answer is that the women had not wielded more influence because they had very little real power to determine the direction of events. There had been a continual tussle between the militarists and the politicians over the question of the acceptance of the Treaty but Cumann na mBan, despite its immediate and forthright rejection of the Treaty settlement, was only marginally considered; its decision was part of the game of political football that was being played as both sides used the women's example to suit their own ends. It was a game that had come to its climax in the franchise debate. Despite this painful experience, Cumann na mBan still failed to realise that they were posing a false question and the real question that needed to be raised was why the organisation was still considered to be subordinate to the main Republican organisation. Instead they berated themselves, as women have done for centuries, for having been 'too retiring, too shy of pushing their views' and urged themselves to combat this 'inferiority complex' by having the courage in the future to lead public opinion.[46] Unfortunately, their criticisms were all self-criticisms, not directed at the political organisations that continued to regard them as little more than useful reservoirs of support.

Nora Connolly's outspoken assessment of the current situation was more to the point, although she too reserved her strongest criticisms for women. As she traced the effects of British conquest over Ireland and the imposition of British laws excluding women from public life, she castigated her sex for having accepted their 'duties' while not claiming their rights, so inducing 'in the minds of our menfolk, of each succeeding generation, a placid acceptance of our inferior status in the nation'. Although women of her generation had finally, through their own efforts, 'won the right to share in the dangers of war', they had 'relinquished their right to share in the dangers of peace' and returned without protest to their domestic role. So, despite all that had been endured over the past decades, progressive and revolutionary women were again content to be 'drudges', without a voice in the revolutionary movement. In quoting from Connolly's analysis of the necessity for women to have equal representation with men ('he saw nothing incongruous in a woman having a seat on an army council, or preferring to bear arms to winding bandages'), she concluded that because of the denial to women of full participation, the movement had lost 'its capacity to withstand the assaults from without and demoralisation from within'.[47]

While Nora avoided direct criticism of the male leadership for its reluctance to promote women's equal rights within the various bodies of the left, and the men studiously avoided the challenge of responding to these public criticisms, content merely to pay lip-service to the concept of women's equality with fulsome praise for their zeal in standing by the men, Cumann na mBan continued to search for some means of expressing their new awareness of their own political importance.

The 1933 Convention

While on their drive to recruit new members Cumann na mBan found themselves handicapped by their constitutional pledge to maintain the Second Dail and to organise the women of Ireland to work for its international recognition. Most of the younger women had barely heard of the Second Dail, which had been elected in 1921, before the Treaty, and its eventual recognition was a remote possibility to say the least. At the 1933 Convention of Cumann na mBan the executive explained its belief that Cumann na mBan, by hanging on to this clause in its constitution, had isolated itself from the new generation of women and were 'taxing their powers of credulity beyond reasonable bounds'. A decision was therefore taken to alter the constitution to a pledge to 'organise and train the women of Ireland to put into effect the ideals and obligations contained in the [1916] Proclamation.'

This was far from being a matter of semantics. Commitment to the social radicalism contained within the Proclamation meant that Cumann na mBan could now embark upon a programme of political education based upon the teachings of Connolly instead of remaining trapped within the sterility of the Second Dail tradition, with its insistence upon the primacy of oaths and allegiances which offered no solution to people's immediate situation. The convention also decided upon an intensive programme of action in the north, based upon the Proclamation, but given the pogroms against Catholics, they were almost immediately forced to alter this to a fervent hope that a revival of Cumann na mBan in the south would light the way for their northern members.[48]

Seven women strongly disagreed with the policy change and despite heartfelt appeals from the entire convention three of them—Mary MacSwiney, Eileen Tubbert and Albinia Broderick—left in protest. The dissidents immediately formed Mna na Poblachta (Women of the Republic), whose leading members were Eileen Tubbert and Noneen Brugha, the daughter of Cathal and Caitlin. It was a right-wing, narrowly nationalistic group of zealots, pledged to pursue its aims 'for the honour of God and the glory of Ireland'. *Irish Freedom*, which had always been strongly pro-Sinn Fein anyway, now decided to give coverage only to Mna na Poblachta. Its pages would never again be contaminated by reference to Cumann na mBan, for whose recent actions Mary MacSwiney declared she could 'find no excuse'. They believed their most important task was to 'break the connection with England—and not to worry too much about economics'.[49] Mna na Poblachta maintained close links with Sinn Fein and broke with the more radical wing of Republicanism. The rift was so complete that *An Phoblacht* refused to publish their notes without payment (normally all organisations had free access) and insisted their assertion that they were the *only* women's organisation standing for the defence of the Irish Republic should be altered. They refused to make the changes required and the few activities of Mna na Poblachta remained confined to the pages of *Irish Freedom*. By 1934 Mary MacSwiney had also broken with Sinn Fein, because it allowed members to accept IRA war pensions. The stern guardian of the Republican conscience was now a lonely figure crying out in the wilderness of intransigent principles.

Everyone deeply regretted Mary's loss. They had all been through so much over the past 20 years and although the dispute had had serious consequences it differed from other splits in that no one disputed their ultimate goal and no one was about to compromise with the existing constitutional set-up. Friendly personal relations were maintained as far as possible by the older members but the resignation of those hostile to the changing direction of Cumann na mBan left the executive free to consolidate the process of radicalisation unhampered by the powerful brake of old-style nationalism.

A new spirit of constructive thought was evident in the notes to members which were regularly published in *An Phoblacht*. The need to study economics was emphasised, so that 'members will understand and be able to explain to others, that a social system suited to the needs of the country can be set up in place of the present system founded on capitalism'.[50] And there were simple articles on such intricate details of socialist economics as the beneficial consequences of abolishing a money-based economy. Executive instructions were sent to all branches and May Laverty appointed organiser, with the responsibility of forming new branches and explaining the new regulations. She often found it necessary to enlist the help of local IRA members who in some areas not only called the first meeting but also explained the duties of branch members.[51] That would seem to indicate a decided lack of women with the confidence to take on such responsibilities. It also emphasises the isolation of many rural women and the limitations of their education.

Too much faith was placed on executive instructions being understood and accepted, and no thorough-going programme of education was initiated. Although debates were arranged by branches, there was little attempt to train women in public speaking. Eithne Coyle admitted that the same people were continually relied upon and because people were so busy with other things no time could be spared in developing the potential of the ordinary member. They just hoped that the debates would 'help a little'. Considering the restrictions on personnel and finance, little else could have been done. It would have been a different situation if Cumann na mBan was still at its peak, but that had long since passed. At their zenith they were preoccupied with fighting a war and few had understood the importance of developing members' capacity for critical thought.

The 1933 Convention elected an executive 'representative of Dublin', an acknowledgement of what had been reality for a considerable time: that Cumann na mBan was now centred around a small group of women who had been activists since the War of Independence and who had struggled through numerous reversals to maintain their organisation as testimony to Irishwomen's commitment to Republicanism. Making that ideal relevant to the majority of women was the problem they faced. This concentration around Dublin accentuated the distance between the executive and the rank and file because those in Dublin had always had close links with the IRA leadership and were therefore privy to all the internal debates that were going on. There were also close personal links with IRA men: Mick Price was the brother of Leslie, formerly the Director of Training of Cumann na mBan and now married to Tom Barry, who was to be the IRA chief-of-staff in 1936-7; Sheila Humphreys was to marry Donal O'Donoghue in 1937—a member of the Army Council, director of the Boycott British Campaign and at one stage editor of *An Phoblacht*. Frank Ryan and Moss Twomey were good friends of many and of course Sean MacBride, chief-of-staff in 1936, was the son of their old friend Maud Gonne.

All these factors—the numerical reduction of Cumann na mBan to a few hundred members dominated by an executive that was politically in advance of the rest; the difficulties involved in educating and disseminating information down through the ranks; the close links between the executive and leading IRA members—were to have important repercussions for Cumann na mBan during the next attempt by Republicans to develop a political organisation.

The Republican Congress

De Valera was going from strength to strength, in the process disarming the Republican opposition. He had called another general election in 1933 (which yielded two women deputies for Fianna Fail, Margaret Mary Pearse and Helena Concannon), increasing Fianna Fail's majority; he had taken the radical sting out of the land annuities campaign, not by abolishing annuities as the left had called for, but by stopping their payment to Britain, so precipitating the economic war; he had dismissed O'Duffy as police commissioner, a man hated by Republicans; he had done away with the oath of allegiance, and he had downgraded the role of governor-general with the clear intention of getting rid of it altogether. The introduction, in 1934, of service pensions for anyone who had participated in the Republican movement up to September 1923 had led to a split in Sinn Fein and the resignation of Mary MacSwiney and Brian O'Higgins (Margaret Buckley now became President of Sinn Fein, remaining in this position until 1949); it also had an effect on the IRA and Cumann na mBan. Although the IRA issued a directive to members not to apply, many were in such economic distress that they did accept a pension, so cutting themselves off from organised Republicanism. Cumann na mBan, more humanely, was concerned about the plight of many of its members and felt morally unable to prevent women from applying but they discovered that in many cases the women faded away afterwards, feeling guilty about compromising.

It was obvious, at least to the left of the IRA, that Fianna Fail was outflanking them, and the IRA, as a purely military body, was irrelevant to the situation. It had a role in challenging the Blueshirt menace, physically driving the fascists off the streets, but in doing so they came into conflict with a government that had begun to insist that the IRA should now disband and leave the final constitutional changes to the politicians. Men like Peadar O'Donnell realised that if it came to renewed military conflict, the IRA would not win the support of the people. What had to be done was to campaign on social issues and expose Fianna Fail as a conservative force. The traditionalists within the IRA, conscious of the debacle of Saor Eire, didn't want to run the risk of another disaster and a split developed. Ryan had already left *An Phoblacht* in protest at the censorship imposed on him by the army executive, Hanna Sheehy Skeffington leaving with him. O'Donoghue took over and Annie O'Farrelly and Aoife Taafe, two executive members of Cumann na mBan, joined its office staff (which probably explains the paper's hostility to Mna na Poblachta).[52]

The Army Convention of 17 March 1934 split down the middle over the question of developing a new social policy. O'Donnell, Gilmore and Ryan proposed the calling of a Republican congress, and secured the backing of the majority of delegates, but the executive and army council voted against and formed, by one vote, a majority. The rebels now left the IRA and spent the next weeks visiting officers around the country to drum up support for the congress.

On 8 April 1934 200 men and women came to Athlone and issued a manifesto calling for an assembly of a congress of Republicans:

> We believe that a Republic of a united Ireland will never be achieved except through a struggle which uproots Capitalism on its way. 'We cannot conceive of a free Ireland with a subject working class; we cannot conceive of a subject Ireland with a free working class.' This teaching of Connolly represents the deepest instinct of the oppressed Irish nation.

After this introduction the manifesto made a detailed analysis of the existing state of Republican thought, part of which made specific reference to the IRA:

> Had the IRA leadership understood that the economic war was not being fought to free Ireland but to serve Irish capitalism they would have carried out this mobilisation first before giving any support to that war. On account of their failure the Republican issue has been pushed further into the background.[53]

IRA members had been forbidden to take part in the congress and there were many who could not countenance such public criticisms; old loyalties were stronger than any radical statements of intent. Many associated with Saor Eire had no links with the congress group, for example, Helena Moloney, Donal O'Donoghue and Mick Fitzpatrick (who drafted most of the Saor Eire manifesto) stayed away. Of the women who signed the Athlone manifesto, three were executive members of Cumann na mBan—Eithne Coyle, Sheila Humphreys and May Laverty. The other two were Cora Hughes, an MA graduate of University College, Dublin, socialist and writer, and also (irrelevantly) god-child of de Valera and Nora Connolly, who had been calling persistently for a new party of the left.

Eithne, Sheila and May in fact attended the Athlone meeting without consulting their executive partly, in Peadar O'Donnell's words, because 'they knew that George, Mick, Frank and I were engaged in a conspiracy which involved half the units of the country, and in order to safeguard our secrets they came to Athlone without breathing a word of it to their own Executive'.[54] They soon found themselves in a very awkward position. Cumann na mBan, an auxiliary organisation to the IRA, had its most prominent members sign a declaration which was explicitly critical of the IRA and had joined a group that also had strong representation from the Communist Party, which was anathema to most Irish people, even if some of them were being propelled to the left. Despite their friendship with men like Ryan and Gilmore, Eithne and Sheila felt uneasy at the rift their action had precipitated with those who had remained loyal to the IRA. They also had to face a huge row within their executive. They were in an intolerable position and as their first allegiance lay with Cumann na mBan they had, by August, both resigned from Congress—before its inaugural meeting the following month.

In their letter of resignation they stated their conviction that the chief aim of the congress was not the ending of capitalism but the destruction of the IRA which they believed did have a social and economic policy. In a significant admission they conceded that their only quarrel with the IRA was 'its tardiness to put its principles into practice'. In other words, as members of an organisation linked to the IRA, they were impatient because their primary function was to act as a support group, left to kick their heels in frustration when no opportunities for action presented themselves. Peadar O'Donnell's reply was scathing. He acidly commented on the relationship between Cumann na mBan and the IRA, tracing the recent history of the two groups with its Bass raids and other 'heedless stunts', all instigated by Cumann na mBan with the intention of 'gingering up the IRA', of 'sticking pins in tardy principles'. To his accusation that the IRA no longer had principles that simply needed activating, Sheila and Eithne made no reply.[55] They refused to enter into a debate and simply withdrew. It was a great pity, because O'Donnell had clearly articulated the dilemma of Cumann na mBan and the vacuum it operated in when there was no clearly defined programme of action initiated by the IRA to which they could give their support. The barrenness of the early 1930s had led them into the directionless militancy typified by the Bass campaign. Even now, while they were struggling to find ways of putting their constitutional commitment to the Republican Proclamation into effect, neither giving active support to working women, or fighting for women's right to political representation formed part of their programme.

Nora Connolly walked out of congress at the Rathmines meeting, together with her brother Roddy and Mick Price, when their call for a Workers' Republic which would be clearly anti-capitalist was defeated by the triumverate of O'Donnell, Ryan and Gilmore, who argued for a united front of Republicans and socialists to challenge the Republican credentials of Fianna Fail before launching a direct attack upon imperialism. The difference lay in opposing views on the method of struggle and form of organisation necessary, rather than in ultimate objectives, but it was enough to ensure a division which signified the end of any hope that the Republican Congress would achieve what its organisers had dreamed of. Although congress staggered on until 1936 it never succeeded in attracting much support, despite a notable success in briefly gathering Belfast Protestants to its banner. But it did take seriously the question of women's oppression and there were many calls for congress to organise the most exploited sections of women—the factory workers, domestic servants and shop assistants—and two women, Mrs Kelly and Mrs Friel, were part of the central bureau, representing factory groups. Cora Hughes and May Laverty remained members. In September 1934, they were arrested in Dublin while helping a woman who was being evicted by her landlord for refusing to pay rent. Her income was 7s 6d per week (relief) and her rent was 10s. Both received one month's hard labour, having refused, as 'members of Cumann na mBan and as members of the Citizen Army' to accept the compromise involved in receiving a suspended sentence.[56] Cora Hughes died in 1940, having contracted tuberculosis as a result of her work in the slums.

Reunited—Cumann na mBan and the IRA

The Republican Congress continued its efforts to build support for its aims through a policy of intervention in the immediate concerns of the working class while Cumann na mBan, after the abortive display of independence by some of its members, returned to its customary position at the side of the IRA. From now on, the two were inseparable and as the Republican momentum waned, so too did that of Cumann na mBan. Their only role now was to protest against the renewed attack upon Republicans and no attempt was made either to enlist the support of other women or to engage in other activities.

When the Bishop of Waterford declared that attendance at a meeting called by the IRA would be 'gravely sinful', the IRA and Cumann na mBan joined forces in organising a meeting of protest.[57] The IRA, late in the day, decided to throw its support behind workers' struggles and intervened in the Dublin train and bus strike which had begun in March. The government used soldiers as scab labour and as soon as army lorries appeared, IRA sniping at tyres began. The government retaliated by rounding up Republicans and the honeymoon with Fianna Fail was well and truly over. The military tribunal, originally reactivated to deal with the Blueshirts, now began to hand out sentences to the IRA—Donal O'Donoghue, Tom Barry and a dozen others were sent to jail. By 20 April, 104 Republicans were in Arbour Hill, *An Phoblacht* was censored and finally suppressed. The Women's Prisoners' Defence League redoubled its efforts in support of the prisoners, with Cora Hughes joining Maud Gonne on the platform, but Cumann na mBan concentrated its efforts on its own Political Prisoners' Committee.[58] Cumann na mBan and the IRA also organised a mass rally of 12,000 to condemn the treatment of prisoners. The women didn't speak but carried placards declaring 'Republican Prisoners Tortured by Fianna Fail', 'Join the Free State Army and Fight for Abyssinia', 'An Phoblacht Suppressed', etc.[59]

The ranks had been firmly closed, the IRA and their allies Cumann na mBan were standing together, fighting the old enemy, now dressed in Fianna Fail clothes. While repression continued, the IRA formed a new political party—Comhairle na Poblachta—their answer to the Republican Congress. Fiona Plunkett, Florence McCarthy and Madge Daly were present at its inaugural meeting on 7 March 1936;[60] those involved in Saor Eire and the Republican Congress do not appear to have been involved. But it was a terrible time to launch a new party. On 21 May, Moss Twomey, the chief-of-staff, was arrested under Article 2A and sentenced to three years and three months. On 18 June, the day before his trial, the IRA was declared an unlawful association. The IRA leaders went on the run. Cumann na mBan wasn't banned, which either reflected on its decreased support or de Valera's chivalry, but its offices were constantly raided. The Bodenstown parade, scheduled for the Sunday following the ban, was itself banned. Although some members of Cumann na mBan and Sinn Fein tried to force their way through the cordon of police, they were unsuccessful and in the end Hanna Sheehy Skeffington had to read Mary MacSwiney's address to the small group gathered round her while they all stood on the roadside.[61]

The prison struggle went its usual way, with hunger strikes and outside protests. When Patrick McKenna was sentenced to 18 months after speaking at a WPDL meeting, Maud Gonne announced that from now on she would invite only women to speak.[62]

But while this familiar act was being replayed yet again, although with a smaller cast, a different attack with no less serious consequences, was being mounted against the rights of women workers, in the shape of the Conditions of Employment Bill. And during this period, Cumann na mBan remained completely apart from all the women's organisations fighting for women's interests.

The Conditions of Employment Bill

In 1926, six out of ten of the 329,000 women in work were either in farming or domestic service, while less than one in ten worked in industry.[63] But between the years of 1926 and 1936, women's share of the industrial workforce rose from 20 per cent to almost 23 per cent, as a result of the establishment of new light industries. The jobs were largely unskilled and concentrated in exclusively female areas, such as clothing, food, drink and tobacco.[64] The majority of workers were single and under 25 years of age. They hardly posed a threat to male workers and nor did they challenge the conventional wisdom of a woman's place being in the home, yet in the atmosphere of economic recession and the growing conservatism of Irish society, the very presence of women workers was an affront to male dignity. Unemployed men used the most convenient scapegoat of all—working women.

The Conditions of Employment Bill of 1935 was partly introduced to improve conditions by imposing a statutory maximum of 48 hours upon the working week, fixing holiday entitlements of one week and imposing restrictions upon the employment of young people. Some people, however, suspected that the beneficial aspects of the bill were mere window-dressing, deliberately introduced to disguise the implications of the provisions affecting women. Section 16 of the bill allowed the Minister for Industry and Commerce, Sean Lemass, to prohibit

the employment of female workers in industry, fixed the proportion of female workers to the number of other workers and forbade employers to employ more women than men in any cases
where a ministerial decision on a specific industry had been
made. No mention was made of particular industries being injurious to women's health as a reason for the section; it was a
clear attempt to alleviate economic depression by removing
women from the workplace and giving their jobs to men. It also
gave unlimited power, with no right of appeal, to the Minister of
Industry and Commerce, which could lead to draconian
measures: a blanket prohibition on women workers, depending
on the prejudices of the particular minister.

The *kinde, kirche, küche* policy so favoured by de Valera
was now being put into effect. The Irish Women Workers'
Union (IWWU), headed by Louie Bennett, which represented
around one-quarter of the 20,000 women trade unionists, immediately began to organise a campaign to protest. In this they
were joined by many other women's organisations and women
members of Fianna Fail, including Dorothy Macardle, one of
the staunchest supporters of de Valera.

At a meeting in the Mansion House on 20 November 1935,
Louie made clear her conviction that Lemass's motive for introducing the bill was not concern for the welfare of women
workers, but was a move to restrict their employment opportunities. Dorothy Macardle, seconding the resolution to delete
Section 16 from the bill, declared their action to be part of a
necessary world-wide campaign for women's independence.
Professor Mary Hayden, representing the National Council of
Women in Ireland, made a strong and constructive speech which
highlighted the reactionary economic policies of the Fianna Fail
government and called for the provision of public works of
national utility to provide further employment. Other speakers
at the meeting (which included a number of female academics)
were Hanna Sheehy Skeffington, who denounced Lemass as a
fascist and declared that any men who would displace women
under such circumstances were nothing short of blacklegs, and
Margaret Buckley and Helena Moloney, both IWWU organisers,
who tried to defend the labour movement over the issue. Helena
said that the Trades Union Congress had fought against the bill

and the section affecting women and that the Labour Party had made representations to get the clause deleted; a delegation which Lemass 'received with politeness and treated with contempt'.[65]

However, both William Norton and Thomas Johnson, Labour Party leaders in the Dail and Senate respectively, gave complete support to the bill, in the process betraying a considerable amount of anti-feminist bias. Within the Senate, Kathleen Clarke and that veteran campaigner Jenny Wyse Power (who had been made a senator when she left Cumann na mBan after the Treaty decision) made a valiant attempt to have the offending section deleted. The two women had been political adversaries for over 20 years but when it came to an attack on the rights of women, all differences were laid aside. Kathleen Clarke based her opposition on nationalist rather than feminist grounds, because she believed the bill was in total contradiction to the 1916 Proclamation, which had given equal rights and opportunities to all citizens. She went to the heart of the malevolent intentions behind the bill when she made the point that if specific industries were mentioned it might then have a constructive purpose and one that would not be simply aimed at putting women out of work:

> I would be perfectly in agreement... if he said 'I am going to prevent women from ever scrubbing floors and I will make men do it instead.' With that aim, I would be in absolute agreement, because scrubbing floors is an ugly, hard and badly paid job, and men do not want it. If he brings in a clause that will prevent women from scrubbing floors, I will be with him.[66]

Her angry witticism left her opponents unmoved. Few would accept the stark reality of working-class life, although Jenny movingly described the vital importance of women's wages to the maintenance of the family. Those in favour of the bill also argued vehemently against the introduction of equal pay for women as a means of ensuring that women would not be used as cheap labour in preference to men. When pressed by the two women, their only riposte was to declare their true feelings, that a woman's place was in the home. Jenny furiously retorted that they should then concentrate their energies into setting up a bureau to supply women with husbands and homes. Lemass airily dismissed the protests from the women's organisations as being completely unrepresentative of the vast majority of women and with that comforting thought the male politicians voted in favour of the bill.[67] As a result, the International Labour Organisation in Geneva placed the Free State on a black list.[68]

An awareness of the spread of fascist ideology and its implications was causing women all over the world great alarm. In Ireland it now appeared that the first non-fascist country was preparing to adopt the same policies and women braced themselves in readiness. The National Council of Women in Ireland announced in December that it had formed a committee to study existing and proposed legislation affecting women, in order to ensure that women's interests were promoted. Louie Bennett became chairwoman and Dorothy Macardle the vice-chairwoman. Other well-known names included Hanna Sheehy Skeffington and Linda Kearns.[69] *Irish Freedom* commented that the new women's organisation 'promises to do excellent work'.[70]

Its formation was an indication that woman suspected what was in store. The final stage in the patriarchal domination of women arrived the following year, under the guise of de Valera's new constitution.

The 1937 Constitution

The initial impetus behind the proposed constitution was the neccessity of establishing the sovereign independence of Ireland, of tearing away the last remnant of the 1922 Treaty Constitution. But de Valera's new constitution was far removed from the liberal-democratic ethos of the 1922 document, being imbued with all the reactionary values of Catholic social teaching, particularly in its insistence upon the primacy of women's role within the family. It echoed many Papal encyclicals, all of which de Valera had studied in detail as he formulated what was to be the climax of his political career. He had refused to admit women into Boland's Mill in 1916 and had disregarded the contribution made by women during the Civil War, finding women activists an anomaly he preferred to ignore in favour of a vision of an Ireland 'whose countryside would be bright with cosy homesteads, whose villages would be joyous with the romping of sturdy children, the contests of athletic youths, the laughter of comely maidens'.[71] Now as president, he took the opportunity to ensure that women, whether they liked it or not, would give priority to their duties as wives and mothers. He had never wanted women in the public sphere and he was going to enshrine these prejudices within the constitution. His attitudes were so well known that no one was taken in by his protestations of concern for women's well-being.

There were several clauses in the proposed constitution which made specific reference to women and which, like Article 16 as it originally stood, had sinister implications:

Article 16

1-1 Every citizen who has reached the age of twenty-one years and who is not placed under disability or incapacity by this Constitution or by law, shall be eligible for membership of Dail Eireann.

1-2 Every citizen who has reached the age of twenty-one years who is not disqualified by law and complies with the provisions of the law relating to the election of members of Dail Eireann, shall have the right to vote at an election for members of Dail Eireann.

Article 40

1 All citizens shall, as human persons, be held equal before the law. This shall not be held to mean that the State shall not in its enactments have due regard to differences of capacity, physical and moral, and of social function.

Article 41

2-1 In particular, the State recognises that by her life within the home, woman gives to the State a support without which the common good cannot be achieved.

2-2 The State shall, therefore, endeavour to ensure that mothers shall not be obliged by economic necessity to engage in labour to the neglect of their duties in the home.

Article 45

4-2 The State shall endeavour to ensure that the inadequate

strength of women and the tender age of children shall not be abused, and that women and children shall not be forced by economic necessity to enter avocations unsuited to their sex, age or strength.

Immediately this draft was made public the Women Graduates Association, led by the three female professors —Mary Hayden, Agnes O'Farrelly and Mary Macken—along with such other notable graduates as Hanna Sheehy Skeffington, joined forces with the Joint Committee of Women's Societies and Social Workers, which was headed by Mary Kettle, Hanna's sister—a staunch feminist who had remained distant from the nationalist movement. Their demand was for the complete deletion of Articles 40, 41 and 45 and the retention of Section 3 of the 1922 Constitution, which simply and unequivocally stated that everyone over the age of 21 who qualified as an Irish citizen was, without distinction of sex, to be accorded that right. In a letter to the *Irish Times* Mary Kettle pointed out that if the constitution, as it stood became law, no woman who worked would have any security whatsoever. The supposed 'protection' offered to women could deprive them of work because laws could be passed in keeping with the spirit of the constitution, declaring such work to be unsuited to their sex.[72]

All the women's organisations were unanimous in denouncing the omission of any statement regarding women's equal rights and opportunities as 'sinister and retrogressive'. They scented a conspiracy, engineered by de Valera, eventually to remove them from all spheres of public life. Section 16 could be used to justify the franchise being taken away from women on the grounds of their 'incapacity' or disability. De Valera protested that he had removed 'without distinction of sex' because he felt it would insult women by reminding them of how recently they had won the right to vote.[73] He eventually gave way and reinserted the clause (after Brigid Redmond had proposed an amendment for the purpose) while making it plain that he believed he was simply accommodating groundless fears fomented by hysterics.

But while de Valera was prepared to grant a formalistic political equality to women, he adamantly refused to be moved on the question of social or economic equality. His introductory remarks when putting the constitution before the Dail made his intention obvious. His aim was that the breadwinner, who is 'normally and naturally the father of the family', should have sufficient income to maintain the whole household. Women should not have to neglect their duties in the home by going out to work. 'I do not care what women's organisations there are... I am going, as long as I live, to try and work for that,' and he defiantly concluded 'I do not care a thraneen who says I am reactionary if I work for that.'[74]

This was almost indistinguishable from Nazi decrees. All de Valera's pious declarations could not obscure the fact that his proposals left the way, at the very least, for the state to legislate against married women going out to work. Dr Rowlette, an Independent from Trinity College, speaking on behalf of Brigid Redmond expressed his concern that the articles could be used in the same way as the Conditions of Employment Act. He reminded the Dail that they had been told that the bill had the aim of simply protecting women at work, but during debate Norton had 'let the cat out of the bag' by insisting the proper use of the section would be to prevent women from competing with men and endangering their livelihood. Rowlette rightly feared the same could happen with the constitution. De Valera stoutly maintained that women's duties in the home were of such importance that the state should not require any further services from them. He peremptorily dismissed his opponents as 'trifling' with his proposals.[75] And in a sense he was right. Only a handful of deputies voiced alarm at the reactionary nature of the sections on women and their amendments, however sincerely put forward, only tinkered with the most objectionable aspects. No one went as far as to demand what the women were calling for: their complete removal.

Several deputations from the various women's organisations met both de Valera and the three women deputies, in an attempt to enlist their support. All that de Valera agreed to was the reinsertion of 'without distinction of sex' to Article 16. Brigid Redmond, the widow of Willie Redmond and a Fine Gael member (the reformed Cumann na nGaedheal) expressed her willingness to put forward further amendments if required, but she was a half-hearted fighter. Her ability to speak in debate was poor, and most of the arguments in support of her amendments were presented by Rowlette as Brigid Redmond, for some reason, was absent from the Dail for most of the time. Margaret Pearse, although present as voting fodder, spoke not a word the entire time. Whatever de Valera said was, presumably, good enough for her. Helena Concannon, as a member of the Women Graduates Association, must have been a disappointment. She readily accepted de Valera's explanations and, unbelievably, went so far as to say 'I sincerely hope that not a comma of this noble declaration will be altered.' When questioned as to why she believed women should be singled out in this paternalistic fashion she introduced the hoary diversion that in the event of conscription ever being imposed, it would serve to prevent women from being called up.[76]

After all the debate, inside and outside the Dail, a few minor (although not insignificant) changes were wrung from de Valera. As well as the already mentioned amendment to Article 16, a new sub-section was inserted:

1-2 No law shall be enacted placing any citizen under disability or incapacity for membership of Dail Eireann on the ground of sex or disqualifying any citizen from voting at an election for members of Dail Eireann on that ground.[77]

Sub-section 2 of Article 45 was also deleted and a new section substituted:

4-2 The State shall endeavour to ensure that the strength and health of workers, men and women, and the tender age of children shall not be abused and that citizens shall not be forced by economic necessity to enter avocations unsuited to their sex, age or strength.[78]

Further than that, de Valera would not go. All objections were taken as personal criticisms of himself as the soul of the man was contained within the document. The basic thrust remained unchanged and in no way alleviated the fears of women. On 14 June, the Dail approved the revised constitution and the date for the election and the referendum was set for 1 July.

Shortly afterwards, a further mass meeting of women was

held in the Mansion House. Now that they had lost the Dail vote they began a campaign to persuade women to reject the constitution when they came to vote in the referendum. The main concern of all the speakers was the necessity of safeguarding the right of women to work. Hanna Sheehy Skeffington also proposed the formation of a women's party to safeguard the interests of women in every sphere of activity. Mrs Keane, in seconding the resolution, proposed that 'equal pay for equal work' would be the party's slogan. The resolution was passed, to loud acclaim.[79]

Three days later, Mary Macken presided at another Mansion House meeting, which Kitty Clive, the *Irish Times* correspondent, described as having been 'splendidly arranged... women of all ages flocked to the meeting which was very representative and included members of the vanguard of old suffrage days'.[80] However, the Irish Women Workers' Union was no longer part of the campaign. They declared that 'their grievances had been adjusted' as a result of the changes in the constitutional draft and although they were in sympathy with the women's meeting, they were withdrawing from the campaign. It was a short-sighted policy, stemming from an overly economistic view of their function as a trade union. They would spearhead a campaign against the Conditions of Employment Bill because that related directly to working women, but they would not give support to a campaign which had as its aim the defeat of a much more wide-ranging attack upon women.

There is no doubt that Louie Bennett, the driving force behind the IWWU, was responsible for that decision. She had an extremely ambivalent attitude towards women going out to work, viewing it as an unfortunate necessity, as her 1932 presidential speech to the Irish Trades Union Congress made clear:

> the modern tendency to draw women into the workforce in increasing numbers is of no real advantage to them. It has not raised their status as workers nor their wage standards. It is a menace to family life and in so far as it has blocked the employment of men it has intensified poverty among the working class.[81]

The ban on married women workers, which started with the ban on national teachers and was then extended to women in the civil service, was therefore not campaigned against by the IWWU. Obviously, the provisions in the constitution would exacerbate the situation, but it was middle-class women outside the trade union movement who consistently argued for an unqualified assertion of women's right to work.

Some nationalist women, while not actively involved in the campaign, did send messages of support to the Mansion House meeting. Kathleen Clarke, in a letter read out at the meeting (she was no longer a senator as de Valera had abolished the upper house in 1936), said: 'I think it is up to every Irish woman to see that no man or group of men robs us of our status enshrined in [the] Proclamation.' Kate O'Callaghan wrote from Limerick: 'These articles I regard as a betrayal of the 1916 promise of "Equal Rights and Equal Opportunities guaranteed to all citizens". They are a grave danger to the future position of women.' Maud Gonne, also referring to the Proclamation, that 'noble, clear, concise document', merged together in her objections the two causes that had motivated her throughout her life:

> If, when Ireland is free, a more detailed Constitution
> were needed, the Articles concerning women, and the Articles providing for special courts in Mr de Valera's Draft
> Constitution would damn it in my eyes.[82]

While some staunch nationalists were prepared to add their voices to the chorus of alarm, Cumann na mBan remained completely silent. And neither did any individual within Cumann na mBan lend her support to the campaign.

While the anti-constitution movement developed, Cumann na mBan was preoccupied with lending its support to Republican protests against the coronation of George V as King of England, Wales, Scotland and Ireland. One meeting, scheduled to be held in College Green, was banned because of the IRA's illegality and held instead outside Liberty Hall, where it was joined by a Cumann na mBan contingent. After police had dispersed the crowd, uniformed women formed in procession and started singing as they marched across O'Connell Bridge.[83] The June 1937 Commemoration at Bodenstown was headed by Cumann na mBan, as the IRA was unable to march. This time there were only 1,500 people present, whereas two years before there had been 30,000, and the handful of police ignored them. Amongst the women present were Mary MacSwiney, Maud Gonne and Leslie Price Barry. In his oration Tom Barry declared that no Republican would vote on the issue of the constitution, as votes polled against it would be open to the interpretation that they were in favour of the 1922 Constitution.[84]

That was the dilemma of Cumann na mBan: as orthodox Republicans first and foremost, they wanted a Constitution of the Republic, and that constitution was not the one formulated by de Valera. The Republic had still not been declared, partition continued, and the new state was to be named 'Eire'. When Margaret Buckley, while speaking at a Sinn Fein meeting, was heckled on her views of the constitution she spiritedly retorted that 'If she were dealing with the constitution she would have something to say about de Valera's treating the women of the country as half-wits.'[85] But she had no intention of dealing with the constitution. Having made their ritual condemnation of the question, Republicans stood aloof. For Cumann na mBan to have entered into the debate concerning its impact on women would have entailed, in their eyes, a compromise with their status as a Republican women's organisation. Although they objected to each article within the constitution they could not, for the reasons outlined by Barry, become involved in the campaign against it. In this they failed, as a women's organisation, to view the issue from a woman's perspective: to see that their abstention from the campaign meant that another voice for women's interests was missing, and it was a voice that had once been very powerful. Many women, from Sheila Dowling and Hanna Sheehy Skeffington, on the nationalist side, to Mary Kettle, on the purely feminist side, had called for a return to the ideals of the Proclamation (the retention of Section 3 of the 1922 Constitution was the last concession they would accept) and within that framework it must have been possible for Cumann na mBan women, without any compromise, to have interjected their views. By deciding to remain with the male Republicans in their total dismissal of the issue, Cumann na mBan failed to give any lead to the women of the country. When faced with the most severe threat yet encountered by Irish women, they could offer only the barren prospect of waiting for the Republic.

The result of the referendum was a lukewarm acceptance of the constitution: 685,105 voted in favour and 526,945 voted against. There was a 31 per cent level of abstention. If Cumann na mBan had mobilised its residual support, the outcome could have been a decisive defeat for de Valera.

Fading away

So the constitution had been accepted and Ireland, after decades of bloodshed and political upheaval settled down into becoming a conservative, inward-looking, rural society. The women's party, so longed for by Hanna Sheehy Skeffington, had a brief appearance as the Women's Social and Progressive League, which campaigned strongly in the 1938 elections but with little result. The Labour Party nominated its first woman candidate for election—Mary O'Connor, who had worked for the Irish Women Workers' Union for 20 years, and who had been a member of the peace delegation during the bombardment of the Four Courts. She polled only 460 votes.

In the 1943 election, four women stood as Independents, on a programme aimed primarily at women, demanding equal pay for equal work, equal opportunities for women, and the removal of all economic, social and domestic restrictions upon women. These were Miss Corbett and Miss Phillips in Tipperary, Margaret Ashe, the chairwoman of Galway Council, in Galway, and Hanna Sheehy Skeffington in Dublin South. They hoped their challenge would form the starting-point for a women's party, but all suffered decisive defeats—Hanna received only 917 votes in a constituency which elected Jim Larkin's son, and only Margaret Ashe, with just over 2,000 votes, managed to retain her deposit. The three women who were elected—the 'silent sisters', Brigid Redmond, Mrs Reynolds and Mrs Rice—were obedient party women and no threat to the status quo. Although disappointed and angry at the result, blaming both the political machines for treating women simply as voting fodder and women themselves for failing to become involved, Hanna continued to believe that the seed they had sown would eventually germinate into a full-blown onslaught by women against the political system that discriminated against them.[86]

But by 1946 Hanna was dead, and with her went the most consistent feminist voice Irish women were to have until a new generation developed its own awareness of women's intolerable oppression.

Within the Republican movement, the impetus changed from the concern with social issues that had characterised the early 1930s, to a renewed militarism which went unchallenged, now that the left wing no longer existed. In 1939 the ill-fated bombing campaign began in Britain, further eroding support for the IRA. Two women—Josephine Brady and Bridie Dolan—were in Armagh Jail in 1938;[87] and when the second world war began, Republicans on both sides of the border were interned, women included. In the north, 18 women were incarcerated in Armagh for three years,[88] and in the south, about 20 women, including Fiona Plunkett, Maeve Phelan, Noneen Brugha and Patsy O'Hagan spent varying periods of time in Mountjoy.[89] But by then, Cumann na mBan existed only in name. It had failed to draw in new members and family responsibilities finally claimed the attention of those who had led the organisation for so long: Eithne Coyle had married in 1935, Sheila Humphreys in 1937. After half a lifetime of putting her Republicanism before any personal considerations, Eithne asked Cumann na mBan to accept her resignation. She had an illness in the family to tie her down and she also admitted to feeling exhausted and war-weary. With great reluctance, in 1941 Cumann na mBan accepted the fact that their president was retiring. Sheila Humphreys took over, but it was really only a gesture to maintain continuity; she never considered herself to have been the president of Cumann na mBan.

Their decline was partly a consequence of their status as an auxiliary organisation to the IRA—once the IRA transferred its activities to England, there was little that Cumann na mBan members in Ireland could do—and once the war started and Republicans were interned, there was no opportunity to engage in any form of political activity other than a muted campaign in support of the prisoners. Younger women could see no point in joining an organisation that appeared to have historical but no contemporary relevance. They were aware that it had played a role in the War of Independence, but that time had passed. When women's rights had come under attack Cumann na mBan, by their 'principled abstentionism', failed to offer any way forward. Republicanism was at its lowest ebb, its ideals a bankrupt travesty of a previous age. The executive members, their 'brains flogged', as Eithne described their state of mind, felt unable to alter their constitution, which to them was a sacrosanct declaration of Republican principles, so that the scope of their activities could be broadened to include a fight for women's equality. As long as partition remained and the Republic yet to win, women would have to wait. To the end, they perceived their role as helping the 'fighting men', and it led to their downfall:

> The Constitution laid it out that we were to help the men and then the men sort of faded away and there was nothing left, unless the Constitution changed. So that was the stumbling block then.[90]

7. Conclusion

Lessons from History

Throughout the long history of women's involvement in the various phases of the struggle for national liberation, a tension has existed between those women who demanded equality of status (and who, on occasion, were more radical than the men in their conception of the political direction to be taken) and women who were content to perform unquestioningly whatever services were demanded of them. But the militant and outspoken individuals never won out. As anomalies within the rigidly masculine tradition of Irish nationalism, they were either deliberately suppressed or eventually compelled to amalgamate with the wider movement where, in a desperate attempt to gain equal status they became hyperactive, constantly dreaming up new schemes to prove their capabilities and justify their existence, but unable to develop any clearly defined programme which would have added cohesion and credibility to these disconnected gestures. Their emotional and ideological identification with nationalism, which always overrode all other considerations, was a crucial factor in preventing them from ever developing a strategy which could have encompassed a broader definition of liberation—one which would have released them from the constraints that ultimately dissipated their radical potential. Relations with their feminist contemporaries were often acrimonious because, while both agreed that women were at a disadvantage within society, the nationalists maintained that to place the needs of women before those of 'the nation' (which was little more than an idealised abstraction, devoid of any social content) would be divisive, and from this perspective they criticised feminism for its implicit lack of commitment to the nationalist cause. Inghinidhe na hEireann, as an autonomous women's group, was the only organisation to attempt a fusion of the two struggles, but as they believed the only legitimate causes to be ones which incorporated some aspect of the fight for political independence, campaigning for women's right to citizenship alone was never part of their programme. Even their school meals campaign, fraught with contradictions as it was, had to be justified on nationalist grounds—a healthy nation needs healthy children—so any movement that insisted upon stressing the primacy of women's needs was heavily criticised.

Few united actions by nationalists and feminists were ever undertaken, and those few were determined by nationalist considerations; there was no reciprocal willingness on the part of nationalist women to fight for feminist demands. For example, women in Sinn Fein and Cumann na mBan refused to raise the question of women's exclusion from the terms of the Home Rule bill until after it had passed through the House of Commons, in case they jeopardised its progress, and criticised feminists for putting the interests of their sex before that of the nation. However, once the bill was on the statute books, they had no hesitation in joining the Irishwomen's Franchise League on a feminist platform, calling for the same demand they had so recently condemned other women for insisting upon. Jenny Wyse Power's explanation for their change of attitude summed up the position of nationalist women:

> Nationalist women refrained from placing their suffrage views before the Irish Parliamentary Party while that Party was carrying the Home Rule Bill through the English House of Commons. Now, however, the situation has quite changed... This is a time when all Irishwomen should come together and put their views forward from an Irish standpoint in the hope that they may be allowed to exercise their right to participate in the government of their own country.[1]

But the IWFL was exasperated at the reasoning behind the nationalist women's new-found willingness to speak on women's behalf and Kathleen Connery impatiently retorted that this attitude showed a false conception of freedom and nationhood

> which is unable to grasp the simple fact that the freedom
> of Irish womanhood is a vital and indispensable factor in
> true Irish Nationhood, not a mere trifling side issue to be
> settled anyhow or anytime at the convenience of men.[2]

No common agreement on the subject was ever reached during all the years of polemic between the two groups. Much later, Maire Comerford sadly mused that it had never occurred to her to doubt that a Republican government would do justice to both sexes equally and she asked, 'Why did Cumann na mBan let down the feminist cause when the war was over?'[3] But Cumann na mBan didn't suddenly and inexplicably let down the feminist cause—because it had never taken it up in the first place. Although it had fought for women at particular moments of crisis, this had always been contingent upon an overall advancement of the nationalist cause. However, as an organisation claiming to represent the nationalist women of Ireland, it did fail to give any lead to Irish women and it was a failure that orginated in their narrow conception of their role as guardians of the Republican conscience, rather than as representatives of the interests of women. When women had their rights as workers and as citizens seriously threatened through the Conditions of Employment Bill of 1935 and the 1937 Constitution, Cumann na mBan either remained silent or put forward the standard Republican case for abstention: if Ireland was not free, it was a fallacy and a contradiction in terms to fight for women's freedom. By remaining outside the widest regroupment of feminist forces that had existed for over 20 years, one that was endeavouring by every means available to fight back against the most serious threat women had yet confronted outside of fascist Europe, Cumann na mBan abandoned its previously affirmed responsibility to Irish women. For their part, feminists discovered they had little popular support in a country which, after the upheavals of years of war, had settled down into a self-sufficient, traditional society, regarding with suspicion and distaste any foreign influence, particularly in areas of morality. Films had already come under a censorship act by 1923 and in 1929 the Censorship of Publications Act set up the zealous censorship board, which was determined to ensure that the Irish way of life would remain uncontaminated by more cosmopolitan values. The Labour Party proved itself to be as rigidly Catholic as the other two main parties and not only offered no radical critique but colluded in the introduction of the Conditions of Employment Bill. The groups on the far left were tiny and bitterly divided, totally unable to establish any significant base within Irish society.

Hanna Sheehy Skeffington was the only woman who attempted to develop an analysis that incorporated the feminist issue into a nationalist framework, but because of the complex political circumstances surrounding the Home Rule crisis, found herself unable to mobilise much support. Although the suffrage movement as a whole consisted of numerous small groups organised throughout the country, only the Irishwomen's Franchise League perceived the importance of the nationalist struggle. Because of the lack of support from nationalist women, however, her strategy remained limited to one of an individualistic intervention into the nationalist arena, arguing for a commitment to women's right to citizenship. While the suffrage movement internationally was divided by the outbreak of the first world war, in Ireland the added factor of the 1916 Rising shattered the remaining groups, and rendered all movements—feminist and labour—irrelevant in comparison with the task of completing the national revolution.

For many years afterwards, Hanna was to devote her energies to the nationalist cause, at the same time using every opportunity to put forward women's issues. On principle, she refused to join Cumann na mBan—the main women's organisation—because of her realisation that its auxiliary role ensured that women would remain of secondary importance. The necessity of fighting against imperialist domination led to the downgrading of her other concerns, which in retrospect was to prove disastrous, but as the new Irish state consolidated its position and the nationalist challenge waned, Hanna's feminism came to the fore once again and her remaining years were devoted to mobilising support against the relentless advance of the patriarchal attack upon women. But by that time Ireland was partitioned and the vital support of northern women, particularly those organised within trade unions, was lost to their southern sisters.

It came as no surprise to those who had consistently criticised the most notorious proponents of women's domestic obligations, that the anti-woman prejudices which had always been a barely concealed undercurrent within the nationalist camp, would surface in a most virulent form once political stability had been achieved. The man who had objected to the participation of women in the 1916 Rising was hardly likely, especially in the conservative, economically depressed climate of the 1930s, to encourage women's participation in the workforce. Only those who had taken at face-value the anti-Treaty advocacy of the extension of the franchise in 1922 could have been caught off-guard by the Fianna Fail policies of the succeeding decade. To the ever-vigilant Hanna, it was simply confirmation of what she had warned against, and evidence of what would happen in the absence of any feminist movement. The tragedy of partition had incalculable consequences in enabling the hegemony of Catholic social doctrine to be implemented almost without challenge. Because the right of women to organise autonomously was never accepted by nationalists—the most that was conceded was the separate organisation of women within the general parameters of nationalist ideological concerns—women were left helpless when faced with a threat to their specific interests that did not engage the concern of nationalists.

The writings and political practice of James Connolly have only been accepted when they have not conflicted with nationalist orthodoxy and nowhere is this more clearly evident than over the controversial issue of women; Connolly's unequivocal support for the suffrage movement has in consequence been completely obscured. When suffragists were pilloried for attacking Prime Minister Asquith on his visit to Dublin in 1912—a visit undertaken to assure Irish people of the Liberal government's determination to pass a Home Rule bill—Connolly made a special trip from Dublin to speak in solidarity at the next public meeting of the IWFL and he declared the following year, when more women had served jail sentences,

> that he had never yet seen or heard of any militant action of theirs that he would not have been fully prepared to

endorse. Suffragettes could only succeed by subordinating everything, regardless of consequences, to the attainment of their object.[4]

In one of his most memorable aphorisms, which is constantly quoted but less consistently acted upon, he reiterated his conviction that women must organise on their own terms, 'None so fitted to break the chains as they who wear them, none so well equipped to decide what is a fetter.'[5]

An example of Connolly's acute awareness of the different economic status of women and men and the political consequences which derived from women's unequal position within the labour force, gains in significance when juxtaposed with what was to occur during the campaign against 'economic conscription'. Connolly had warned in 1915 of the dangers of women being used in place of men and he correctly argued that if they had equal pay and franchise rights, this problem could not arise:

> Sex distinctions must go. Women must protect themselves. Sex distinctions are harmful alike to men and women... Women must organise. They must ask for a minimum wage; and insist upon having it. They must ask for war bonuses. They must give the employers even more trouble than do the men. They must make a row about the parliamentary vote![6]

Two years later, there was a government decree that vacant civilian positions should not be filled by men between the ages of 16 and 62, and the economic conscription of which Connolly had warned was a reality. But in 1918, when nationalist Ireland organised against conscription, no voice was raised in support of these exploited female workers, the only concern being the creation of a united campaign against the introduction of conscription and the use of cheap female labour in the place of men. Women signed pledges of resistance and members of the Irish Women Workers' Union carried placards declaring 'Women won't blackleg', suppressing any protests about their abysmal pay and conditions in order to maintain a united front. As one of the few occasions when an issue assumed such importance that it brought together church leaders, trade unionists and nationalists, and where women's support was essential for success and therefore actively courted, the anti-conscription campaign has great significance, but its enduring legacy was a symbolic reaffirmation of women's acceptance of their inferior economic status.

It would undoubtedly have been almost impossible in that context for anyone to have put forward an appeal on women's behalf, a difficulty compounded by the fact that the feminist movement was split in political allegiance with only the IWFL supporting the Sinn Fein cause and their chief spokeswoman, Hanna, was still in America. Although the women's pledge might have been tactically necessary, it was not far removed from the ethos surrounding the Conditions of Employment Bill less than 20 years later, which deliberately sought to exclude women from areas of the labour force because of a fear that they were taking work away from men. It could be argued that 1918 set a precedent for 1935, when feminists and female trade unionists finally came to realise what was happening.

New beginnings?

Historical events in Ireland appear constantly to reproduce themselves as the next generation rises up to fight for the final resolution of the intractable national question. In some periods, a commitment to social change has been embodied within the political programme, while at other times an uncompromising straightforward physical force mentality has been predominant. But until recently, the Republican movement has never included within its programme a strategy for the liberation of women.[7] At best, the constant referral to the traditions of Gaelic Ireland has contained the implication that the as yet unborn Ireland would unshackle the chains of centuries from the necks of grateful women. There is also another and more insidious element to this affirmation of a past egalitarian culture: if the subjection of Irish women was directly related to the foreign conquest of Ireland, then Irish*men*, who had also suffered from foreign domination, could not be blamed for what had occurred over the intervening centuries. As they were fighting for freedom, in some unexpressed manner it was always assumed that they must also be fighting for the freedom of women. In Republican mythology, Irish men used to be non-oppressive and this dubious proposition somehow becomes transmuted into an assurance that they will automatically become so again—as soon as the contaminating effects of 'foreign influence' are removed. Apart from the fact that this sleight-of-hand conveniently ignores any analysis of the root causes of women's oppression, the political consequences of this nonsensical position—whereby life in a pre-industrial society is equated with the complexities of modern capitalist development—has been to instil a false sense of security into the female supporters of the nationalist movement. Only in the last few years, as a result of both internal and external pressures, has Provisional Sinn Fein accepted that this was hardly an adequate scenario for the present day.

In 1979, a full ten years after the start of the latest round in the nationalist campaign, Sinn Fein was forced to admit that 'apart from a few articles in the Draft Charter of Rights and a short declaration made at a press conference in 1972, nothing has ever been said or written on the subject [of women].'[8]

In 1971, *Eire Nua*, the social and economic programme of Sinn Fein, had detailed (in replica of the protectionist nationalism of Arthur Griffith and the early Sinn Fein) laboriously worked-out policies on agriculture, fishing, trade, industry, forestry, transport, etc., with the startling omission of any mention of women. Even the section on the social services contained no reference to the needs of women or children as it discussed such issues as pensions and the handicapped. On education, much was made of proposals for a five-year university course, while children were dismissed with the statement that pre-primary schools for the three-to-six age group would enable children to learn 'social responsibility'. There was to be no day-care for younger children and the 'rights of the family as the primary and natural educator of the child' was affirmed.[9]

Challenges by feminists both inside and outside the Republican movement exposed the bankruptcy of such reactionary and out-dated notions, so obviously suffused with Catholic social thought, leading finally to Sinn Fein women holding a meeting in Belfast in November 1979, their intention being to formulate policies on women which would be placed on the agenda of the next *ard fheis*. Although only 22 women attended, an indication that many women within the organisation failed to see the necessity of Sinn Fein developing a programme on women, a tentative start was made.

It was obvious from the report of the meeting that certain criticisms and campaigns by women's groups had had an effect in highlighting the inadequacies of the Sinn Fein position. They admitted that when women activists were asked for their policy on such issues as violence against women, contraception and childcare, they ended up giving their personal views, forced to confess that Sinn Fein had no policy in these areas. The Sinn Fein women were also concerned that their leadership might be supplanted by Women Against Imperialism. Their fear had been accentuated by pickets on West Belfast drinking clubs, initiated by Women Against Imperialism in protest against the exclusion of women, and supported by local women and other women's groups—but not by members of Sinn Fein, who did not want publicly to criticise male Republicans. Recapturing the initiative from Women Against Imperialism was a strong motivating factor in this new move.

One point, made in a speech by Martha McClelland of Derry during the conference, signified a reversal of a previously held position. Only three years before, Sinn Fein women had argued against the Belfast Socialist Women's Group who were calling for the state provision of nurseries, repeating the standard Republican line that no nationalist would ask the state for anything; now the fact that no nurseries were provided by the state was condemned, and the meeting called for a state policy on the issue. The implications of this are reminiscent of the difficulties encountered by Inghinidhe na hEireann in their school meals campaign of 1911 and demonstrate a new-found understanding on the part of some nationalists that political gains have to be constantly fought for, and cannot be postponed until the creation of the ideal state.[10]

The policy document which was eventually accepted in 1980, while an advance on any previous policy, contains little that advanced western capitalism has not already implemented. Radical alternatives to the existing sexual division of labour are ignored, the focus centring exclusively on heterosexuality with an emphasis upon marriage, albeit with a proviso that 'childcare must be shared as an equal responsibility between both parents.' There is no acceptance of a woman's right to control her fertility; contraception, a contentious issue even within Sinn Fein, is 'a matter of conscience for the couple involved' while abortion in the 'new Ireland' will still be illegal. An attempt to appease feminist criticism is made with the statement 'we are opposed to the attitudes and forces in society that impel women to have abortions', but this is immediately negated by the categorical assertion 'we are totally opposed to abortion'. Within the preamble, the existence of divorce in Celtic Ireland is deliberately included to disarm potential dissent, but while they accept 'in principle' the introduction of divorce 'for those who wish to avail of it', divorce and contraception continue to be moral issues and are therefore left to the individual conscience—an indication of the tensions inherent within Sinn Fein, containing as it does a wide spectrum of social groups and political interests. There is no analysis of the origins of women's oppression in this document, whose basic thrust is aimed at legislative change so limited as barely to advance women's status to that achieved by Scandinavian countries. Once again, imperialist domination becomes a convenient scapegoat to which all subsequent ills can be attributed, being 'mainly inherited from Victorian England [as] in Celtic Ireland women had more equality with men that at any time since'.[11]

As part of this newly discovered concern for women, a Sinn Fein Women's Affairs Department was formed, but this remains the province of a few committed women, who see their function primarily as agitating within the movement to raise members' awareness of the realities of women's oppression, and to formulate further policies when required. They appear to be fully preoccupied with the arduous task of convincing the rank and file of the fundamental importance of taking women's issues seriously and have not, as yet, campaigned on behalf of women who would not necessarily be in sympathy with Provisional Sinn Fein. The continuing internal power struggle between the radicals and the traditionalists has had repercussions here, in that it has only been reluctantly accepted that Sinn Fein should broaden its concerns and work for a greater degree of popular support through engaging in social and economic issues. For that reason, a more overtly interventionist role on the part of Sinn Fein women contains innumerable problems.

The controversy surrounding Sinn Fein's attitude towards the proposed constitutional amendment on abortion clearly reveals all these underlying tensions. The 'right to life' groups, by seeking a constitutional prohibition on abortion (which is already illegal anyway), intend to forestall any possibility of future legislative reform. The issues involved concern not only a woman's right to control her fertility, but also the future position of Catholic social teaching within the entire range of state policies. If the Amendment campaigners are successful, an onslaught on the hard-won and still unsatisfactory reform of the contraception law will undoubtedly be their next target.

The present campaign, conducted with all the hysterical fervour that religious fanatics are capable of mobilising, has been denounced by all major Protestant churches, by some eminent Catholic theologians, a proportion of trade unionists and, of course, by all feminists. It is highly significant that Sinn Fein hesitated a considerable length of time before issuing a statement of condemnation—and equally significant that it announced it would not be participating in the anti-Amendment campaign. The rationale for this was that opposition to a constitutional amendment entailed recognition of the political structures of the 26 counties. Irishwomen, in the cause of doctrinal purity, are left —as they were in 1937—to fight without any assistance from the Republican movement. The Sinn Fein Women's Department, which took so long to come into being, may in consequence be rendered all but irrelevant when confronted with the first major crisis of its existence.[12]

One major innovation of the present military campaign is the presence of female volunteers: the result of a combination of female insistence and male recognition of the necessity of having some militarily trained women. In the late 1960s, younger women who were joining Cumann na mBan began to express their disillusionment and disaffection with their subsidiary role and argued strongly for their integration into the IRA. As a result of these pressures, sympathetic IRA officers finally agreed to give them military training, but this was conducted without the knowledge of the older women. The younger radicals remained within the ranks of Cumann na mBan, attempting to inject a new political dimension into what had become a highly conservative organisation and one that was completely under the control of the IRA executive. The days of conventions which debated policy changes at length were over; there was no military campaign for them to assist and the annual general meetings of Cumann na mBan were attended by only 30 delegates, an observer from the Army council in attendance. All constitutional changes had to be ratified by the IRA. In this situation, relations between the women and the men were often strained. On one occasion, money raised for uniforms by Cumann na mBan as part of its efforts to celebrate the fiftieth anniversary of the 1916 Rising, was commandeered by the IRA. After protests, the women were told that half of all the funds they collected were to go to the IRA. It was to become obvious, in the changed atmosphere of the Civil Rights era, that not many of the new recruits would put up with such arrogance.

At the time of the Republican split of 1969-70 many women joined what they perceived to be the socialist wing—the Officials —who then disbanded Cumann na mBan and accepted women into the Official IRA. But women were soon complaining that they were discriminated against in training and promotion and were regarded with hostility by many of the men—particularly those from rural areas. A formal acceptance of women's equality which didn't also include the political education of the male membership, meant that, in real terms, women continued to be regarded as inferior. The Provisionals, on the other hand, maintained Cumann na mBan as a separate organisation but allowed women to be seconded into the IRA—which meant that they were militarily active but without the status of full members. Although women are now accepted on an equal basis with men into the revised unit structure of the IRA, it is unlikely that many have attained high military ranking: they can be given a role without that implying any power within the organisation. But the outcome of this change has been that those most impatient with the subordinate role of Cumann na mBan have joined the IRA, leaving Cumann na mBan to be dominated by the most traditional elements.[13]

The attitudes of the female volunteers—as soldiers first and foremost—reveal an identification with the Republican movement which is so complete that it precludes any awareness of their own position as women. In a recent interview[14] women members of the IRA declared the role of the Women's Department to be 'politicising and educating the women in the movement on women's issues', a stereotypical dismissal of its radical potential which duplicates the male relegation of the women's section to 'women's issues'—as if men had no need for education or politicisation! For this, they were severely rebuked by Rita O'Hare in her capacity as head of the Women's Affairs Department, who was at pains to correct the 'misconception'.[15]

The interview with the IRA women disclosed the activists' incomprehension of the reasons why anyone should find it necessary to prioritise women's demands. As women working militarily alongside men, they stood on their individual merits, neither expecting nor wanting preferential treatment. And as people fully committeed to armed struggle, they found it contradictory to have a separate organisation for women—although they patronisingly accepted that Cumann na mBan still provided essential back-up by servicing their needs. The suggestion that the Republican movement might be male-dominated and anti-woman was ignored, except for a brief comment on the cordial relations they experienced with the men they worked with, while the 'flimsy excuse for a woman's movement' was dismissed without further comment. One married woman volunteer interjected that although she had the added pressures of family responsibilities, 'for me personally, my family life is secondary... and incidental to my commitment to the struggle'. She did, however, think that the organisation could help by supplying crèche facilities.

Such attitudes, although at variance with the policies of the Women's Department, are far removed from those of the present members of Cumann na mBan. In many respects, these contemporary women echo their predecessors in the earlier Cumann na mBan. They express the self-confidence of women who, because of their actions, believe they have transcended their traditional role. Accordingly, they find it retrogressive for a section of women to continue making the point that all women remain oppressed, and that far-reaching structural changes will have to be implemented before any genuine equality of the sexes can be created.

The distinction between the two groups is clearly evident in the reaction provoked by the interview. Angry letters reminded readers of the 'proud tradition of service' of Cumann na mBan, while Cumann na mBan itself replied by issuing a statement detailing their historical and present role. Unwittingly, this confirmed the reservations voiced by those who had left the confines of Cumann na mBan, reinforcing their suspicions of its secondary and traditional role. By denying their own oppression as women, through their insistence that Cumann na mBan needed no extra facilities, they also denied the crucial importance of the Women's Department—'We need no one to organise crèches for us, we are a self-sufficient organisation to which any Irish woman should feel proud to belong'—and they jealously discounted the future potential of any organisation other than their own. On the attainment of a 32-county Ireland:

> Cumann na mBan will remain as the organisation to
> which Irish women will want to belong... We see
> ourselves as the women of Ireland, the mothers of future
> generations of Irish men and women and we consider this
> no mean role in life. We consider the family as the basic
> unit of society and it is as the defenders of all that is
> good in society that we have acted.

Further elaboration of their conception of the role of women provides depressing evidence of the internal obstacles encountered by those attempting to introduce some degree of feminist awareness into the movement:

> we see our role in society as equal to men's, though
> naturally not the same, and it will be towards the fulfil-
> ment of womanhood and the acceptance of the value of
> women in society that we will strive.[16]

The alliance of interests contained within any national liberation movement will almost inevitably give rise to acute differences of opinion, and international experience has demonstrated time and again that when it comes to the question

262 / Unmanageable revolutionaries

of women's oppression, these contradictions may erupt in a most virulent fashion. Whether Irishwomen can develop the strength to guard against this remains to be seen.

Although Sinn Fein Women's Affairs Department, the IRA and Cumann na mBan all belong to the same movement, their attitudes towards women's participation within the movement and within the wider society are completely divergent, while the male leadership has made no statements concerning their policies on women, other than occasional brief references to the struggle of the prisoners in Armagh Jail. But despite the efforts of groups like Women Against Imperialism to create a climate of opinion which would have accorded equal status to the struggle of the women political prisoners, they have remained a secondary element in the overall prison campaign. For their part, the 30 women in Armagh Jail understandably see themselves as an integral part of the Republican tradition, and, although they had to exert considerable pressure in order to receive permission for three women to join the first hunger strike in December 1980, as prisoners of war they are obviously in total solidarity with the male prisoners and the movement outside.

The accounts by Margaretta D'Arcy and Liz La Grua, the two members of Women Against Imperialism who went to jail in solidarity with the struggle of the Armagh women, revealed the extent of the Republican women's hostility towards the organised feminist movement—hostility originating in what they perceive to be the failure of feminism to support the national struggle unconditionally.[17] But can feminism offer such unqualified support and retain its ability to encompass the reality of all women's oppression, to fight without compromise for women's interests?

We again have, as we had decades ago, two groups of politically active women: one a part of the anti-imperialist struggle, the other a fragile collection of individuals attempting to develop a space for women's voices to be heard. We have also seen that although Irishwomen have been politically active for more than 100 years, this involvement has not necessarily led to an improvement in women's lives. It is true that participation in political movements has often had the consequence of altering women's consciousness, creating an awareness of their own oppression and engendering a desire to fight for their own demands as well. However, if there is no strong feminist movement to give expression to these demands then they are unlikely to be translated into action. History shows us that it has been the persistent campaigning by groups on the margins of what has normally been recognised as 'political life' which enabled that initial discourse on women to be developed; we also know that feminists have had to fight for the space in which to articulate women's demands, refusing to be deflected by other considerations. There will always, in the long struggle for human liberation, be a need for a movement that will fight for an authentic feminist vision of the future, just as there will also be a need for a movement that unites the working class in common struggle. While relations between the two will never be uncomplicated, the priority for Irish feminists must be to learn the lessons of history and to develop a strategy that will unite women in a fight for our own liberation.

Notes

Introduction
1. Adrienne Rich, *On Lies, Secrets, and Silence: Selected Prose 1966-1978*, London, Virago, 1980, p.11.
2. Elizabeth Fox-Genovese, 'Placing Women's History in History', *New Left Review*, no.133, May/June 1982, p.29.

1. The Ladies' Land League, 1881-82
1. Michael Davitt, *The Fall of Feudalism in Ireland*, London and New York, Harper & Row, 1904, p.310.
2. Anna Parnell, 'The Land League: Tale of a Great Sham', National Library of Ireland, MS. 12144. Anna wrote this in 1907 and spent the last years of her life trying to get it published. Helena Moloney met Anna in Dublin in 1909, at the time when Helena was editor of *Bean na hEireann*, journal of Inghinidhe na hEireann, but Helena was forced to tell Anna that the journal was too small and had too much to say on current affairs to be able to publish Anna's manuscript. Shortly afterwards, the offices of *Bean na hEireann* in Westmoreland Street were raided and the manuscript disappeared. On 7 July 1910, Anna wrote to Helena, 'I have no money to pay for lodgings except for a short time.' But Helena appears to have been reluctant to explain about the disappearance of the manuscript. On 23 November 1911, after Anna's death, her sister, Theodosia Paget, wrote to Helena that she was anxious to get the MS. published, but Anna had left no money which could be used for that purpose. In the 1950s, Maeve Cavanagh McDowell found a parcel addressed to Helena Moloney amongst the possessions of her sister, Mrs Frazer, who had just died. It contained the long-lost manuscript. Helena put the notes at the disposal of Professor T.W. Moody, and it was then deposited in the National Library. The version I have was shown to me by Maire Comerford, who copied it from the original, lent to her by Helena. I am also indebted to Maire Comerford for the saga of the manuscript's history.

Anna explained her method of writing history to Helena, in a letter dated 7 July 1910.

> I have avoided personalities as much as possible in the History as I consider the actions of particular individuals are unimportant in history, while the action of groups, classes, etc. of persons are most important because the former are not met with again and the latter are—I do not mean, of course that the actions are unimportant, only that it does not matter what particular individual does them except in so far as he or she represents others.

While this is true, it is little consolation for the feminist historian attempting to create a whole picture.

3. T.W. Moody, 'Anna Parnell and the Land League', *Hermathena*, 117, Summer 1974, pp.5-17.
4. R.F. Foster, *Charles Stewart Parnell: The Man and His Family*, Sussex, Harvester Press, 1976, p.246.
5. Marie Hughes, 'The Parnell Sisters', *Dublin Historical Record*, vol.20, no.1, March 1966, pp.14-27.
6. Anna Parnell, *op.cit.* Any quotations in the text which are un-attributed, come from Anna's remarks in her MS.
7. Anna Parnell, 'How They Do in the House of Commons: Notes From the Ladies' Cage', *Celtic Monthly*, May-June 1880, as quoted in Foster, *op.cit.*, p.104.
8. N.D. Palmer, *The Irish National Land League Crisis*, Yale University Press, 1940, p.110; Joseph Lee, *The Modernisation of Irish Society*, Dublin, Gill & Macmillan, 1973, p.89.
9. Davitt, *op.cit.*, p.164.
10. A.M. Sullivan, *New Ireland*, Glasgow, Cameron & Ferguson, 1882, p.138.
11. Paul Bew, *Land and the National Question in Ireland 1858-82*, Dublin, Gill & Macmillan, 1978, p.25. Between 1852 and 1868, the government commissioned a valuation of land, for the purposes of estimating taxation. This had been carried out by Sir Richard Griffith, and it was used by the League as a standard to assess fair rent.
12. A full version of 'Hold The Harvest' is published in Foster, *op.cit.*, pp.323-5. For an account of the trial, see Davitt, *op.cit.*, p.294.
13. Foster, *op.cit.*, p.245, quoting from 'Fanny Parnell' (anonymous), in *Celtic Magazine*, vol.1, no.2, September 1882. Fanny's remarks were contained in a letter she wrote to Helen Sullivan.

14. Davitt, *op.cit.*, p.256.
15. Foster, *op.cit.*, p.246.
16. Davitt, *op.cit.*, p.299.
17. A.J. Kettle, *The Material for Victory* (ed. L.J. Kettle), Dublin, Fallon, 1958, p.48.
18. *Nation* 2 April, 1881. This statement was used in evidence when Davitt was called upon to give evidence at the Parnell Special Commission, which was appointed in 1888 by the House of Commons to enquire into the possible connections between Parnell and Irish crime. *The Special Commission Act, 1888: reprint of the shorthand notes of the speeches, proceedings and evidence taken before the commissioners appointed under the above-named Act*, 12 vols, London, 1890, (vol.ix, 3 July 1899, 88, 368).
19. This was a letter from Parnell. It all appears to have been conducted on extremely formal and impersonal terms; another indication of Parnell's personal antipathy to the scheme.
20. D.B. Cashman, *The Life of Michael Davitt and the Secret History of the Land League*, Glasgow, Washbourne, 1883 or 1884, p.230.
21. *Ibid*.
22. Jenny Wyse Power, 'The Political Influence of Women in Modern Ireland', in W. Fitzgerald (ed.), *The Voice of Ireland*, Dublin and London, Virtue, 1924, pp.158-61.
23. Katharine Tynan, *Twenty-Five Years: Reminiscences*, London, Smith, Elder, 1913, pp.75-7.
24. *Nation*, 19 February 1881.
25. *Ibid.*, 2 April 1881.
26. *Ibid.*, 26 March 1881.
27. F.S.L. Lyons, *Charles Stewart Parnell*, Suffolk, Fontana, 1977, p.174.
28. Cashman, *op.cit.*, p.230.
29. *Parnell Special Commission*, *op.cit.*, 'Testimony of Davitt', 88, 371. 'From general conversation amongst the parties charged, your impresion is that the books of the Ladies' Land League have been destroyed.—That is my impression. I may be wrong, and I hope I am wrong. I would be very glad if they have not been destroyed.'
30. Cashman, *op.cit.*, p.231.
31. Bew, *op.cit.*, p.236.
32. William O'Brien, *Recollections*, London, Macmillan, 1905, p.332.
33. Katharine O'Shea, *Charles Stewart Parnell: His Love Story and Political Life*, vol.1, London, Cassell, 1914, p.207.
34. Bew, *op.cit.*, p.200.

35. Cashman, *op.cit.*, p.231. The breakdown of expenditure is as follows:

Evicted tenants to date	£20,849 19s 4d
Families of coercion prisoners	£5,123 2s 0d
Families of ordinary law prisoners	£1,449 11s 11d
Building	£9,469 3s 5d
Providing for coercion prisoners and ordinary law prisoners from 26 December to date	£21,637 16s 4d
Ordinary law prisoners from 26 December to date	£1,603 12s 1d
Legal costs by LLL	£1,508 17s 7d
Miscellaneous grants	£187 7s 0d
Grants made by Land League since its suppression	£7,542 16s 2d
Total:	£69,372 5s 10d

In *United Ireland*, 7 January 1882, the treasurer, Mrs Moloney, details grants to evicted tenants of £1,972 4s 9d; prisoners' families £81; with contributions received for the General Fund of £107 7s 7d and for the Political Prisoners' Fund £408 4s 3d.

36. Bew, *op.cit.*, p.278.
37. *Freeman's Journal*, 3 November 1881. The officers of the Political Prisoners' Aid Society were listed as: President, Miss Helen Taylor; General Secretary, Miss Kennedy; Recording Secretary, Miss V. Lynch; Financial Secretary, Miss Stritch; Accountant, Miss Mahoney; Treasurers, Mrs Moloney and Miss Parnell.
38. Quoted in *Freeman's Journal*, 24 October 1881.
39. Quoted in *Belfast News-Letter*, 14 March 1881.
40. *Ibid.*, 18 March 1881.
41. *Ibid.*, 15 March 1881.
42. *United Ireland*, 19 November 1881. Report of a meeting at the Exchange Hall, Bradford.
43. In 'The Land League: Tale of a Great Sham', *op.cit.*, Anna Parnell, describing the decline of nationalism in Ireland, which she attributes to the dominance of the Irish party, talks about the loss of the 'infinitesimally small chance... of a minority being able to seize some unexpectedly magnificent opportunity and by its aid turn the national rudder against the dead weight of the majority.' Foster, *op.cit.*, p.282, believes that this reveals the elitism of her approach, but if that is the case, then Connolly's participation in the Easter Rising was also elitist.
44. Tynan, *op.cit.*, p.84. The father referred to owned a Dublin bakery and the husband was a partner in a wholesale grocery business.

45. *United Ireland*, 12 November 1881.
46. Quoted in *United Ireland*, 10 December 1881.
47. Cashman, *op.cit.*, p.231.
48. *United Ireland*, 3 September 1881.
49. *Ibid.*, 7 January 1882.
50. Foster, *op.cit.*, p.274.
51. *United Ireland*, 12 November 1881.
52. *Ibid.*, 5 November 1881.
53. *Ibid.*, 26 November 1881.
54. Contained in a collection of songs (the Kidson Collection) held in the Mitchell Library, Glasgow. With many thanks to Sean Corcoran for bringing it to my notice.
55. Foster, *op.cit.*, p.274.
56. Lord Cowper to the cabinet, 19 April 1881; cited in R.B. O'Brien, *Life of Charles Stewart Parnell*, vol.1, London, Smith, Elder, 1898, p.326.
57. *United Ireland*, 31 December 1881.
58. *Ibid.*
59. Jenny Wyse Power, 'The Political Influence of Women in Modern Ireland', in W. Fitzgerald (ed.), *op.cit.*, pp.158-61.
60. Cashman, *op.cit.*, p.233.
61. *United Ireland*, 28 January 1882.
62. *Ibid.*
63. T.P. O'Connor, *Memoirs of an Old Parliamentarian*, vol.1, London, Benn, 1929, p.244. William O'Brien, *Recollections*, London, Macmillan, 1905, p.377, states that the women were imprisoned under statutes of Edward III, directed against 'persons of evil fame'.
64. *United Ireland*, 18 February 1881.
65. Tynan, *op.cit.*, p.83.
66. Davitt, *op.cit.*, p.349.
67. *Ibid.*
68. R.B. O'Brien, *op.cit.*, p.329, gives a list of crimes committed: March-December 1880: 7 homicides, 21 firing at persons, 62 firing at dwellings; March-December 1881: 20 homicides, 63 firing at persons, 122 firing into dwellings.
69. Davitt, *op.cit.*, p.340.
70. *Ibid.*, p.355.
71. Tynan, *op.cit.*, p.89.
72. Lyons, *op.cit.*, p.228. Parnell to Dillon, 9 August 1882.
73. Cashman, *op.cit.*, p.235.
74. W. O'Brien, *op.cit.*, p.463.
75. *United Ireland*, 12 August 1882.

76. Lyons, *op.cit.*, p.288. Parnell to Dillon, 11 August 1882.
77. *United Ireland*, 5 August 1882.
78. Foster, *op.cit.*, p.281.
79. Maud Gonne MacBride, *A Servant of the Queen*, London, Victor Gollancz, 1974 (1st edn 1938) p.91.
80. Foster, *op.cit.*, p.284.
81. Richard P. Davis, *Arthur Griffith and Non-Violent Sinn Fein*, Dundalk, Dundalgan Press, 1974, p.46.
82. William O'Brien, *Recollections*, London, Macmillan, 1905, p.382 and p.463.
83. Tim Healy, *Letters and Leaders of My Day*, vol.1, New York, Stokes, 1929, p.157.

2. Inghinidhe na hEireann, 1900-14

1. P.T. MacGinley, 'The Language Movement and the Gaelic Soul', in W. Fitzgerald (ed.), *The Voice of Ireland*, Dublin and London, Virtue, 1924, p.450.
2. *United Irishman*, 20 April 1901.
3. Maud Gonne MacBride, *A Servant of the Queen*, London, Victor Gollancz, 1974 (1st edn 1938), pp.41-2.
4. Conrad A. Balliett, 'The Lives—And Lies—Of Maud Gonne', *Eire-Ireland*, Autumn 1979, pp.17-44, for a scathing review of Maud's portrayal of herself.
5. Gonne MacBride, *op.cit.*, p.83.
6. *Ibid.*, p.89.
7. Professor Mary Macken, 'W.B. Yeats, John O'Leary and the Contemporary Club', *Studies*, vol.28, 1939, pp.136-42.
8. Gonne MacBride, *op.cit.*, p.95.
9. Padraic Colum, *Arthur Griffith*, Dublin, Browne & Nolan, 1959, p.50.
10. Gonne MacBride, *op.cit.*, p.95.
11. Balliett, *op.cit.*, p.27.
12. Gonne MacBride, *op.cit.*, p.233.
13. *Shan Van Vocht*, August 1896.
14. *Ibid.*, June 1896.
15. *United Irishman*, 7 October 1899.
16. For the origins of Inghinidhe na hEireann, see *United Irishman*, 21 April 1900; *Bean na hEireann*, May 1910; Gonne MacBride *op.cit.,,* p.291.
17. Gonne MacBride, *op.cit.*, p.295.
18. Details of the preparations were contained in each issue of *United Ireland*, May 1900. £248 8s 4d. was spent, leaving a balance of £8 17s 3d., *United Irishman*, 3 November 1900.

19. *United Irishman*, 7 July 1900.
20. Gonne MacBride, *op.cit.*, p.295.
21. *United Irishman*, 7 July 1900.
22. W.B. Yeats, *Autobiographies*, London, Macmillan, 1955, p.368.
23. *United Irishman*, 7 July 1900.
24. *Bean na hEireann*, March 1911; *United Irishman*, 13 October 1900.
25. *United Irishman*, 27 October 1900.
26. Ella Young, *Flowering Dusk*, London, Dobson, 1947, p.70.
27. *United Irishman*, 5 January 1901.
28. R.P Davis, *Arthur Griffith and Non-Violent Sinn Fein*, Dundalk, Dundalgan Press, 1974, p.14.
29. Gonne MacBride, *op.cit.*, p.292.
30. *The Irish Worker*, 6 January 1912.
31. IRIAL, 'Men, Women and Morals', *United Irishman*, 26 January 1901.
32. W.B. Yeats, *op.cit.*, p.396.
33. *United Irishman*, 13 April 1901.
34. *Ibid.*, 31 August, 7 September 1901.
35. W.B. Yeats, *op.cit.*, p.449.
36. Allan Wade (ed.), *The Letters of W.B. Yeats*, London, Rupert Hart-Davis, 1954, pp.367-8.
37. Maire nic Shiubhlaigh, *The Splendid Years*, Dublin, Duffy, 1955, pp.12-19.
38. *United Irishman*, 26 October 1901.
39. *Ibid.*, 29 March 1902; Gonne MacBride, *op.cit.*, p.317.
40. *United Irishman*, 18 April 1903; first annual report of the Cork branch.
41. Sydney Gifford Czira ('John Brennan'), *The Years Flew By*, Dublin, Gifford & Craven, 1974, p.48.
42. IER, 'Inghinidhe na hEireann', *United Irishman*, 24 August 1901. The anonymous correspondent is obviously male, i.e. 'We men...' But Brian Farrell, 'Markievicz and the Women of the Revolution', in F.X. Martin (ed.), *Leaders and Men of the 1916 Rising*, London, Methuen, 1967, p.230, misleadingly attributes this report to the actual annual report of the Inghinidhe—'The slangy record of its first year... catches the flavour of Inghinidhe.' Although it is tempting to agree with him, the evidence does not support Farrell's contention. Also, few women at that time would have had the self-confidence to indulge publicly in such denunciations of male ineptitude.
43. *United Irishman*, 20 July 1901.
44. *United Irishman*, 18 January 1902, claims the *Freeman's Journal* and *Evening Telegraph* printed it in mutilated form, while the

Herald and *Independent* suppressed it.

45. Chantal Deutsch-Brady, 'The King's Visit and the People's Protection Committee 1903', *Eire-Ireland*, vol.10, no.3, 1975, pp.3-10.

46. Gonne MacBride, *op.cit.*, p.335.

47. *Ibid*. pp.336-7.

48. Deutsch-Brady, *op.cit.*, report of press statement issued by the committee, and published in *Irish Independent*, Freeman's Journal, and the *Evening Telegraph*, 18 May 1903.

49. *United Irishman*, 23 May 1903.

50. Deutsch-Brady, *op.cit.* Statement by Redmond published in *Express*, 20 May 1903.

51. Gonne MacBride, *op.cit.*, p.338.

52. Samuel Levenson, *Maud Gonne*, London, Cassell, 1977, p.209.

53. Nancy Cardozo, *Maud Gonne: Lucky Eyes and a High Heart*, London, Victor Gollancz, 1979, p.234.

54. Levenson, *op.cit.*, p.211, quoting from an article by Maud Gonne written for *Our Nation* c. 1940s.

55. *United Irishman*, 25 July 1903.

56. Levenson, *op.cit.*, pp.211-12.

57. R.M. Fox, *Rebel Irishwomen*, Dublin and Cork, Talbot Press, 1935, pp.120-1.

58. *United Irishman*, 1 August 1903.

59. *Ibid*.

60. *Ibid*. 25 July 1903. Appeal by Inghinidhe na hEireann, signed by 'Mrs Gonne MacBride—President; Mrs James Egan—Vice-President; Miss Macken—Hon. Secretary; Miss Maggie Quinn—Hon. Treasurer.'

61. *Ibid.*, 1 August 1903.

62. *Ibid*. 31 October 1903. Annual report for 1902-3.

63. *Ibid*.

64. *Ibid.*, 5 November 1903.

65. R.P. Davis, *op.cit.*, Appendix 1.

66. R.M. Fox, *op.cit.*, p.58.

67. *Ibid.*, p.121.

68. S. Czira ('John Brennan'), *op.cit.*, pp.48-9.

69. Jacqueline Van Voris, *Constance de Markievicz in the Cause of Ireland*, University of Massachusetts Press, 1967, p.61.

70. *Bean na hEireann*, April 1909.

71. *Ibid.*, September 1909.

72. *Ibid.*, May 1909.

73. *Ibid.*, 'Fergus' replies to Mary MacSwiney. It is not known who 'Fergus' is.

74. *Ibid.*, November 1909. 'Sinn Fein and Irish Women', Hanna

Sheehy Skeffington.

75. *Ibid.*, January 1910. Pearse did start a girls' school—St
    Ita's—but the women who appear to have been most active in
    giving their support were women like Louise Gavan Duffy and
    Mary Colum, both of whom were prominent in Cumann na
    mBan. After the Rising, Louise established her own St. Ita's,
    and Mary and Annie MacSwiney set up a girls' school in Cork.
76. Dorothy Macardle, *The Irish Republic*, London, Victor
    Gollancz, 1937, p.67.
77. Jenny Wyse Power 'The Political Influence of Women in
    Modern Ireland' in W. Fitzgerald (ed.), *The Voice of Ireland*,
    op.cit., pp.158-61.
78. *Sinn Fein*, 19 March 1910.
79. *Ibid.*, 8 April 1911.
80. Samuel Levenson, *James Connolly*, London, Martin Brian &
    O'Keefe, 1973, p.162.
81. *Sinn Fein*, 22 April, 6 May 1911.
82. *Annual Register*, 1911, p.293.
83. Countess Markievicz, 'The King's Visit: Memories', *Eire*, 14 July
    1923.
84. *Sinn Fein*, 15 July 1911.
85. *Eire*, 14 July 1923.
86. R.M. Fox, *op.cit.*, p.123.
87. *Sinn Fein*, 15 July 1911.
88. *Irish Freedom*, August 1911.
89. Van Voris, *op.cit.*, p.89.
90. *Eire*, 14 July 1923.
91. S. Czira ('John Brennan'), *op.cit.*, p.53.
92. *Irish Review*, December 1911, pp.483-5.
93. *The Irish Worker*, 2 November 1912.
94. Levenson (1977), *op.cit.*, p.275. Levenson reports that Gwynn
    found the draft so well prepared, he had only to present it.
    However, the Education Act lists Brady, not Gwynn, as the
    presenter.
95. *The Irish Worker*, 7 November 1914.
96. 'On Franchise', *Bean na hEireann*, April 1909.
97. *Bean na hEireann*, April 1910.
98. *Sinn Fein*, 27 March 1909.
99. *Ibid.*, 5 July 1913.
100. *Ibid.*, 13 April 1912.
101. Countess Markievicz, 'Women, Ideals and the Nation', In-
    ghinidhe na hEireann, 1909, National Library of Ireland.
    Transcript of a lecture delivered to the Students' National

Literary Society, Dublin. When the meeting was advertised, it was announced that the meeting would be held at 7 o'clock, instead of the usual hour, 'so all the ladies might be present for all the discussion on the paper' (*Sinn Fein*, 27 March 1909).

3. Cumann na mBan, 1914-16

1. *Belfast News-Letter*, 21 January 1914.
2. *The Irish Citizen*, 5 July 1913. The Cat and Mouse Act (Prisoners' Temporary Discharge for Ill-Health Act) was introduced to outwit the hunger-striking tactic and eliminate the need for forcible feeding. Under its provisions a prisoner could be released and rearrested almost indefinitely. For more details of the Irish suffrage movement, see Margaret Ward, ' "Suffrage First—Above All Else!": An Account of the Irish Suffrage Movement', *Feminist Review*, 10, Spring 1982.
3. F.X. Martin, *The Irish Volunteers 1913-1915*, Dublin, Duffy, 1963, p.114. Subsequent quotations are also taken from this book, which is a compilation of documents relating to the Volunteers.
4. *Ibid.*, quoting from *The National Student*, December 1913, p.121.
5. *Irish Freedom*, September 1914.
6. *Ibid.*, November 1913.
7. *The Irish Citizen*, 28 March 1914.
8. *The Irish Volunteer*, 18 April 1914.
9. *The Irish Citizen*, 13 December 1913.
10. *The Irish Volunteer*, 23 May 1914.
11. Elizabeth Coxhead, *Daughters of Erin*, Gerrards Cross, Colin Smythe, 1979, p.62.
12. Maire nic Shiubhlaigh, *The Splendid Years*, Dublin, Duffy, 1955, pp.159-60.
13. Mary Colum, *Life and the Dream*, Dublin, Dolmen Press, 1966 (1st edn 1947), p.164.
14. *The Irish Citizen*, 25 July 1914.
15. *Ibid.*, 30 May 1914.
16. *Ibid.*, 7 November 1914.
17. *Ibid.*
18. *Ibid.*, 22 May 1915.
19. *Irish Freedom*, September 1914.
20. *The Irish Citizen*, 23 October 1915.
21. Frank Robbins, *Under the Starry Plough*, Dublin, Academy Press, 1977, p.40.
22. Cumann na mBan, leaflet, 1914, National Library of Ireland.
23. Eithne Coyle, interview, Dublin, 1975.

24. *The Irish Citizen*, 4, 11, 25 July 1914.
25. *The Irish Volunteer*, 17 October 1914.
26. Eithne Coyle, 'The History of Cumann na mBan', *An Phoblacht*, 8 April 1933.
27. Lil Conlon, *Cumann na mBan and the Women of Ireland 1913-25*, Kilkenny, Kilkenny People, 1969, p.13. Conlon took the Treaty side. Mary MacSwiney, another Cork Cumann na mBan member, strongly opposed the Rising because of what she considered to be Pearse's too close association with Connolly. Her brother shared her views, considering it to be not a Volunteer, but a Citizen Army rising. See Moirin Chavasse, *Terence MacSwiney*, Dublin, Clonmore & Reynolds, 1961, p.85.
28. *The Irish Volunteer*, 1 May 1915.
29. *Ibid.*, 1 January 1916.
30. Bulmer Hobson, *Ireland Yesterday and Tomorrow*, Tralee, Anvil Books, 1968, p.16. Countess Markievicz was elected president of the Fianna in 1910.
31. *Irish Freedom*, August 1912.
32. *The Irish Volunteer*, 8 January 1916.
33. *Ibid.*, 1 January 1916.
34. Ina Connolly Heron, 'James Connolly—A Biography', *Liberty*, August 1966. Journal of the Irish Transport and General Workers' Union.
35. *Ibid*.
36. *Ibid*.
37. *The Irish Citizen*, 7 August 1915.
38. Maire nic Shiubhlaigh, *op.cit.*, p.161.
39. Nora Connolly O'Brien, *Portrait of a Rebel Father*, Dublin, Four Masters, 1975 (1st edn 1935), pp.298-300.
41. R.M. Fox, *Rebel Irishwomen*, Dublin and Cork, Talbot Press, 1935, p.140. According to Hanna, Connolly said, 'We were practically unanimous, only one questioned it.' It's impossible to speculate upon the identity of the dissident.
42. William O'Brien, *Forth The Banners Go*, Dublin, The Three Candles, 1969, p.278.
43. Maire nic Shiubhlaigh, *op.cit.*, p.166.
44. Eilis bean Ui Chonail, 'A Cumann na mBan Recalls Easter Week', *Capuchin Annual*, 1966, pp.271-8.
45. Eithne Coyle, 'The History of Cumann na mBan', *An Phoblacht*, 8 April 1933. Also, questionnaires compiled by Eithne Coyle and other members of the Cumann na mBan executive and filled in by branch members. Completed questionnaires were kindly shown to the author by Eithne Coyle.

46. Commandant Joseph O'Connor, 'Boland's Mill Area', *Capuchin Annual*, 1966.
47. Dail Eireann, *Official Report*, vols.67-8, 13 May 1937, p.462.
48. *An Phoblacht*, 16 July 1932; also *Prison Bars*, July 1937.
49. Eilis bean Ui Chonail, *op.cit.*.
50. Helena Moloney, radio interview (no date), issued by Ceiruini Claddagh, 1966.
51. Esther Roper (ed.), *Prison Letters of Countess Markievicz*, London, Longman, Green, 1934, pp.37-41.
52. Margaret Skinnider, *Doing My Bit For Ireland*, New York, Century, 1917, p.52.
53. *Ibid.*, p.143.
54. *Catholic Bulletin*, May 1918; *An Phoblacht*, 25 June 1932.
55. Louise Gavan Duffy, 'Insan GPO: Cumann na mBan', in F.X. Martin (ed.), *1916 and University College Dublin*, Dublin, Duffy, 1967, pp.91-5. With thanks to Brendan O Fiach for his translation.
56. Nic Shiubhlaigh, *op.cit.*, pp.174-6.
57. *Ibid.*, p.184.
58. Evidence of Mary Byrne, a member of the Inghinidhe branch of Cumann na mBan and a member of the Marrowbone Lane garrison, Eithne Coyle Questionnaire. Also, R.M. Fox, *Green Banners*, London, Secker & Warburg, 1938, pp.257-8.
59. *Irish Times, Sinn Fein Rebellion Handbook Easter 1916*, Dublin, 1916, pp. 16-7.
60. *Catholic Bulletin*, February 1917-May 1918. Each month carried a further instalment of the experiences of Elizabeth and Julia.
61. Anne Marreco, *The Rebel Countess*, London, Weidenfeld & Nicolson, 1967, pp.212-26. Her main concern when she was first arrested was the welfare of Michael Mallin's wife, who was expecting a baby any day. Although Eva and her friend Esther searched for Una Mallin, they were unable to find her; however, when Markievicz was baptised a Catholic in 1917, Una Mallin attended the ceremony.
62. Tim Pat Coogan, *Ireland Since the Rising*, London, Pall Mall Press, 1966, pp.20-1.
63. *Belfast Telegraph*, 8 May 1916. Reprinted from the *Glasgow Herald*.
64. Piaras F. MacLochlainn, *Last Words*, Dublin, Kilmainham Jail Restoration Society, 1971, p.61.
65. *The Irish Citizen*, August 1917.
66. MacLochlainn, *op.cit.*, p.141.
67. Chrissie M. Doyle, *Women in Ancient and Modern Ireland*, Dublin, Kilkenny Press, 1917, p.4.

4. Cumann na mBan, 1916-21

1. *Sinn Fein Rebellion Handbook Easter 1916*, Dublin, Irish Times, 1916, p.223.
2. Sydney Gifford Czira ('John Brennan'), *The Years Flew By*, Dublin, Gifford Craven, 1974, p.85.
3. Hanna Sheehy Skeffington, 'A Pacifist Dies', in Roger McHugh (ed.), *Dublin 1916*, London, Arlington, 1966, pp.276-88.
4. *Eire*, 16 February 1924.
5. Margery Forester, *Michael Collins—The Lost Leader*, London, Sphere 1971, p.66.
6. R.M. Fox, *History of the Irish Citizen Army*, Dublin, Duffy, 1943, pp.193-5. Maire Comerford in her memoirs states that Helena Moloney told her that the ICA protest was originally planned jointly with the IRB, but that Mimi Plunkett was sent to tell Helena that it had been cancelled. Mimi also told Helena that the order imposed secrecy upon her and that she could say no more.
7. Ella Young, *Flowering Dusk*, London, Dobson, 1945, p.133.
8. Dail Eireann, *Official Report. For periods 16 August 1921 to 26 August 1921, and 28 February 1922 to 8 June 1922*, Dublin, no date; for 22 March, p.208.
9. Michael Laffan, 'The Unification of Sinn Fein in 1917', *Historical Studies*, vol.17, September 1971, pp.353-79.
10. Thomas Dillon, 'Birth of the New Sinn Fein and the Ard Fheis 1917', *Capuchin Annual*, 1967, p.394.
11. Dorothy Macardle, *The Irish Republic*, London, Victor Gollancz, 1937, Appendix 4, pp.951-2.
12. *The Irish Citizen*, November 1917.
13. *Ibid.*
14. Cumann na mBan, leaflet (no date), National Library of Ireland (NLI).
15. Cumann na mBan executive, 'The Present Duty of Irishwomen', leaflet (no date) NLI.
16. Cumann na mBan Convention, September 28-9 1918. Conference Report, NLI. The pledge is contained in point 4 of policy for 1918-19: 'To organise opposition to conscription along the lines laid down in the two Anti-Conscription Pledges.'
17. T.M. Healy, *Letters and Leaders of My Day*, London, Butterworth, 1928, p.599.
18. Esther Roper (ed.), *Prison Letters of Countess Markievicz*, London, Longman, Green, 1934, p.205.
19. Elizabeth Coxhead, *Daughters of Erin*, Gerrards Cross, Colin Smythe, 1979 (1st edn 1965), p.103.

20. Cumann na mBan Convention, 1918, NLI. The letter was quoted in full in the minutes, as 'considerable misunderstanding' arose as a result of the disbandment of the committee.
21. Information on the recruitment drive of Cumann na mBan contained in the report of the executive to the 1918 Convention.
22. *Ibid.*
23. David Fitzpatrick, *Politics and Irish Life 1913-21*, Dublin, Gill & Macmillan, 1977, p.145.
24. Cumann na mBan, National Series: no.1, *Why Ireland is Poor*; no.2, *The Spanish War by Wolfe Tone*; no.3, *Dean Swift on the Situation*. NLI.
25. Macardle, *op.cit.*, p.275.
26. Brian Farrell, *The Founding of Dail Eireann*, Dublin, Gill & Macmillan, 1971, p.27.
27. Helga Woggon, 'Winnie Carney', Berlin, June 1982. An unpublished biographical article. With many thanks to Helga for sending me a copy.
28. *The Irish Citizen*, January 1919.
29. Cumann na mBan questionnaire, compiled by Eithne Coyle and other members of Cumann na mBan and kindly shown to author.
30. *The Irish Citizen*, December 1918.
31. Jacqueline Van Voris, *Constance de Markievicz in the Cause of Ireland*, University of Massachusetts Press, 1967, p.250.
32. Macardle, *op.cit.*, p.288.
33. Fitzpatrick, *op.cit.*, p.167, quoting from Mrs J.R. Green, *The Government of Ireland*, London, 1921.
34. Dan Breen, *My Fight for Irish Freedom*, Kerry, Anvil, 1973 (1st edn 1924), p.38.
35. *Irish Bulletin*, 19 October 1919. For the policy of Cumann na mBan 1919-20, see Lil Conlon, *Cumann na mBan and the Women of Ireland 1913-25*, Kilkenny, Kilkenny People, 1969, pp.301-8.
36. Maire Comerford, unpublished memoirs in the possession of Ms Comerford and shown to author by Ms Comerford; an extended version was also shown to the author by Janet Martin of Arlen House. Henceforth, referred simply as 'Maire Comerford, unpublished memoirs'.
37. Esther Roper (ed.), *op.cit.*, pp.218-19. For details of the numbers of women elected in January, see Conlon, *op.cit.*, p.108. So far, I have not been able to calculate the numbers of women elected in June.
38. Ernie O'Malley, *Army Without Banners*, London, Four Square, (1st edn, *On Another Man's Wound*, 1936), p.151.

39. An invaluable source of information on the 1920 period is contained in *Capuchin Annual*, 1970.
40. Dail Eireann, *Minutes of Proceedings of the First Parliament of the Republic of Ireland, 1919-21*, Dublin, Stationery Office, no date; for 29 June, 1920.
41. R.M. Fox, *Green Banners*, London, Secker & Warburg, 1938, p.313.
42. Fitzgerald, *op.cit.*, p.182.
43. Conor Maguire, 'The Republican Courts', *Capuchin Annual*, 1969, pp.378-88.
44. Countess Markievicz, 'What Irish Republicans Stand For', leaflet, no date, NLI. Reprinted from *Forward*, Glasgow, 1923.
45. Maguire, *op.cit.*, p.380.
46. Maire Comerford, unpublished memoirs. Based on the account related to her by Aine Ceannt. Few women left any details of their work in the courts or local government.
47. American Commission on Conditions in Ireland, Interim Report, 'Memorandum on British Atrocities in Ireland 1916-20', Washington, no date (c.1921). The report was compiled by the Committee of One Hundred, which included Jane Addams, Frederick C. Howe, James H. Maurer, Oliver P. Newman, George W. Norrs, Norman Thomas and others. Part one is compiled from court records, newspapers and the official reports of Dail Eireann; part two of the submission summarises persons assassinated by the British Armed Forces, 1917-20. The commission interviewed a number of witnesses, the women who gave evidence being Mary MacSwiney; Muriel MacSwiney; Anna Murphy; Ruth Russell, correspondent for the Chicago *Daily News*; Susanna Walsh, sister-in-law of Tomas MacCurtain, murdered Mayor of Cork; Ellen Wilkinson; and Louie Bennett.
48. *Ibid*. Testimony of Mary MacSwiney, given 9 December 1920, p.339.
49. *Ibid*. Testimony of Ellen Wilkinson, given 21 December 1920, p.600.
50. Tom Barry, *Guerrilla Days in Ireland*, Kerry, Anvil, no date (1st edn 1949), p.191.
51. O'Malley, *op.cit.*, pp.274-5.
52. American Commission on Conditions in Ireland, *op.cit.*. Testimony of Muriel MacSwiney, 9 December 1920, p.282.
53. Eithne Coyle, interview, Dublin 1975.
54. Van Voris, *op.cit.*, p.316; Conlon, *op.cit.*, pp.220-4. She states that three women were also in Armagh Jail at this time. Cumann na mBan Convention Report 1921 gives the figure of 50 women imprisoned.

55. Roper (ed.), *op.cit.*, p.266. Letter dated 1 January 1921.
56. Annie Smithson (ed.), *In Times of Peril: Leaves from the Diary of Nurse Linda Kearns, from Easter Week 1916 to Mountjoy 1921*, Dublin, Talbot Press, 1922, for a breathless account of the whole period; Conlon, *op.cit.*, pp.220-4.
57. Margaret Buckley, *The Jangle of the Keys*, Dublin, Duffy, 1938, pp.7-8.
58. Eithne Coyle O'Donnell, unpublished memoirs. Eithne provocatively adds 'Women's Lib take note!' when she states her success in avoiding detection for so long. In the late 1940s she had a statement on her involvement taken by the Bureau of Military History, which had been set up to compile a history of the nationalist movement from 1913 to 1921. All the participants were interviewed and the work finally completed in 1959, when it was transferred to a government archive. It is now, unfortunately, under a 50-year embargo, which makes me all the more grateful to Eithne Coyle O'Donnell for kindly showing me her copy of her original deposition. For brevity's sake I describe this as her unpublished memoirs.
59. Macardle, *op.cit.*, p.359.
60. *Irish Bulletin*, 1 January 1920.
61. Maire Comerford, unpublished memoirs; also, Conlon, *op.cit.*, p.204.
62. Maire Comerford, unpublished memoirs.
63. Maire Comerford, interview, Dublin 1975.
64. Maire Comerford, unpublished memoirs.
65. Macardle, *op.cit.*, pp.434-5. Also, Revolutionary Communist Tendency, *Ireland's Victory Means Britain's Defeat*, Revolutionary Communist Pamphlet, no.7, London, 1980, pp.18-19.
66. Nancy Cardozo, *Maud Gonne: Lucky Eyes and a High Heart*, London, Victor Gollancz, 1979, p.343; also, Andro Linklater, *An Unhusbanded Life—Charlotte Despard: Suffragette, Socialist and Sinn Feiner*, London, Hutchinson, 1980, pp.217-18.
67. Cardozo, *op.cit.*, p.343.
68. Kathleen McKenna, 'The Irish Bulletin', *Capuchin Annual*, 1970, pp.503-26. Also extracts from the autobiography of Kathleen Napoli McKenna in the *Irish Times*, 24-7 December 1979. Her father's aunt was Agnes O'Farrelly, who chaired the inaugural meeting of Cumann na mBan. Kathleen later worked as secretary to the Dail. She took the pro-Treaty side and on meeting Anna Fitzsimons (who was strongly anti-Treaty) in a train compartment, the two former friends felt unable even to catch the other's eye—a common experience amongst many during the bitterness of

the Civil War. Una Brennan, formerly Una Bolgar, had been secretary of the Enniscorthy branch of Inghinidhe na hEireann.

69. Van Voris, *op.cit.*, p.294, quotes the estimate of Major Florence O'Donoghue, that the total in all ranks was 112,650 in autumn 1921, but not all were active. Tom Barry, *op.cit.*, pp.189-90, estimated the ratio between the IRA and the British in terms of armed men to be on a scale of 1:40 and from his experience, the whole of County Cork had only 310 rifles. Estimates of the strength of Cumann na mBan from a discussion with Eithne Coyle.

70. Macardle, *op.cit.*, p.561.

71. Uinseann MacEoin, *Survivors*, Dublin, Argenta Publications, 1980, pp.153-4; Conlon, *op.cit.*, p.238; Smithson (ed.), *op.cit.*, pp.54-60.

72. Eithne Coyle, unpublished memoirs (see note 58, this chapter).

5. Cumann na mBan, 1921-23

1. Cumann na mBan Convention Report, 22-3 October 1921, National Library of Ireland (NLI).

2. Lil Conlon, *Cumann na mBan and the Women of Ireland 1913-25*, Kilkenny, Kilkenny People, 1969, pp.238-42. In reporting the convention, she omits this section of Markievicz's speech. She and her branch (Shandon, Cork) of Cumann na mBan took the pro-Treaty side, and so indications that Cumann na mBan was going to hold out for 'the Republic' are carefully expunged from her account of events.

3. Conlon, *op.cit.*, p.121. Reporting a request from Eglinton Asylum to Cork District Council of Cumann na mBan for permission to have a branch established there. The decision was that two branches of Cumann na mBan already existed, and until a company of Volunteers was formed there, permission could not be granted. Intending members could join an existing branch instead. The organisers' report to the convention also made the point that Cumann na mBan was best where the fight was keenest—surely an indication that women in those places had a clearly defined role.

4. Commandant of First Western Division. Ironically, this was Michael Brennan, who took the pro-Treaty line.

5. Officer-in-Charge, Longford Area. Possibly Sean MacEan, who was also pro-Treaty.

6. There were four other sections relating to the organisation, outlining the duties of the officers of each branch—captain, secretary, and treasurer.

7. Interview, Dublin, 1975.
8. Dail Eireann, *Official Report. For Periods 16 August 1921 to 26 August 1921 and 28 February 1922 to 8 June 1922.* Dublin, Stationery Office, no date. On 23 August, Mrs O'Callaghan introduced her motion of regret, p.56. Maire Comerford in her memoirs makes the point that there was no public notification of the cabinet changes and, as far as she knew, the ministry set up in open session by the Dail in 1919 was still the government of the Republic. She greatly disapproved of the downgrading of Markievicz.
9. Dail Eireann, *Official Report Debate on the Treaty Between Great Britain and Ireland signed in London on the 6th December, 1921.* Dublin, Stationery Office, no date. On 21 December, Professor Stockley read out Muriel MacSwiney's letter, pp.90-1. All references following in the text were taken from the published reports of the Dail.
10. Maire Comerford, unpublished memoirs.
11. *Ibid.*
12. Maire Comerford, interview, Dublin 1975.
13. Conlon, *op.cit.*, pp.225-6.
14. *Ibid.*, p.257.
15. Maire Comerford, interview, Dublin 1975. Mike Farrell has mentioned hearing reports that Mabel and her husband actually separated for a time, because of disagreement over the Treaty.
16. Uinseann MacEoin, *Survivors*, Dublin, Argenta Publications, 1980, p.340.
17. *Ibid.*, p.49.
18. Conlon, *op.cit.*, p.260.
19. The debate over the franchise occurred on 2 March 1922, Dail Eireann, *Official Report*, *op.cit.*, pp.197-214.
20. Esther Roper (ed.), *Prison Letters of Countess Markievicz*, London, Longman, Green, 1934, p.298.
21. P.S. O'Hegarty, *The Victory of Sinn Fein*, Dublin, Talbot Press, 1924, pp.104-5.
22. Maire Comerford, unpublished memoirs.
23. Conlon, *op.cit.*, p.300.
24. Dail Eireann, *Official Report*, 28 April 1922, p.337.
25. Dorothy Macardle, *The Irish Republic*, London, Victor Gollancz, 1937, p.721.
26. For more details of this period, see Carlton Younger, *Ireland's Civil War*, London, Fontana Books, 1970.
27. *Ibid.*, p.316.
28. *Ibid.*, p.334.

29. Jacqueline Van Voris, *Constance de Markievicz in the Cause of Ireland*, University of Massachusetts Press, 1967, p.323.
30. Annie Smithson, *Myself—and Others*, Dublin, Talbot Press, 1944, p.251.
31. MacEoin, *op.cit.*, p.211.
32. C. Desmond Greaves, *Liam Mellows and the Irish Revolution*, London, Lawrence & Wishart, 1971, p.211.
33. *Eire: The Irish Nation*, 22 September 1923. Letter from Maud Gonne MacBride. Also included on the deputation was Dr Gertrude Webb. She claims that Nora Connolly was also present, but this is obviously an error. See also, R.M. Fox, *Louie Bennett: Her Life and Times*, Dublin, Talbot Press, no date (c.1958), pp.76-8, for Louie's own account of the peace delegation. She had independently decided, inspired by the Women's International League for Peace and Freedom, to try to avert war and states she sent a message to her friends to meet at the Mansion House the next day. Who actually instigated the peace move is difficult to determine. The Irish Women Workers' Union, on 15 October 1922, also addressed an open letter to the provisional government and the Republicans to agree to an unconditional truce as the first step towards a peace conference.
34. Maire Comerford, unpublished memoirs.
35. Ernie O'Malley, *The Singing Flame*, Dublin, Anvil, 1978, p.130.
36. Younger, *op.cit.*, p.339.
37. O'Malley, *op.cit.*, p.131.
38. MacEoin, *op.cit.*, p.47. Maire Comerford mentions only Linda Kearns and Kathleen Barry in this account, but in her unpublished memoirs she also mentions Muriel MacSwiney's presence. Younger, *op.cit.*, p.342, says on the other hand that it was Mary MacSwiney, her sister-in-law. However, Robert Briscoe (with Alden Hatch), *For the Life of Me*, London, Longman, Green, 1959, p.176, says that when escaping from Ireland to England during the Civil War he met Muriel MacSwiney and Linda Kearns on board, both women on their way to America to try to arouse sympathy for the Republican cause. This evidence would seem to substantiate the claim that both were in the Hammam Hotel.

    Muriel MacSwiney was a very interesting woman. In an affidavit made in Dublin, August 1944, she told of the kidnapping of her daughter Maire, by Mary MacSwiney, on the grounds that as Muriel had joined the Irish Communist Party and was a declared atheist, she was not a fit mother. Muriel had joined the Irish Communist Party in 1922. She then lived in Germany where, in 1932, her daughter was kidnapped by Mary MacSwiney.

Although Muriel came straight back to Ireland and tried to enlist the help of Linda Kearns and de Valera, anti-communist feeling was strong enough for a court order to be made, giving Mary MacSwiney legal rights over the child. Muriel never regained custody and subsequently went to England, where she joined the British Communist Party. Her daughter Maire later married Ruairi Brugha, Fianna Fail TD and son of Cathal Brugha. (With many thanks to Jeff Dudgeon for this information and for showing me the affidavit of Muriel MacSwiney.)

39. Macardle, *op.cit.*, p.784.
40. O'Malley, *op.cit.*, p.152.
41. Dail Eireann, *Minutes of Proceedings of the First Parliament of the Republic of Ireland, 1919-1921*, Dublin, Stationery Office, no date. Proceedings of 11 March 1921 and 10 May 1921.
42. Eithne Coyle, unpublished memoirs (see ch.4, n.58). In Dail Eireann, *Official Report*, *op.cit.*, Griffith complained on 26 April that 'Within eight days after the Pact making for peace and unity had been signed, an effort was made to smash it by the opponents of the Treaty. Forty-five seizures of Belfast goods were made within those eight days on the Great Northern Railway by unauthorised persons who pretended to reimpose the Belfast Boycott' (p.236).
43. Eithne Coyle, unpublished memoirs (see ch.4, n.58). However, in MacEoin, *op.cit.*, she unaccountably makes no mention of this period in her life, although she confirmed it to the present author in conversation.
44. MacEoin, *op.cit.*, pp.342-6.
45. Younger, *op.cit.*, p.450.
46. MacEoin, *op.cit.*, p.48. Eithne Coyle complained when sent to meet Liam Pilkington in Sligo without being given any indication of how she could meet him, 'But that was the sort of GHQ organisation we had then; we would send a woman from Dublin to Sligo, where I had never been before, and with no hint or clue of where I might bring my message' (*ibid.*, p.155).
47. O'Malley, *op.cit.*, p.106.
48. *Ibid.*, p.148.
49. *Ibid.*, p.175.
50. *Ibid.*, p.185.
51. R.M. Fox, *Green Banners*, London, Secker & Warburg, 1938, p.327.
52. O'Malley, *op.cit.*, p.174.
53. Eoin Neesan, *The Civil War in Ireland*, Cork, Mercier, 1966, pp.186-8.

54. *Ibid.*, p.193.
55. *Eire*, 17 February 1923.
56. Eithne Coyle, interview, Dublin, 1975. Peadar O'Donnell, *The Gates Flew Open*, Cork, Mercier, 1966, p.24, in discussing the anti-clerical attitudes of the Republicans says 'even girls were abusively anti-clerical and many old-time reverences were blasted'. Dorothy Macardle is the only woman to have publicly renounced her religion.
57. *Eire*, 12 May 1923.
58. *Ibid.* 19 May 1923.
59. Margaret Buckley, *The Jangle of the Keys*, Dublin, Duffy, 1938, p.25.
60. Greaves, *op.cit.*, p.372.
61. Macardle, *op.cit.*, p.891.
62. *Eire*, 23 June 1923. The editor's first comment on Maire's action was, 'It is like her.'
63. O'Donnell, *op.cit.*, p.91.
64. *Eire*, 10 November 1923 mentions that 50 women were released and 8 were still on the protest. Macardle, *op.cit.*, p.902 simply says all the women were released.
65. MacEoin, *op.cit.*, p.347.

6. Cumann na mBan, 1924-40

1. Conor Cruise O'Brien, *States of Ireland*, Hertfordshire, Panther, 1974 p.103; Andro Linklater, *An Unhusbanded Life*, London, Hutchinson, 1980, p.230.
2. *Eire*, 31 May 1924.
3. With thanks to Mike Farrell, who was shown the letter by Maire Comerford.
4. *An Phoblacht*, 16 July 1933.
5. Eithne Coyle interview, Dublin, 1975.
6. *Irish Freedom*, October 1926. The paper was owned by Albinia Broderick and managed by Sheila McInerney, both Cumann na mBan members.
7. Uinseann MacEoin, *Survivors*, Dublin, Argenta Publications, 1980, p.52.
8. Sean Cronin, *Frank Ryan*, Dublin, Repsol, 1980, p.45.
9. Sean O'Casey, *Autobiography: Book 4. Inishfallen, Fare Thee Well*, London, Pan Books, 1972 (lst edn 1949), pp.178-9. 'Poor Old Woman' is a reference to Maud's role as Kathleen ni Houlihan, the personification of Ireland.
10. *Irish Freedom*, January 1927.
11. *Ibid*, November 1927.

12. J. Bowyer Bell, *The Secret Army*, London, Sphere, 1972, p.119.
13. Leaflet, National Library of Ireland.
14. MacEoin, *op. cit.*, pp.348-9.
15. *Irish Freedom*, June 1928.
16. *Dail Eireann Debates, Official Reports*, Dublin Stationery Office, vol.24, 7 June 1928, pp.291-304.
17. *Irish Freedom*, July 1931.
18. *Ibid.*, September 1931.
19. MacEoin, *op. cit.*, p.158.
20. *Irish Freedom*, July 1931.
21. *Ibid.*
22. Tim Pat Coogan, *The IRA*, London, Fontana Books, 1971, p.84.
23. MacEoin, *op. cit.*, p.158.
24. Cronin, *op. cit.*, p.36.
25. *Workers' Voice*, 7 November 1931.
26. Bell, *op. cit.*, p.109.
27. *Republican File*, 28 November 1931.
28. *Ibid.* 23 January 1932. Kathleen Merrigan was married to an IRA officer, Maeve Phelan had a fruit and flower shop.
29. *An Phoblacht*, 12 November 1932.
30. *Republican File*, 13 February 1931.
31. *Ibid.*, 28 November 1931. I wonder if this is a misprint for Rosamund Jacob, an early (and critical) member of Cumann na mBan. She now devoted her time to writing.
32. *Workers' Voice*, 21 March 1931.
33. *Republican File*, 2 January 1932.
34. Michael McInerney, *Peadar O'Donnell, Irish Social Rebel*, Dublin, O'Brien Press, 1974, p.131.
35. *Republican File*, 13 February 1932. Mary Reynolds's husband Patrick, chairman of Leitrim Board of Health, was shot dead on the eve of the 1932 election. She was elected at a delayed poll but defeated in the 1933 election, having remained silent the entire time within the Dail. She was elected in 1937 (*Irish Times*, 25 June 1937).
36. *An Phoblacht*, 19 March 1932.
37. Maire Comerford interview, Dublin 1975.
38. *Irish Freedom*, May 1932.
39. *An Phoblacht*, May 1932.
40. MacEoin, *op. cit.* p.350.
41. Michael Farrell, *Northern Ireland: The Orange State*, London, Pluto Press, 1976, p.129.
42. *An Phoblacht*, 28 January 1933.
43. *Ibid.*

44. Linklater, *op. cit.*, p.257.
45. *An Phoblacht*, 15 November 1932.
46. *Ibid.*
47. *Ibid.*, 25 June 1932.
48. *An Phoblacht*, 23 September 1933; *Irish Freedom*, June 1933.
49. *Irish Freedom*, April 1934.
50. *An Phoblacht*, 23 September 1933.
51. *Ibid.*, 14 October 1933.
52. Cronin, *op. cit.*, p.46.
53. George Gilmore, *The Irish Republican Congress*, Cork Workers' Club, Cork, 1974 (1st edn 1934), pp.16-17.
54. *Republican Congress*, 11 August 1934.
55. *Ibid.*
56. *Ibid.*, 15 and 22 September 1934.
57. Bell, *op. cit.*, p.149.
58. *Republican Congress*, 28 September 1935.
59. *Ibid.*, 5 October 1935.
60. Coogan, *op. cit.*, p.115.
61. Bell, *op. cit.*, p.156.
62. *Irish Freedom*, September 1936.
63. Mary Daly, 'Women, Work and Trade Unionism', in Margaret MacCurtain and Donncha O'Corrain (eds), *Women in Irish Society: The Historical Dimension*, Dublin, Arlen House, 1978, pp.71-81.
64. Mary Daly, 'Women in the Irish Workforce from Pre-Industrial to Modern Times', *Saothar*, 7, 1981 (Journal of the Irish Labour History Society), pp.74-82.
65. *Republican Congress*, 30 November 1935.
66. *Seanad Eireann*, *Official Report*, Dublin Stationery Office, vol. 20, 11 December 1935, p.1399.
67. *Ibid.*, p.1426. The vote was lost by 19 to 14. Within the Dail, Section 12 was vigorously argued against by Patrick McGilligan, who later made a strong speech against the provisions relating the women in the 1937 Constitution. Helena Concannon and Bridget Redmond, the two female deputies, did not speak. Dail Eireann, *Official Report*, vol.57, 27 June 1935, pp.1206-33.
68. Reported in speech by Mary Hayden during the debate on the constitution (*Irish Times*, 22 June 1937).
69. *Republican Congress*, 21 December 1935. Other members of the committee were: Dr Angela Russell, Mrs K. Reddin, Miss D. Browne, Mrs Robert Childers, Miss Barrett.
70. *Irish Freedom*, January 1936.
71. Radio broadcast, 1943, Tim Pat Coogan, *Ireland Since the Ris-*

ing, London, Pall Mall Press, 1966, p.72. De Valera's early years must account in part for his subsequent attitudes. His mother Catherine was widowed when he was three and she was forced to place the child in the care of another woman while she went out to work. He remembered his mother on the occasions when she came from work to visit him. Shortly afterwards he was sent back from America to live with relatives in a small village in Ireland, a simple life he later romanticised. His mother remarried and, as Catherine Wheelwright, became a prominent figure in Irish nationalist circles within America. By a strange irony, Hanna Sheehy Skeffington became close to her when she visited America on propaganda tours. She wrote a warm obituary of Catherine for *An Phoblacht*, 25 June 1932. De Valera's marriage to Sinead O'Flanagan exemplified his vision of women's true role: she bore him seven children and was rarely to be seen at any public occasion, even waiting at home for him when he was released from jail after the Rising.

72. *Irish Times*, 11 May 1937. Letter by Mary Kettle.
73. Dail Eireann, Parliamentary Debates, *Official Report*, Dublin Stationery Office, vol.67, 11 May 1937, p.64. See also speech by John Costello, 12 May 1937, p.311, for an acute account of the consequences of the de Valera proposals; 'it seemed to me to fit in completely with the idea that it was intended to allow... women, if it were thought fit, or any section of women, to be deprived of their right to vote or their right to be members of Dail Eireann.'
74. Dail Eireann, *Official Report*, vols. 67-8, 11 May 1937, p.67.
75. *Ibid.*, 4 June 1937, p.1870, and *Irish Times*, 3 June 1937. As an interesting sidelight, at one stage during the debate, when Dillon taunted de Valera as to what might happen if Cumann na mBan got on to his trail because he would not allow women into the army, de Valera ruefully replied 'That may be the beginning of all my trouble.' He then proceeded to give a laborious explanation of his reasons for not allowing women into Boland's Mill. Dail Eireane, *Official Report*, *op. cit.*, 13 May 1937, p.462.
76. *Ibid.*, 12 May 1937, p.244.
77. *Ibid.*, 9 June 1937, p.153.
78. *Ibid.*, 9 June 1937, p.242.
79. *Irish Times*, 22 June 1937.
80. *Ibid.*, 25 June 1937.
81. Daly (1978), *op. cit.*, p.75.
82. *Prison Bars*, July 1937. The newspaper of the Women's Prisoners' Defence League (1937-8), edited by Maud Gonne.

83. *Irish Times*, 12 May 1937.
84. *Ibid*., 21 June 1937.
85. *Ibid*., 30 June 1937.
86. A leaflet produced by the Women's Social and Progressive League, *Open Letter to Women Voters,* National Library of Ireland, no date, would appear to have been produced for the 1938 election. It listed examples of the deterioration in the position of women in the tailoring trade, as teachers, within the civil service, agricultural workers, etc. Hanna's account of the 1943 election is contained in Hanna Sheehy Skeffington, 'Women in Politics', *The Bell*, vol.7, no.2, 1943, pp.143-8. With thanks to Bill Rolston for bringing this to my notice.
87. *Prisons Bar*, July 1938.
88. John McGuffin, *Internment!*, Kerry, Anvil Books, 1973, pp.81-3. Betty Sinclair, as a Communist Party member, was also interned.
89. MacEoin, *op. cit.*, pp.170-1. Testimony of Mrs Patsy O'Hagan.
90. Eithne Coyle, interview, Dublin, 1975.

7. Conclusion

1. *Irish Independent*, 28 May 1914, quoted in Rosemary Owens, 'Votes for Women: Irishwomen's Campaign for the Vote, 1876-1915' M.A. thesis, University College, Dublin, 1977.
2. *Irish Citizen*, 8 August 1914.
3. Maire Comerford, unpublished memoirs.
4. *Evening Telegraph*, 12 November 1913, quoted in Owens, *op. cit.*
5. James Connolly, *The Reconquest of Ireland*, Dublin and Belfast, New Books Publications, 1972 (1st edn c.1914), p.45.
6. 'Women and Wartime Conscription' *Workers' Republic*, 18 December 1915.
7. From this charge I am excluding an examination of the programme of the Republican Congress, which took very seriously the position of women workers, and the Official Republicans (now the Workers' Party), both of whom are outside the mainstream of Irish Republicanism.
8. *An Phoblacht/Republican News*, 17 November 1979, in the introduction to the report on the Sinn Fein Women's Conference.
9. Sinn Fein, *Eire Nua: The Social and Economic Programme of Sinn Fein*, Dublin, 1971.
10. Report by Teresa Kelly, *An Phoblacht/Republican News*, 17 November 1979.
11. *Iris*, Sinn Fein Foreign Affairs Bureau, vol.1, no.2, November 1981, pp.57-9.
12. An Phoblacht/Republican News, 4 November 1982. One interest-

ing issue arising out of the debate on the Amendment concerned the question of whether the Republican movement should give such token recognition to Free State institutions so that they could more effectively be campaigned against. The report and the ard fheis remarked that this issue occurred on several occasions and 'will indoubtedly become an increasingly relevant debate in the future'. It will be instructive to discover whether or not the impetus for this originated within the feminist current of Sinn Fein.

13. This information was gained in private conversation with a former member.
14. *An Phoblacht/Republican News*, 27 May 1982.
15. *Ibid*. 27 May 1982.
16. *Ibid*.
17. Margaretta D'Arcy, *Tell Them Everything*, London, Pluto Press, 1981, pp.107-12; Nell McCafferty, *The Armagh Women*, Dublin, Co-op Books, 1981, p.14.

Index